THE MAJOR
LATIN POEMS
OF
JACOPO
SANNAZARO

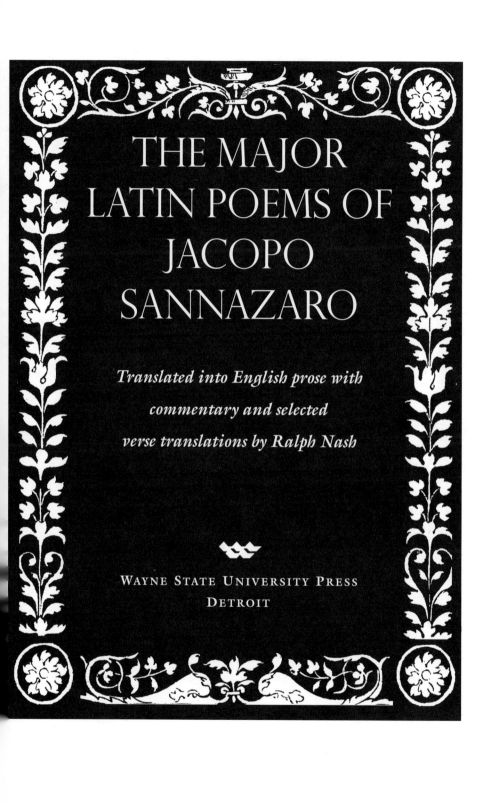

THE MAJOR
LATIN POEMS OF
JACOPO
SANNAZARO

Translated into English prose with
commentary and selected
verse translations by Ralph Nash

WAYNE STATE UNIVERSITY PRESS
DETROIT

Library of Congress Cataloging-in-Publication Data

SANNAZARO, JACOPO, 1458–1530.
    THE MAJOR LATIN POEMS OF JACOPO SANNAZARO / TRANSLATED INTO
ENGLISH PROSE WITH COMMENTARY AND SELECTED VERSE TRANSLATIONS BY
RALPH NASH.
    P. CM.
    INCLUDES BIBLIOGRAPHICAL REFERENCES.
    ISBN 0-8143-2549-1 (ALK. PAPER). — ISBN 0-8143-2576-9
(PBK. : ALK. PAPER)
    1. LATIN POETRY, MEDIEVAL AND MODERN—TRANSLATIONS INTO ENGLISH.
I. NASH, RALPH, 1925–   . II. TITLE.
PA8570.S3A25 1996
871'.04—DC20   95-22615

DESIGNER: MARY KRZEWINSKI

Contents

5

Chronological Table

1443	Alfonso of Aragon becomes King of Sicily and Naples
1451(?)	Birth of Frederick of Aragon, Sannazaro's future king and patron
1458	Ferdinand I (Ferrante) succeeds Alfonso the Magnanimous. Birth of Jacopo Sannazaro, July 28
1462(?)	Death of Sannazaro's father
1475	Death of Sannazaro's mother
1481	Alfonso, Duke of Calabria, heads the allied expedition that expels the Turks from Otranto
1483–85	Sannazaro twice campaigns with Alfonso in expeditions against papal forces near Rome
1489	Sannazaro completes most of *Arcadia* and thereafter concentrates on Latin poetry
1494	Death of Ferrante, succeeded by Alfonso I. Charles VIII of France invades the kingdom
1495	Abdication of Alfonso, succeeded by Ferdinand II (Ferrandino)
1496	Death of Ferrandino, succeeded by Frederick I
1499	Sannazaro receives his villa Mergellina from Frederick
1501	Frederick capitulates to France and Spain. Sannazaro accompanies him into exile in France
1503	Death of Pontano, Sannazaro's friend and mentor
1504	Death of Frederick, at Tours. Sannazaro sanctions publication of *Arcadia*, returns to Mergellina
1506–12	Sannazaro devotes much time to assisting Summonte in publication of Pontano's *Opera*
1516	Machiavelli's *Prince*, Ariosto's *Orlando Furioso*. Martin Luther openly breaks with Rome

1517–19   Sannazaro increases his exertions in behalf of his friend, Cassandra Marchese, in her unsuccessful defense against her husband's divorce suit

1519–21   Sannazaro engages in extensive revision of *De Partu Virginis*

1525   Sannazaro succeeds Summonte as leader of the Pontanian Academy

1526   First publication of *De Partu Virginis* and *Piscatoriae*

1527   The Sack of Rome

1530   Death of Sannazaro, August 6. Sannazaro's Italian *Rime* published posthumously

1535   First publication of the *Elegies* and *Epigrams*

1543   The Spanish viceroy shuts down the Pontanian Academy

General Introduction

"Shall these bones live?" A twentieth-century reader of Sannazaro's Latin poems may well respond, with Ezekiel, that the bones are very dry. The work of some forty years, in the life of a serious and meticulous craftsman, cannot easily be dismissed as a mere aberration in literary history. But to appreciate the accomplishment we need to make out something of the poet's method, and to at least speculate about his motivations.

Motive and Method in Sannazaro's Imitatio

A fundamental problem appears at once. Neither method nor motive can be quite disentangled from the rather bizarre undertaking of Neo-Latin humanist poetry—to recreate, in an acquired language, a facsimile of the sound and sense of poems written in that language, but for an alien culture and by poets who were natives of that culture. Almost any discussion of method and motive will involve questions of the echoing, or modifying, or direct replicating of words and phrases from the Roman poets. Inevitably these discussions will be clearer for those with some command of Latin. Still, the intention here is to supply an English version of Sannazaro's text (with the usual provisos about the inadequacies of translation), from which a reader may get a sense of the kind of poetry that resulted from Sannazaro's methods in applying the humanist doctrine of *imitatio*—the imitation of classical models.

That doctrine arose very naturally, for Dante and Petrarch and their followers, out of their steadily increasing awareness of how Latin literature and educational method had been consciously formed, in large part, through imitation of the Greek *paideia*. The chief instrument in that process of transmitting Greek literary culture to Rome had been the elaborate system of rhetorically-based education long ago traced lucidly and fully by H. I. Marrou (*A History of Education in Antiquity,* trans. George Lamb, New York, 1956), and perceived by Ernst R. Curtius as underlying a great many quite specific developments in the medieval literature treated in the wide-ranging pages of his *European Literature and the Latin Middle Ages,* trans. Willard Trask (Princeton, 1953). These two

9

scholars will give their readers an excellent overview of some of the broad implications in a system of education that encouraged production of literature through imitation of "classical" models from an earlier literature. For more recent scholarship, more directly connected with Sannazaro and his age, one may consult Thomas M. Greene, *The Light in Troy* (New Haven, 1982), and David Quint, *Origin and Originality in Renaissance Literature* (New Haven, 1983).

This book, however, is concerned only with a small segment from the whole spectrum of *imitatio* in the Renaissance and later. That spectrum, almost of necessity, is in very large part a matter of translation in one form or another—Spenser's Englishing of a passage from Ariosto or Tasso that in turn was modelled on Catullus's Latin, say, or Ovid's, with perhaps a Greek original in the background, and so forth. In his youth, Sannazaro exploited this method to the hilt, assimilating to the Italian of his *Arcadia* virtually all the pastoralists, in verse or prose, within the Graeco-Roman tradition. But the *imitatio* of his Neo-Latin poetry is almost exclusively a matter of Latin verses imitating other Latin verses. His practice does occasionally deviate from this general rule. In the *Piscatorial Eclogues* his Latin renders a Greek original here and there; in *De Partu Virginis* his version of Mary's Magnificat clearly adumbrates the Latin prose of the Vulgate; and in the *Elegies* fairly often he adapts another Latin meter to his elegiacs—usually hexameters from Virgil or Ovid, but in one striking instance even a Sapphic stanza from Statius's *Silvae* (see below, pp. 20–21), and not infrequently locutions from poems in lyric meters, for example Horace. In general, however, when practicing this particular form of humanist *imitatio*, he is modelling his verses on Roman verses in the same genre and the same meter.

Naturally Sannazaro's actual employment of this *imitatio* varies widely as to the extent of its application. Some poems are virtually without reminiscences of Roman originals; others are clearly intended as formal exercises in imitating a particular poet, such as Tibullus. A major aim in providing this translation and commentary is to enable readers to assess the extent of Sannazaro's *imitatio*, in the restricted sense just described, and the overall effect achieved by this peculiar process, in which a poet from one culture sets himself the problem of making his statement almost always in the same tongue, usually in the same meter, and frequently in the same words as an earlier poet from an essentially disparate culture. The situation should at least pique our curiosity. What is Sannazaro doing, and why is he doing it?

Answers for the second question are the more speculative, but also they can be advanced more briefly, with less need for illustrative detail. There are, of course, some obvious motivations that need not detain us long. Latin was in high repute, as the universal language for learned

men, so that a poet who hoped to be famed throughout Europe for serious poetry on serious subjects might readily think of polishing his
skills at Latin verse. In Naples this elitist attitude was reinforced by the
state's deliberate encouragement of Latin literature in various genres
through the renowned Academy founded by Alfonso the Magnanimous
soon after he established his government at Naples. For Sannazaro this
encouragement was reinforced when the Academy came under the leadership of the remarkable Giovanni Pontano, himself a skilled and intelligent writer of Latin verse. Sannazaro's connection with the Pontanian
Academy clearly must have influenced his manner of practicing his skills
as a Neo-Latin poet. Then as now the academies encouraged their members in reading papers to one another, sometimes approximating modern efforts at literary analysis. For the Pontanian Academy specifically,
we can get some idea of the nature of their efforts through Pontano's
Dialoghi (ed. Carmelo Previtera, Florence, 1943), as when Pontano presents Hieronymus Carbo and Francesco Pucci making observations
comparing the strategies of Virgil, Lucretius, and others in opening
major sections of their poems ("Aegidius," Previtera, pp. 260–63). In
"Actius" Pontano devotes more than forty pages to a presentation, by
Sannazaro himself, of an extensive survey of varieties of rhythmic effect
in the Virgilian hexameter (Previtera, 146–90). We have no way to tell
whether the selection of examples is genuinely by Sannazaro, by
Pontano, or both, but the essential point here is that Sannazaro is accustomed to look at Roman poems as artifacts susceptible of analysis. This
attitude seems to carry over into such elegies as *To His Mistress* (1.3) and
To Bacchus (2.5), which become almost a commentary on themes selected from several elegies by Propertius and Tibullus, as discussed in
the Introductory Notes, below. Somewhat akin to this is the deliberate
and extensive use of Virgil's "Messianic" eclogue in *De Partu Virginis*
(3.174–202, discussed below, pp. 14, 17), although this example may
adumbrate literary history more than criticism.

Indeed, the very concept of history can be considered another motivating force behind the imitation of classical models. Here the modern
reader will need to take account of two aspects of Renaissance historiog-
raphy, inherited from the Graeco-Roman culture. One is its very common view of human history as a kind of proving-ground. The individual
is to measure himself against heroic examples from the past, striving to
outdo, equal, or at least resemble them. The life-blood of this view is
emulation, its social outlook is aristocratic and elitist, its measure of
value is excellence—the *aretē* of Werner Jaeger's monumental *Paideia*
(e.g., 1.13–23), to which the reader is referred for a comprehensive account of the subject. Its motto, one might say, is *Go thou and do likewise;*
and thus by an easy gradation we arrive at *imitatio*—whether *imitatio*

Christi or *imitatio Virgili* is perhaps not irrelevant, but for the moment we are following the footsteps of Sannazaro and his fellow humanists.

Another aspect to be taken into account is much more tied to particulars. We may follow Spenser in calling it *Troynovant*—the reshaping of legendary history to make the fugitives from fallen Troy the founders of new nations in the West. This whole matter of validating a culture by finding its roots in another has obvious relationship to the general subject of this introduction. But our immediate concern is with a sub-variation in Virgil's treatment of the theme. The broad scheme of the *Aeneid* has Aeneas replacing Troy by founding Rome, or at least laying the groundwork for the founding of Rome. Virgil is patently conscious of this theme, even to the very end, where Juno's last speech in the poem says "Troy is fallen: let the name be fallen too" (12.828). But along the way, in Book Three, Aeneas has already encountered a striking example of the willed replication of past history as he and his fellow-fugitives land at Buthrotum, where he meets Andromache, formerly Hector's wife, who tells him that she is now the wife of Helenus, Priam's son. Helenus, having inherited a small princedom, "named the plains Chaonian, and called all the land Chaonia after Chaon of Troy, and built withal a Pergama and this Ilian citadel on the hills" (*Aen.* 3.334–36, trans. Mackail). Aeneas goes with Andromache to her home. As he later recounts this episode to Dido, he says, "I advance and recognize a little Troy, and a copy of the great Pergama, and a dry brook with the name of Xanthus, and clasp a Scaean gateway" (3.349–51). After a few days Helenus (who is both king and priest) makes an inspired prophecy of Aeneas's further travels. Aeneas departs, saying to Helenus: "For you rest is won, and no ocean floor to furrow, no ever-retreating Ausonian fields to pursue. You see a pictured Xanthus, and a Troy your own hands have built" (3.495–98).

This curious and minor episode has significant repercussions in Book Five when Juno, through her messenger Iris, takes advantage of the homesickness aroused in the Trojan women by their brief visit to the "little Troy" at Buthrotum. Disguised as one of the Trojan women, Iris cries out: "Shall there never be a Trojan town to tell of? Shall I nowhere see a Xanthus and a Simois, the rivers of Hector" (5.633–34)? Thereupon the Trojan women actually burn almost the entire Trojan fleet. In the upshot, Aeneas agrees to let those stay behind who wish: "Meanwhile Aeneas traces the town with the plough and allots the homesteads; this he bids be Ilium, and these lands Troy" (5.755–57). After this, he and his chosen band set sail again.

Aeneas and Helenus are diametrically opposed in their responses to the fall of Troy. A modern reader may be inclined to see here Virgil's paradigm of two responses to the demands of history: the heroic resolve to navigate unpathed waters, following one's star come what may, versus the non-heroic impulse to be content with replication of the past. This may not be quite the way Sannazaro would have read these passages, but certainly he was aware of the "little Troy" in Books Three and Five, as were many generations after him. Why should he *not* take Virgil's invention as validating the human impulse to create a replica of the past, whether in politics or in poetry? He nowhere calls his *De Partu Virginis* a "little Aeneid," but the poem is as Virgilian as he could make it. Nobody is going to claim a cause-effect relationship here, but the episode at Buthrotum does supply one vivid example among many of an impulse lying behind a great deal of poetic activity from the Alexandrian Age to the Renaissance—and beyond.

Perhaps other motivating attitudes ought to be explored, but introductions should try to be brief. In turning to a survey of Sannazaro's methods of *imitatio*, we may reasonably proceed by moving from some clear examples that ask the reader to be able to recall the original in order to appreciate its contribution to Sannazaro's poem, to imitations of less familiar lines, made clear and demonstrable through a device that I call the "signature line," and then on to a sampling of imitations in which the original is blended into the imitation less visibly and demonstrably, and so on to the realm of echoes and allusion, sometimes too faint to be demonstrated convincingly, but still available for the reader's private sense of the poem.

The first of these four categories will be, for readers of twentieth-century English poetry, the most familiar survival of the method of *imitatio*. T. S. Eliot and Ezra Pound made vigorous attempts to restore a fading sense for the continuity of literary tradition, by studding their poems with familiar quotations from earlier English poets—to say nothing of extension of the method (for example, prose bits left as prose amid the surrounding verse; fragments of Greek, Latin, French, Italian, German, even Chinese, with or without translation, and so on). Most of their readers will have recognized such lines as "Those are pearls that were his eyes," "This music crept by me upon the waters," "Your eyen two wol sleye me sodenly," "Sweet Thames, run softly, till I end my song," and so forth; and they will have had some immediate sense of the relevance of the recognized original to its new context. *Mutatis mutandis* (that is, with Latin substituted for English), the same situation obtains for many passages in Sannazaro, especially in *De Partu Virginis*. As with Pound and Eliot, so with Sannazaro—the line quoted is not always familiar and the relevance not always crystal clear, but still the method and its aim are recognizable.

Examples from Virgil presumably have the best chance of being familiar to modern readers. We may begin with Sannazaro's extensive use of Virgil's Fourth Eclogue (the "Messianic" eclogue) in *De Partu Virginis*. Sannazaro attempted to make his poem Virgilian in its diction, syntax, rhythm, and decorum; and in the song of the shepherds Aegon and Lycidas, celebrating the divine birth (3.196–232), more than anywhere else in his Latin poems, he insists on making the reader aware of his model by echoing line after line with no change at all, or virtually none:

(1) ultima Cumaei venit iam carminis aetas (*Ecl.* 4.4; *De Partu* Lat. 3.200)

(2) iam nova progenies caelo demittitur alto (4.7; 3.203)

(3) [desinet] ac toto surget gens aurea mundo (4.9; 3.204–5)

(4) te duce, si qua manent sceleris vestigia nostri,
inrita perpetua solvent formidine terras (4.13–14; 3.206–7)

(5) ille deum vitam accipiet divisque videbit
permixtos heroas et ipse videbitur illis,
pacatumque reget patriis virtutibus orbem
(4.15–17; 3.211–13)

(6) ipsae lacte domum referent distenta capellae
ubera, nec magnos metuent armenta leones
(4.21–22; 3.217–18)

(7) et durae quercus sudabunt roscida mella (4.30; 3.224)

(8) alter erit tum Tiphys, et altera quae vehat Argo
delectos heroas; erunt etiam altera bella (4.34–35; 3.228–29)

(9) cara deum soboles, magnum Jovis incrementum (4.49; 3.232)

(10) incipe, parve puer, risu cognoscere matrem (4.60; 3.231)

Thus fifteen of the thirty-six lines in Sannazaro's song of Aegon and Lycidas are transcribed directly from Virgil with virtually no changes beyond a shift from polytheism to monotheism. Omission of the three introductory lines, plus inclusion of transcribed phrases and half-lines, would easily raise the proportion to more than fifty percent. Obviously Sannazaro wants his reader thoroughly aware that his savior's birth was prophetically sung not only by the great Jewish poet David, but also by the great Roman poet Virgil.

In itself, the example is misleading, and perhaps unfair to Sannazaro, since a reader may be inclined to shrug and go off in search of poets less slavish. But it certainly does demonstrate that Sannazaro is quite willing to import into his poetry unaltered, and virtually unaltered, lines from his classical models—an important aspect of his method when the source in question is not so widely known to his general public, as will be shown below when we consider his use of "signature lines." First, however, as a kind of antidote to the above example, consider the effectiveness of his slight, but definite, allusion to one of Virgil's most famous lines, as he pleads with the grand chancellor of France to persuade the French king to show clemency toward vanquished Naples. After portraying the haplessness of the Neapolitan nobility under French rule, Sannazaro bursts out: "The treasury gets riches from the wretched. Alas, is it this 'to spare the conquered peoples'!" (*El.* 1.8.25). When he asks *hoc est, heu, parcere victis?* one cannot doubt that Sannazaro is echoing Virgil's praise of the art that is to be Rome's special gift: *parcere subjectis et debellare superbos* (*Aen.* 6.853)—to spare the vanquished and subdue the proud. Yet the "imitation" here is hardly more than the echo of a single word and the substitution of an equivalent for another: its effectiveness lies in the total context surrounding Virgil's phrase and Sannazaro's (plus that drive to emulate great historical exemplars, mentioned above).

We proceed to our second category. Time and again, in imitating a particular Roman poet by pulling together images and phrasings from diverse passages in that poet's work, Sannazaro appears to acknowledge his source by importing into his poem an entire line (or more) from that poet, exactly duplicated or virtually unaltered. These lines, which we may call "signature lines," have the effect of confirming (or in modern phrase "highlighting") the presence, in this section of Sannazaro's poem, of one of his classical models—usually Tibullus, Propertius, Virgil, or Ovid. Most of them are, of course, less immediately recognizable than the kind of "familiar quotation" which I have offered as a separate category in the preceding paragraphs, but it seems pointless to speculate on just how much Sannazaro counted on such recognition. Signature lines occur so often throughout the Elegies and the *De Partu Virginis* that one can scarcely doubt that they constitute a deliberate method in Sannazaro's practice of *imitatio*. Quite possibly he had noted that Greek and Roman poets employ a similar method of quoting directly from their sources, so as to make what Jaeger calls "a literary allusion in the Hellenistic manner" (*Paideia*, 1.25). I have tried (unsuccessfully doubtless) to identify all examples from the Elegies, usually with some commentary, in my Introductory Notes for each of the elegies, without attempting equal treatment for all the other poems. The following examples of "signature lines," selected from the Elegies, are placed here in the General Introduction partly because they seem, in one way or another, to call for more comment than is suitable for the limited space of the Introductory Notes.

Elegy 1.9 begins as an exercise in imitating Tibullus and Propertius, but after some thirty lines it becomes a relatively lengthy encomium of the man whom the Academy at Naples called its "Old Man" (Senex), Giovanni Pontano. The opening lines of the poem reject "the weariness of the long road, and the sea" in favor of Sannazaro's quiet life at home, frequenting "the holy haunts of Phoebus." By living thus, says Sannazaro, he will not be forgotten when he dies, "and my celebrated shade may wax proud over my sepulcher" (*Et nostro celebrata superbiat umbra sepulcro*—1.9.17). These words very clearly echo the sound of a line from the Umbrian poet Propertius:

> Vt nostris tumefacta superbiat Vmbria libris
> That swelling Umbria may wax proud over my
> poems (4.1.63).

Of itself this echo seems no more, perhaps, than a clever adaptation, avoiding an unwanted topical reference by replacing *Vmbria* with *umbra* ("shade," or "spirit"). But after line 32 Sannazaro turns to praise of Pontano, also a native of Umbria, and drives the point home, in his poem's closing lines, by scoffing at Umbria's hopes for claiming Pontano as her own: "Why, Umbria, are you hoping to have for yourself the palms of his victory? He has fetched them back to the walls of my native land" (1.9.103–4). The play on *Vmbria-umbra*, by which Sannazaro had appropriated for his own persona the boast of Propertius, is made to bear fruit by providing an indirect compliment to Pontano, as another Propertius, and a direct compliment to Naples, as a city that fosters poets. Poetry courts dangers when it becomes a game not readily accessible to the general reader: but wit and subtlety have their rewards also, once the key is discovered.

Let us pause for a moment, however, to acknowledge that the reader's wit and subtlety may easily be over-exercised. The *Vmbria-umbra* wordplay just sketched out here had few implications, as long as Sannazaro's poem was merely one more imitation of Tibullus and Propertius; only when the Umbrian Pontano became the true subject of the poem did the further ramifications become possible. Quite possibly Sannazaro had made his substitution *before* his elegy became a tribute to Pontano, so that the appropriateness of replacing *Vmbria* with *umbra* becomes a happy accident—a "found form," so to speak.

A further caveat is in order here. In his elegy addressed to King Frederick, Sannazaro appears to supply a signature line by echoing Propertius as he asks the gods of the Etruscan sea to speed Frederick's voyage:

> Sann.: Candida felici solvite vela Noto
> Shake out his shining sails with a favoring breeze
> (3.1.166)

> Prop.: Candida felici solvite vela choro (1.17.26)
> Give prosperous escort and unfurl our white sails
> (tr. Butler, LCL)

I suggest in the Introductory Note to this elegy some reasons for considering this a signature line providing a clue to the presence of Propertius in this part of the poem. Yet the seventeenth-century editor Broekhuizen explicitly cites this line as an example of Sannazaro's accidentally echoing one of the many lines stored away in the treasure-house of his memory (Amsterdam, 1689, p. 212). And we do have a letter to Antonio Seripando in which Sannazaro says that he has sometimes forgotten from what author he took a certain turn of phrase (*Opere Volgari*, ed. Mauro, p. 376; in Fantazzi-Perosa, Appendix, p. 96).

For virtually any particular example a claim of accidental echoing can scarcely be refuted. But cumulatively the number of these echoes results in convincing one that deliberate method is at work. In addition to the overwhelming obviousness of the examples cited above from Virgil's Messianic eclogue, consider a further example that immediately follows them (*De Partu* Lat. 3.233–36):

Talia dum referunt pastores: avia longe
Responsant nemora: & voces ad sidera jactant
Intonsi montes: ipsae per confraga rupes,
Ipsa sonant arbusta: Deus, Deus ille, Menalca.

The latter three lines come straight from Virgil:

ipsi laetitia voces ad sidera iactant
intonsi montes; ipsae iam carmina rupes,
ipsa sonant arbusta: 'deus, deus ille, Menalca'

The unshorn mountains themselves cast echoes of
gladness to the skies; the very copses now resound
in song: "A god, a god is he, O Menalcas." (*Ecl.* 5.62–64,
trans. Mackail)

I cite this example because there is only one reason for Sannazaro to introduce the name of Menalcas here and nowhere else in his poem—he and his readers both know that he is quoting Virgil.

An additional example of a surely intentional echo occurs in Sannazaro's very late autobiographical elegy addressed to Cassandra Marchese. While summarizing his career as poet and as courtier, he alludes to the composition of his Piscatorial Eclogues:

I was the first to go down to the salty waves, daring
to utter my song in styles not tried before

. . . salsas descendi ego primus ad undas,
Ausus inexpertis reddere verba sonis. (*Elegies* 3.2.57–58)

The couplet is unmistakably an adaptation of the hexameters of Sannazaro's own Fourth Piscatorial:

... salsas deduxi primus ad undas,
Ausus inexperta tentare pericula cymba. (*Pisc.* 4.19–20)

We can no more believe that Sannazaro is accidentally echoing his own verses than we can believe that Virgil closed the fourth and final book of his *Georgics* by accidentally repeating the opening line of his *Eclogues*.

The eighteenth-century Cominian editions of Sannazaro's Latin poems print a biographical sketch, by J. A. Vulpius, which tells us that in his old age Sannazaro was accustomed to spend an entire morning with his friend Francesco Poderico, now old and blind, reading aloud a verse from the manuscript of *De Partu Virginis,* and then discussing it, rephrasing it, polishing cadence and structure, until sometimes the two old men had arrived at as many as ten variants for the single line before going on to the next (*Poemata,* Padua, 1751, p. xxvii). Such an approach to artistic composition may lead to some stiffness and formality, but it is not likely to lead very often to accidental echoes.

Of course Sannazaro does not always supply a signature line to verify the reader's sense that a particular Roman model lies behind a given passage. A good example of a third category, of less visible and demonstrable *imitatio,* is provided by Elegy 2.1, a patronage poem addressed to Alfonso II during the brief period of his reign (1494–95). Structurally this elegy is modelled almost entirely on the first elegy in Propertius's second book, yet there is scarcely one verbal resemblance between the two poems. This kind of *imitatio* virtually defies any attempt at point-by-point comparison, but perhaps it will suffice to summarize Propertius's eighty lines here.

Propertius 2.1 is addressed to Maecenas. It begins with Propertius's standard pose as the singer of "smooth" elegy, whose subject matter is all centered on his mistress. "From a mere nothing springs a mighty tale," he says (2.1.16), having already claimed, however, that if his mistress flings away her robes and enters the lists with him naked, then he is inspired to write whole Iliads. The poem moves on to say that if fate had granted Propertius the ability to write heroic verse, he would sing not Troy, nor Thebes, nor the wars of the Titans, nor the struggles of Rome's early history, but rather the deeds of Maecenas's master, Caesar (2.1.17–38). Propertius then reverts to the theme that each man must limit himself to what his skill can encompass (2.1.39–70), closing his poem with a vignette of Maecenas some day mourning the news of Propertius's death:

si te forte meo ducet via proxima busto,
    esseda caelatis siste Britanna iugis,
taliaque illacrimans mutae iace verba favillae:
    "Huic misero fatum dura puella fuit"

If perchance thy journeying lead thee near my tomb, stay
awhile thy British chariot with carven yoke, and weeping pay
this tribute to the silent dust: "An unrelenting maid wrought
this poor mortal's death." (2.1.75–78, trans. Butler, LCL)

A cursory reading of Sannazaro's elegy addressed to Alfonso will
reveal the essentially similar structure: the poet's stance as a singer of
non-heroic subjects, confined to a narrow circuit; his preference, if he
were able to rise to the heroic, for taking as his subject Alfonso's mighty
deeds; and at the close a reversion to his stance as the poet of love whose
early death, caused by his mistress's harshness, is to be wept by the great
man whose triumphant chariot comes to a stand while he pays tribute to
the buried poet:

Quare si nostri veniet tibi nuncia lethi
    Fama, triumphales jam prope siste rotas:
Atque haec ad cineres moerens effare sepultos:
    Saevitia dominae rapte Poeta jaces. (2.1.115–18)

Wherefore if Fame shall come to you as the messenger of my
death, let your triumphal wheels come to a stand nearby, and
as you shed a tear say to my buried ashes: *Lie quiet, poet,*
taken from us by the harshness of your mistress.

I have quoted here the last four lines of each poem as evidence of a decisive similarity in concept that seems nonetheless to avoid deliberately any
verbal echo beyond the single imperative, *siste.* The elegy is an impressive
example of Sannazaro's skill in varying the method of his *imitatio.*

We need not linger long over examples of my fourth and final category, of echoes and allusions too faint to be confidently proclaimed.
They are undeniably there, for it is simply impossible in this poetic
world that they should not be, and their effect can be an important part
of a reader's experience of Sannazaro's poems, but it will not necessarily
be a part of that shared experience which is vital to a sense of poetry as
cultural tradition. For example, in an elegy that may well be the last
poem of his life, Sannazaro once more imagines himself as the dead
poet, mourned this time by his beloved Cassandra Marchese. The poem
has begun with an attractive sketch of himself as a child in the Picentian
mountains, surrounded by the harmony of birds and learning to sing to

the flocks and the wild creatures of the place. As his autobiographical sketch proceeds, its tones become more and more somber, until in its final section Sannazaro accuses himself of the sin of Sloth and seems ready to succumb to the sin of Despair. He breaks off his poem with a strangled cry to Cassandra:

> Parce tamen scisso seu me, mea vita, capillo,
> Sive: sed heu prohibet dicere plura dolor

> Yet forebear (my life) to mourn me with tresses shorn, or—
> but alas my sorrow forbids me to say more. (3.2.115–16)

There may be no conscious allusion here at all, for one's impression is that the poet's late work shows a perceptibly reduced interest in *imitatio*. Yet I like to think that this outcry echoes a love in Sannazaro's life far older than his love for Cassandra. Fifty years before, he had canvassed every inch of Tibullus's elegies, and no motif in the Roman elegists could be more familiar to him than the mistress who cuts or pulls out her hair in mourning for the death of the elegist, as in Tibullus 1.1.67–68: "Do my shade no injury, but (Delia) spare your flowing locks, and spare your tender cheeks."

And as a final example, illustrating at least the potential fallibility of one's memory in capturing these echoes and allusions, consider a passage from the exordium to the elegy for Sannazaro's king, Frederick:

> Now will I drink from springs untouched and wander the sacred wood where pathway there is none. . . . Boldly I shall pluck my greening laurels on Parnassus peak, or in your forest groves, melodious Pindus. (3.1.9–10, 15–16)

Having for some years been plagued with what seemed a memory that these lines appear somewhere in Statius, I finally decided that they must be an echo from the *Silvae*, indeed, but from a poem written in sapphics, not elegiacs. I quote the passage from the pleasantly cadenced prose of Kathleen Coleman's recent translation:

> And do you, monarch of the lyric band, grant me rights awhile over a novel plectrum, if, Pindar, I have sanctified your Thebes with Latian song. . . . Now I must take my garland from untrimmed myrtle, now the greater source is running dry and I must drink from a purer stream.
> (*Silvae* 4.7.5–12)

The language sounds somewhat similar, but the content is exactly reversed, since Sannazaro is turning from the amatory to the heroic, whereas Statius is turning from heroic verse to the "purer stream" of lyric. Is this imitation, echo, allusion, or chimaera? I leave it to yourself to determine. . . .

The four "categories" outlined above are characterized by differences not so much in kind as in degree—the degree to which the *imitatio* strikes a reader as overt and obvious. Inevitably that degree will vary with each reader, and indeed will also vary within each reader as he becomes more (or less) familiar with the materials imitated. That is of no great concern, since something like it is a necessary part of all Writer-to-Reader relationships, and we learn to live with insoluble problems, such as the "authorship" of *Iliad* and *Odyssey*, rival "states" of the text of *Hamlet*, and so on. But it is perhaps useful to have given here some indication of the range of *imitatio* as practiced by Sannazaro.

The Achievement of the Method

In the foregoing discussion, the illustrative examples are restricted to two sources: the *De Partu* and the elegies. Thus the examples exclude the *Piscatorial Eclogues*, the *Salices*, the *Lamentatio de Morte Christi*, and the *Epigrams* (which are for the most part too brief to allow the kind of *imitatio* with which we have been concerned). This suggests the interesting, though highly speculative, possibility that the method of *imitatio*, as it has been discussed here, may be in large part an aspect of Sannazaro's early work as Neo-Latin poet, appearing most prominently in work done between c. 1485–95.

There seems no inherent improbability in the suggestion. The whole approach of imitation of classical models grew out of the methods of the schoolroom, and Sannazaro always had just the right mixture of seriousness and humility about learning his craft, so that he thought of himself as a student in the presence of the great Roman poets—an "ephebe," as Wallace Stevens would say. The major difficulty lies not in general consideration of probabilities, but in the practical question of determining what is early and what is late in his production. Sannazaro has not helped us much in that respect. He was not in the habit of dating his manuscripts, and he notoriously *was* in the habit of keeping his poems by him, to be revised, recombined with earlier productions, dedicated to friends whom he had not even known when the poem was first written, and so on. Still, there is some possibility for reasonably accurate dating of coterie poems like the elegies, with their relative profusion of personal and topical reference, and it does indeed seem that the later elegies show diminished interest in the kind of close *imitatio* illustrated in the first section of this introduction. We will consider these elegies first, with a reminder that the Introductory Notes to individual elegies often give a somewhat fuller discussion of dates than is sketched out here.

The entire third book (comprising only three elegies) can surely be dated after 1495, and Elegies Two and Three after Sannazaro's return to Naples in 1505, inasmuch as that return is the explicit subject of Elegy Three, and the autobiographical Elegy Two not only is dedicated to Cassandra Marchese (whom Sannazaro scarcely knew before his return in 1505) but also makes her an integral part of the poem itself. Both these poems show a mature skill, but faint interest in any kind of *imitatio*. Elegy One of Book Three, in praise of Frederick after he became King of Naples in 1496, resembles its counterpart in Book Two (i.e., the introductory elegy in praise of Alfonso II, king in 1494–95), in that both poems show an adroit and subtle use of themes from Propertius. Alfonso's elegy seems otherwise virtually devoid of explicit *imitatio*, whereas Elegy 3.1 ranges rather widely through allusions to Virgil, Propertius, Statius, Tibullus, and Ovid, thus constituting a notable exception to the suggestion that interest in *imitatio* dwindles in the later poetry.

Elegy 2.6 addresses Lodovico Montalto as Magister Scrinii for the Emperor Charles (i.e., Charles V), and is thus conceivably to be dated after 1520, although Sannazaro might have updated Montalto's official title as he (or an editor) updates Troiano Cavaniglia's titles when dedicating the *Salices* to him (see the Introductory Note to *Willows*, below). This poem to Montalto seems completely devoid of *imitatio*.

Elegy Eight, in Book One, was quite probably written in the winter of 1501–2 (see its Introductory Note), and certainly is to be dated after Guy de Rochefort's appointment as grand chancellor of France, in 1497. It seems virtually devoid of imitation also, like the poem addressed to Montalto. In both instances, Sannazaro may have thought that close imitation of classical models did not suit the decorum of politically-oriented poems addressed to important figures in the bureaucracy. In Book One, the fifth elegy, addressed to an unknown "Julius of Siena," can be pretty certainly dated after 1497, for reasons stated in its Introductory Note, and may indeed even be post-exilic, if we are to take seriously the poet's complaint that Apollo has abandoned him. It too shows very little direct *imitatio*, although saturated with classical allusion. And Elegy 1.4 can be dated by the birthdate of Antonio Garlon's first-born, which Altamura gives as c. 1500 (*Sannazaro*, 1951, p. 174). Like Elegy 3.1, this poem would be an exception to my general proposition, being a skillful blend of Tibullus, Propertius, and Virgil.

The overall picture, then, shows at least eight of the twenty-four elegies having some external evidence to suggest a date of 1495 or later, and six of these (1.5,8; 2.1,6; 3.2,3) with remarkably little *imitatio* of the kind being discussed here. In addition, the Cumae elegy (2.9) and the Ovidian poem about Morinna (2.4) are noticeably lacking in such *imitatio,* but yield no clues about date of composition other than a general appearance of mature poetic skill. Two other elegies (1.7 and 1.11) show little evidence of close imitation but are probably early productions, nonetheless.

Beyond the elegies, we have Sannazaro's work in dactylic hexameter—the *Lamentatio* and *Salices,* plus five Piscatorial Eclogues and a fragmentary sixth, with *De Partu Virginis* reserved for discussion in the next section. The *Piscatorials* I have left without Introductory Notes, but W. P. Mustard's extensive annotations (in an edition for which we need a photographic reprint) can give the reader materials for exercising his own judgment about the nature of the *imitatio* exercised in those poems. *Salices* seems much like the Morinna elegy (2.4), obviously imitative of Ovidian technique but not frequently concerned with direct textual echoes and allusions. The *Lamentatio* seems still more to avoid close imitation, perhaps for considerations of decorum. These poems are generally viewed today as having been written after King Frederick made Sannazaro the gift of his villa at Mergellina (June 12, 1499). It has always been known, indeed, that Sannazaro had the *Piscatorials* with him while in France with Frederick, reportedly losing four of them on the return trip; and in this century we have long known that Sannazaro showed Fausto Andrelini the *Lamentatio* when visiting him in Paris. Andrelini, a careerist of the worst kind, later allowed it to be published without authorization, in *Pia et emuncta opuscula,* Paris, 1513. (For the most recent account, see Carlo Vecce, *Iacopo Sannazaro in Francia,* Padova, 1988, pp. 46–50.) Thus we can generalize that most of the work in heroic meter, other than *De Partu Virginis,* is relatively late (i.e., 1495 and after), and that it either shows (like most of the late elegies) a diminished interest in close imitation, or moves away from that style of echoing the language of the Roman poets, into a more abstract kind of imitation, reflecting an Ovidian subject matter and narrative technique or translating the flytings and love plaints of Theocritean-Virgilian shepherds to the topography and local deities of the Bay of Naples.

The foregoing survey of Sannazaro's short poems in elegiac and heroic meters accommodates a speculation that he deliberately set himself to learn from poets such as Tibullus, Propertius, and Statius by leaving outcroppings of their very language here and there in his poems, while also performing variations on their themes and modes of expression—what I have been calling "close imitation." About the last thing one would want to suggest is that suddenly came a day (in 1495 or some such arbitrary date) when Sannazaro decided to be his own man, no longer apprenticed to the past. That Walt Whitman approach is not in the cards. But one can believe that a poet might accept the challenge of blending his own language with language taken directly from his masters, and that eventually he might say to himself: "I have proved that I can do it. More is unnecessary." And one can certainly believe that while accepting that challenge Sannazaro, with an unsurpassed ear for the cadences of Latin verse, could learn a great deal in the process.

These remarks have been directed toward what Sannazaro might have achieved for himself through close imitation, what he "got out of it." But there is also the question of what the poems achieved in their effect on their readers. For this we need to shake free of preoccupation with the particular technique of close imitation and consider the total effect of his poetic production. Overwhelmingly, that total effect is of virtuosity in the *construction* of poems, the selecting and crafting of their materials. The reader of *De Partu Virginis*, for example, will be struck at once by the parallel closing of each book with a prophetic song—the Song of David, the Song of Joseph, and the Song of Jordan—each developed to whatever length seemed right to the poet and each reflecting a separate aspect of the effect of the miraculous birth on its audience, both human and divine. In *The Willows* (*Salices*) Sannazaro shows splendid instinct for adjusting the narrative tempo, as he begins with the tranquil pastoral scene, moves on to the slow Pavanne of the Nymphs, disrupts it with the discordant Assault of the Satyrs, scattering the harmonious dance into desperate flight toward the hills, then brings all back to the riverside, graceful still but rooted forever. Not every imitator of Ovid has understood his master's art this well. So also with *Piscatorials* and *Elegies*—poem after poem leaves us with a sense that the poet has arranged his materials and composed his scene and left it standing there, satisfying in its own completeness. If at times the materials are from the realm of close imitation—fragments from Propertius and Tibullus woven together into an elegy addressed to Bacchus, for instance, or to the poet's mistress, or to his own birthday—then we can see how the discipline of that weaving might teach a poet how to control and shape another, less imitative poem—to Cumae, for example. But more important than the learning process is the result; and for Sannazaro the result was a considerable number of poems that attest to the intelligent, hard-working craftsmanship of their author.

Remarks on De Partu Virginis

As we turn to Sannazaro's major work, it is time to reduce the emphasis on *imitatio*, in favor of remarks on more general qualities of a poem whose excellence deserves recognition and respect.

Sannazaro's autobiographical elegy 3.2 ("How He Spent His Childhood in the Picentians") gives the impression that he turned to a poem on the birth of Christ immediately after writing his *Arcadia* (which was virtually completed by 1489). The poet's reason for placing *De Partu* first among the works following *Arcadia* is likely, however, to be hierarchical rather than chronological, for the sequence of the Latin works cited in Elegy 3.2 is *De Partu, Piscatorials, Elegies,* and *Epigrams* — i.e., hexameters, elegiacs, and mixed meters. It is not flatly impossible that *De Partu Virginis* was under way in the early 1490s or conceivably earlier, but Sannazaro is still speaking in terms of preparing to write a major poem when he dedicates *Salices* to Troiano Cavaniglia (b. 1479). That statement, unless we choose to treat it purely as poetic fiction, suggests actual composition of *De Partu* beginning not earlier than c. 1495, and probably a few years later than that.

The poem's most recent editors have meticulously examined the available external evidence about the stages in Sannazaro's long process of composition and revision (*De Partu Virginis,* ed. Charles Fantazzi and Alessandro Perosa, Florence 1988, pp. lvii–xc). Without attempting a résumé of their lengthy discussion, and without necessarily claiming their authority for the observations, I offer here four more or less unrelated generalizations based on reviewing the extensive data that these editors provide:

(1) The extant mss. preceding the *editio princeps* (1526) are, generally speaking, fair copies of "finished" states of the poem — not material from the poet's workshop, reflecting the additions and deletions of ongoing composition.

(2) Sannazaro's revisions appear to have been in large part incremental, adding new material with relatively little deletion of old material. This observation is based chiefly on roughly collating Book One of the *editio princeps* (462 lines), with the Forma Antiquior (359 lines). A major contribution of the Fantazzi-Perosa edition is its presentation of this earlier version of Book One.

(3) The editors amply demonstrate how arduous and extensive a revision was going on between 1518 and 1521, as reflected in the letters to Seripando which they reprint with minute annotation of their many references to classical texts used by Sannazaro.

(4) There appear to be no strong objections to assuming that Sannazaro began serious composition at about the time he came into possession of his villa at Mergellina. I think general probabilities favor this assumption.

In 1546 Paolo Giovio stated that Sannazaro spent twenty years revising the *De Partu* (Fantazzi-Perosa, pp. lviii–lix). The long delay in the poem's publication resulted not only from Sannazaro's personal circumstances (chronic ill health, a tendency to perfectionism, and evidently a severely depressed psyche after 1505) but also from his deliberate commitment to the Horatian ideal of meticulous revision, word by word and line by line—and year by year. Since the *De Partu* contains fewer than fifteen hundred hexameters, revision usually involved single words and phrases, there being little scope for large-scale insertions and deletions. In 1521 the poet remarked wryly, in a letter to Antonio Seripando (March 23, in Mauro, p. 370; Fantazzi-Perosa, Appendix, p. 89), that he might have done better to go fishing, rather than spend so much of the past three years revising the same passages over and over. But the process benefited the poem, which has been consistently admired for the purity of its Latinity, criticism usually being reserved for such matters as the suitability of embellishing a Christian subject with a pagan décor, and other such questions that no longer much engage our interest.

One notable revision was the change of title to *De Partu Virginis* from *Cristias* or *Cristeide* (Fantazzi-Perosa, pp. lix–lxi). In electing to emphasize through the title that his subject is the birth of a divine child from a virgin, Sannazaro is insisting on his own daring in choosing a subject that will leave him, at its crucial moment, without a model in Virgil, Homer, or the other stars in his classical galaxy: *stat ferre pedem, qua nulla priorum / obvia sint oculis vatum vestigia nostris*—I am resolved to set foot where no tracks of earlier poets can be visible to our eyes (2.264–65). In these very lines, it is true, *stat ferre pedem* is a Virgilian locution (*Aen.* 2.750; cf. 2.660, 12.678), no doubt consciously employed. But that is merely the poet's clever way of saying to his reader, "No matter how many swans of Cayster, no matter how many Virgilian locutions, or epic similes, or quoted lines, this is a poem about the Mystery of mysteries, God become man in ways that Nature cannot understand." Sannazaro makes room in his poem, of course, for the sermons and the miracles, the crucifixion and the resurrection: but he keeps his eye unwaveringly on that central tenet of godhead become flesh, even when the tenet is being expressed through a Virgilian "A god, he is a god, Menalcas" (3.205–6).

This choice of subject has significant consequences. The essential action covers less than ten months, most of which time transpires while the poem is calling the roll of the provinces of the Roman Empire. The hero is a new-born infant, and all the drama of his later development and accomplishment must be relegated to the indirect discourse of prophecy. The forces opposing the hero are given no voice and no plan of action, other than the Slaughter of the Innocents. In short, the subject resists being modelled on the traditional heroic poem narrating the significant actions of kings and princes, although it still affords some room for councils, exhortations, and embassies.

Sannazaro copes with this paucity of action by devoting about six hundred lines to set speeches calling for minimal response, or none. Of these, about a third are based directly on texts from scripture or from Virgil: Mary's Magnificat, 2.43–66; the Song of Lycidas and Aegon, 3.174–202; and Gabriel's Annunciation, 1.101–14, 126–39, 147–59 — plus God's addresses to himself, to Gabriel, and to the assembled angels (1.39–50, 53–76; 3.30–76), which are less oriented to a specific text, but are of course based on Christian orthodoxy. The rest of the six hundred lines is comprised in the three prophetic songs. Nearly 200 lines are devoted to the Song of David (1.221–399) and the Song of Joseph (2.380–402), both addressed to the Divine Child, and each closing its respective book. A third set speech, the Song of Jordan, comprising some 150 lines, is addressed to the Creator, and devoted largely to the Prophecy of Proteus (3.290–434). This Song of Jordan in turn closes the book in which it appears, so that the three songs receive special emphasis through the symmetry of their structural function, although in length and content they are far from symmetrical.

Another three hundred lines may be said to be devoted to half a dozen journies: the descent and return of Gabriel (1.77–101, 183–88), the descent of Joyfulness (3.81–126), Mary's journey to Elizabeth and her return (2.1–42, 86–102), the journey to Bethlehem (2.205–45), the journey of the shepherds to the manger (3.126–46), and the "journey" of Augustus's decree through all the provinces of the Roman Empire (2.104–204).

Another hundred lines are devoted to set passages of description: the streets of Bethlehem (2.231–45); the manger (2.246–51); the Courts of Heaven (3.1–12); the robe of God (3.15–27); the Cave of Jordan (3.246–59) and its Urn (3.260–77). When we add some 150 lines of narrated action—the conception, 1.167–82; the birth, 2.295–323; the adorations of Joseph and the shepherds, 2.351–79 and 3.161–73; and the angelic celebration in the skies over Bethlehem, 3.206–44—these four general categories have accounted for very nearly the entire poem.

Along with this rather enumerative analysis, we may make some observations about the relationship of segments. Preeminently, one notes the apparent care to balance Christian and classical in the development of the poem. One passage translates Mary's Magnificat into polished Latin hexameters: another integrates bodily into the poem the already polished hexameters of Virgil's Pollio eclogue. The material based on the Pollio eclogue allows the shepherds to welcome the Child through the language of the poet-shepherd Tityrus (i.e., Virgil): the Child has already been welcomed by the poet-shepherd-prophet David. The Song of David incorporates a prophetic account of much of the gospels: the Song of Jordan incorporates yet more in the Prophecy of Proteus, shepherd of the sea. Jordan's Cave, with its attendant nymphs, is balanced by the Courts of Heaven, with their attendant angels. Or, for a final example, consider how Sannazaro provides two Annunciation scenes. Gabriel's annunciation to Mary, an inescapable part of his poem because of its Scriptural sanction, is deliberately given the familiar dress of annunciations by messenger gods and goddesses in Homer, Virgil, and lesser poets. But the much lengthier scene of Joyfulness making her annunciation to the shepherds, based on only a verse or two in Luke, is the poem's premier example of Christian allegorizing. In one of his letters to Seripando (April 13, 1521), Sannazaro justifies his invention only on the grounds of variety, but it seems clear enough that he decided he should provide his military and masculine Gabriel-Hermes with a feminine counterpart stressing the Christian message of his subject—the Good News for Earth's poor and insignificant. Incidentally, this invention of the character Joyfulness harks back to the Letizia who brings the good news of the fall of Granada in Sannazaro's *La Presa di Granata,* performed March 4, 1492 (*Opere Volgari,* ed. Mauro, pp. 282–84, especially lines 216–19).

A concomitant observation may be made. This balancing of Christian and classical seems intentional and demonstrable, but it is not done in the spirit of the poet's renowned design for his own tomb, with symmetrical and regular oppositions. Indeed, throughout his Latin poems Sannazaro is willing to develop passages as he pleases, without the aids of symmetry. It is true that this is a characteristic encouraged by the whole corpus of Greek and Latin poetry, free of the troublesome bondage of rhyme and virtually free of the allied convention of stanzaic division: but whatever its cause, the result is what our ancestors might have called a pleasing irregularity.

Reflection on Sannazaro's choice of subject leads to considering two other aspects of his aesthetics. Manifestly, he chose a subject congenial to the pastoral *stasis*—that freezing of human action and passion into a single "freeze frame," nowhere more brilliantly achieved than in the closing scene of Idyll Seven of Theocritus, and familiar to all English readers through the "cold Pastoral" of Keats's ode. From the time that he first came to the attention of Naples' *literati,* Sannazaro adopted the pose of the shepherd-poet-lover under the name of Sincero in his *Arcadia,* or Actius Syncerus when he was admitted to the Pontanian Academy. (English readers will think of Sir Philip Sidney as Astrophil, and Edmund Spenser as Colin Clout—the latter a remarkably exact parallel to Sannazaro's use of the convention.) He kept up this persona throughout his poetic career, and even adroitly manages to insinuate that the Lycidas who sings in praise of the Child (*De Partu,* 3.169–70) is somehow the counterpart of Actius Syncerus. From its very beginnings, moreover, the pastoral genre had been consciously non-heroic (cf. the explicit rejection of epic subjects by Theocritus in the above-mentioned Idyll 7), and when Sannazaro decided to venture on a "brief epic" (the term is Milton's, not his own) we may say that he chose well in selecting a subject that totally avoided the need for representing human action in combat, or even debate, in favor of a succession of highly pictorial scenes suited to treatment in the vein of pastoral.

This predilection for the pictorial extends far beyond *De Partu Virginis*—into the *Epigrams,* for instance, where the epigram on the equestrian statue of the Angevin king Ladislao (*Epigrams,* 1.4) is one of Sannazaro's most widely known poems. Even more indicative are two other epigrams. One of these (2.44 in the Cominian edition of 1751), which is addressed to Anna, mother of the Virgin, and was printed under the title *In Picturam,* utilizes the Renaissance painter's technique of cutting away the walls of a house to reveal the actions transpiring in its several rooms. The other (*In Gemmam Suam,* 1.16) describes a cameo of Aeneas carrying Anchises—evidently the poet's own "find" in one of the ruins around Naples. But the *De Partu* is evidence enough, for one's memory of the poem is almost inevitably filled with brilliantly executed scenes: the winding torchlight procession of the shepherds in search of the manger (3.129–35); the simile of the Virgin Mary as a barefoot maiden frozen silent and motionless (*silet . . . immobilis haeret,* Lat. 1.131); the dwindling figure of the messenger-angel Gabriel returning to his heavenly home (1.183–88); the crowded streets of Bethlehem at dusk (2.232–42); the consciously pagan reminiscences in the scene of the rivergod Jordan flanked by his lovely daughters (3.246–59); the dogs and cattle awakening at the descent of Joyfulness from Heaven (3.113–17). All these and many more strike one as written by a poet alive to the greatness of the visual arts in his own day.

Hactenus . . . sit satis. "Let this much suffice," as Sannazaro says in his masterly conclusion of *De Partu Virginis.* This is not a book on *imitatio* in the Renaissance. It is a translation attempting to make Sannazaro's achievement in that mode accessible, within the limits of translation.[1]

Note

The text for all poems translated here, including Altilio's epithalamion, has been my copy of *Jacobi . . . Sannazarii Poemata* (Patavia, 1751)—the Cominian edition, sufficiently reliable for most purposes. For *De Partu Virginis* the best edition is that by Fantazzi and Perosa (Florence, 1988), and I have followed it in the few instances of variant readings other than those of spelling and punctuation. The Cominian editions do expurgate half a dozen anti-papal epigrams, which can be found in the Dutch Protestant edition annotated by Jan Broekhuizen (Broukhusius). My copy was printed in Amsterdam, 1689.

Readers of the translations offered here should remain at all times aware that the versified translations may be unscrupulous about compressing and omitting material when that seemed to improve the total effect.

DE PARTU
VIRGINIS/
ON
THE VIRGIN'S
CHILDBEARING

BOOK I

The offspring of a virgin birth, and coeval with his great Father, who (being sent down from heaven's upper air) washed away for hapless mortals their race's ancient stain, and opened the path to barred Olympus—let this, ye denizens of Heaven, be my first task: from this let my chiefest work arise. From the beginning make clear the causes as you have understood them, and (if it be lawful) the sequential chain of such a deed.

And here no less, ye Muses the poets' glory, would I desire your springs, your cliffs, the groves not easily attained. For you from heaven
10 derive your lineage, and your delight is in virginity, and reverence for Holy Writ. Show then the way (whether moved by concern for Heaven or for its Virgin's honor) by which I shall prevail against the clouds: and jointly with me throw open the portals of illimitable Heaven. Great matters indeed, Aonian maidens—great matters I require, but justly so, and not unknown to you. For you were able to look upon the cave and the singing choirs: and it cannot be supposed that you failed to note the signs growing visible in the sky, and the Eastern kings.

But chiefly you, o Gracious Mother, the certain hope of men, the certain hope of the gods, whom a thousand armed bands attend, and the
20 whole militia of high heaven with all their chariots, their standards, their clarions and trumpets, joining their multitudes to the singing circle about you—if to your shining temple I bring the garlands that are due; if for you I establish abiding altars in the carven rock, whence lovely Mergellina rising high from her steep summit looks down on the foaming waves, and comes in view for the approaching sailor while yet he is far away; if rightly I sing your praises, if I bear witness to your rituals and offerings and your day, and your assemblies everywhere renowned, when yearly we observe the celebration of the blessed birth; Goddess, instruct your poet ignorant of the way and unaccustomed to the work,
30 and aid him now benignly in his fearsome enterprise.

From his eminence in Heaven the ruler of the gods had seen borne off to Tartarus the spoils acquired from every corner of the earth, and Tisiphone seeking to overturn all things in the deep abyss, urging her savage sisters to dreadful deeds. Nothing now it availed mankind that he

could trace his descent from high heaven, or could refine his mind to various skills; such power had the contagious infection of mortal sin! Then thus to himself the Father, his breast suffused with eternal love: "Shall there be no end? shall late-born descendants expiate with such
40 sufferings those ancient acts committed by their parents? Shall I allow those whom I created to eternal life, and almost equal to the angels, to succumb to gloomy death, entering into hideous dwellings and the realms of darkness? Not so: but rather let them be recalled to the realms of the gods, as is fitting, and as my noble handiwork requires. And let them at once prepare to fill the abandoned forums and the seats of empty heaven—from which that legion, driven by its impious insolence, fell through the frighted air in banishment. And since a single woman was spring and fount of so many evils, bringing death and lamentation upon the earth, now let that sex bring aid, and set such limit as may be,
50 to their unfortunate state."

So he speaks: and for carrying his divine commission to the chaste maiden he addresses a swift messenger,[1] in starry vesture clad, remarkable for his face and glittering wings: "For you whom they call the certain prologue of great things to come, my faithful sentinel, the strongest link of my army—it is time for you to go and establish a new covenant for the ages. Now turn your attention here, and store these things in your breast.

"There lies between the Phoenician cities and wide-spreading
60 Jordan a region well-known for our religion, they call it Judaea, powerful for its arms and for its Law. Here lives a chaste Virgin sprung from famous ancestors, an ancient lineage of kings and prophets; and though blessed with a suitable marriage, she preserves me yet unimpaired (who will preserve for some years more) her heart's modesty. And (marvellous love!) to honor her husband's old age she lives in narrow chambers and a house of poverty, she who deserves to rule the sky and to shine forth in the high council of the gods and dwell in my house forever. From among all virgins this one alone have I chosen long since, and with foreknowledge have settled in my most secret mind, that she it would be
70 who untouched should receive the Holy Spirit in her womb, and without seed should be with child divine.

"Go then, through space make your cloud-wandering way and, when you have come to the place, speak these things as commanded to her chaste ears. And ply her, if reluctant, with gracious exhortations, for I have willed to snatch from Stygian shades the race of mortals, and put an end to their cruel sufferings."

[1] See Glossary, s.v. Gabriel.

He had spoken. The angel, when he had called up the zephyrs, pursues his journey through upper space, he cleaves the clouds, and swims along seeking out the lower atmosphere, and gliding down scarce
80 moves his agile wings. As when from on high the swan has seen before him the depths of Maeander between their familiar banks, or the spreading pools of quiet Cayster, he hurls himself headlong, his body gleaming, and all the while seems to his very self unfledged and slow until at last he can drink in triumph from their beloved waters—so did he cleave the winds and clouds. But when from his height he turns toward the plains of palmy Judaea, he sees our queen revolving in her breast no petty cares, and the ancient Sibyls in her hand, as was her custom, if from their holy hearts prophetic poets had sung any matters to be revealed thereafter in their descendants' era. You could see that her confi-
90 dent and happy soul was living in hope of its Creator; for she had understood that the time was drawing near when the Holy Spirit descended from the aethereal stars should fill the unspotted womb of some blessed Mother. Ah what reverence for high heaven appears in her maidenly face! She breathes a sigh, casting down her modest eyes, and honors the mother of the God who is to come, repeatedly calling her blessed and created free from subjection to mortal law, as yet unaware that the honor is her own.

Then of a sudden the youth sent down from heaven's height reveals his radiant countenance, and (in his dress and bearing manifesting his divinity) displays his mighty wings, and all through the house dif-
100 fuses an exotic odor. Then first these words: "Hail, Virgin Supreme, the destined light of our eyes, the sun long since familiar in our heaven, on whose just merit so many gifts, so many heavenly riches lavish themselves, all that flows forth of Good and Just from the eternal mind, all that purest Wisdom brings with her, descending to earth from highest heaven, and Grace abounding in full-flowing streams. Thee the Creator by his unalterable law has firmly consecrated to himself—the Creator who sets for the stars their eternal courses—and within your heart has established his abiding presence. Wherefore revered among the unspot-
110 ted bands, you alone are she whom untold choirs of angels will one day celebrate throughout the broad fields of heaven. Ah, how many joys will you bestow upon earth! how many prayers from mortal men will you undertake to assist."

The frightened virgin forthwith was stunned, she cast down her eyes, her every limb grew pale. Even so the barefoot maiden, her fortunate mother's freshest pride, intent on gathering shells along the rocky coast of Seriphos perhaps, or tiny Myco, if she sees a sailing ship approach the neighboring shore, she is afraid, and dares not now tuck up her skirts to make a safe retreat to her companions, but warily holds her

120 peace, suspended in a long, unwavering gaze. The ship (that is carrying
Arabian wares and the rich offerings of Canopus) intends no harm to
any men but with innocent tackle gleams upon the water.

Then spoke the swift-winged glittering messenger from heaven,
from whose breast flows smooth copiousness of speech and ambrosial
dews divine, by which he has power to calm the bitter tempest and drive
from the sea the angry winds: "Put away fear from your mind, Goddess:
you are to bear a Power revered in heaven, and through your blood bestow on earth a welcome joy and peace eternal, world without end. I
from my starry height am sent to you the messenger of these matters,
130 whose soaring wing has borne me along the rapid winds: I speak true
prophecy, unskilled to weave deceits, or treacheries. Deceit is banished
far distant from our realms. For you yourself, Virgin, will one day see
great changes throughout broad earth from this your progeny and
blessed birth. He will surpass his ancestors and extend their Law with
far-flung dominion; when he has called his people to his throne he will
govern mighty cities everywhere, and there will be no limit to his rule,
nor ending to his reign. But by degrees will arise in the souls of the just
the loveliest of religions, in whose holy temples without dire slaughter-
ings chaste altars will please not monsters, but true gods."

140   He had spoken. She, mastering her emotions in her quiet breast,
stood still and with placid countenance spoke thus, succinctly: "You tell
me then (heavenly creature) of conception, and a birth to follow? Do
you think that I can endure the embrace of man—I for whom, from the
very womb of my dear mother, virginity alone has been my constant and
unalterable vow? Nor is there reason why I should desire to repeal the
laws of my beloved chastity, or break that pledge."

"Not so (the messenger continues), but through your very ears—
what now you can scarcely imagine—the Spirit descending from fiery
heaven and the glittering stars will steal within the fertile womb and fill
150 your being with His mighty progeny. But you when you see your virgin
belly swollen will stand fear-struck: then at length, when fear has been
dispelled, you will enjoy delights unlooked-for, your chastity yet preserved. And lest you think these matters vain, or doubt them in your terror at my words, place before your eyes the gifts that were granted just
now to advanced old age. For a woman joined to you by your ancestral
blood (sterile though she be, and stooped with heavy age) is carrying at
this moment a child who was totally unforeseen, and all is well as she enters her sixth month. To such extent is nothing impossible to mighty
Heaven."

160   Upon these words, lifting her eyes to the stars and to the supernal
dwellings and golden mansions of the gods, our Queen nodded and
loosed these words from her breast: "Now have the mastery, faith: have

the mastery, my obedient will. Lo, here am I. Reverently I accept your commands, almighty Father, and your beloved Law. Nor is it in you, sky-dweller, to deceive. I acknowledge the hair, I acknowledge the face, and the hands and the words, and the winged scion of eternal Heaven."

When she had said this, of a sudden she sees the whole interior gleam with a strange light; behold, its shining filled the house. Then she felt fear the more, unable to bear the burning rays and sparkling flames. But her womb (marvelous to relate! things not unknown I sing), without forcing, without discredit of her modesty, began to swell with the arcane Word. A radiant Power, sent from on high, a Power almighty descends, a Power that floods all things, God Himself, very God—it gives of itself through all her limbs and intermingles with her womb, so that at once her vitals contracted at the touch. Nature is silent and fearful, as if stunned; and confused at this unprecedented revolution in Her affairs, She tries to seek out the hidden causes. But it is far other strength She feels, and a greater divinity. The earth is shaken; and on the left from an unclouded sky the Father whose power is over all gave voice in thunder, in witness of the advent of His Son, that far and wide it might be heard by all the peoples whom greatest Ocean encircles, and Tethys, and the hoarse-voiced Amphitrite.

Amid these thunderings of earth and heaven (while all was in alarm), the gorgeous winged messenger had made his departure, speeding on balanced wings, and was flying high up when the Virgin sees him alternating his shoulders through the lofty clouds and cleaving the vasty regions of the winds, and soon with multicolored plumage shining through the upper air and seeking out the dome of heaven. At length while she watched she pursued him with such speech as this: "Oh mighty winged one, high heaven's glory, who enter upon pathless ways and leave the clouds far behind, and fly before the winds: whether stars of good omen in their happy stations and the constellations revolving in their orbits are awaiting your return; or whether you are claimed by an established home of noble crystal, and the bright regions of the realm of glass; or whether chambers nearer the Supreme Thunderer are calling you, where lies the highest region of fiery Olympus, and you are nourished by love and the burning breeze from translucent flames: go, I pray thee, go and bear witness in defense of my chastity."

No more than this. But then she turns her vision downward and at once scans all the mountains with a careful eye, and considering many things she revolves in her mind her kinswoman and the child by her conceived, marvelling at the late-come honor of her womb.

Meanwhile Fame descends to the shades below and fills their pale dwellings with rumors that are true: that the long-awaited day is coming

when they may abandon gloomy Tartarus, fleeing from Acheron, its shadows vanquished, and from the savage howls and sinister growling of the three-headed dog[1] who lies ever-wakeful in his cave outside their prison,
210 dreadful with his triple-throated jaws, and fills the deep night with noise when he is pricked with hunger, and tries to bite the arriving shades. Then did the joyous Heroes and the souls of the just begin to lift their noble palms to heaven. And one of the Elders, famous for the sling, and skilled at the harp, and for his scepter renowned—while he goes wandering through the shadowy regions and binds with a chaplet his holy locks, while he is gathering withered flowers among the grasses of Lethe, where secret waters glide and the songless birds observe an eternal silence among the sterile branches—he conceived a sudden inspiration, and the divine spirit in his astonished mind: and rolling his eyes, filled with the familiar
220 power, he recounts the fated things that are drawing near:

[*The Song of David*]

Come to your hour of birth, o mighty Child, whom the Father has willed to loose our bonds and undergo such labors. O mighty Child, by whom these realms at last stand ready to be despoiled—realms enriched (alas!) by the ruin of so many wretched mortals—come to your hour of birth, if once from my heart's truth I promised mankind your coming, as the fiery heat that stole within my being kept driving me on, inspired by its heavenly power; if I have performed your rites and by my report have published your Law through all this wide world. See how blessed Peace is smiling upon you; and see how powerful kings from another
230 part of the world are hastening here, set on by heaven and driven by divine promptings. Hail, blessed Ethiopes, holy race of men, who have followed your star—it is right that you bring hither the gifts from your kingdoms. Receive them, Child; and you, most holy Mother, be of good cheer: peoples and their princes visit you even now from the farthest shores and the fragrant Nabatheans.

But that priest resplendent in his gilded vestment,[2] hoary and venerable in his ripe old age—what means he, that he places the Child before the sacred altar, in such wise worshipping, and gazing into the heavens with joyous countenance? And cries aloud that from this mo-
240 ment he is ready to close his eyes in a quiet death, since (filled with desire and for that reason staving off old age and Fate) he has been allowed to see by the rising of this sun the gift awaited through the ages, the peace long promised and sure salvation of the world.

---

[1] See Glossary, s.v. Cerberus.
[2] See Glossary, s.v. Simeon.

But what am I seeing (alas), houses bespattered with a cruel slaughter of infants, and rivers suddenly running with their blood? and what sad wailing is carried to my ears? Ah, it is criminal to murder the newborn. Cruel man, what are you doing? These have deserved nothing; and you will never be allowed to destroy with your mindless sword the child you are seeking. Now, mothers, now, while you can, take flight from that
250 wicked land, hiding your sons within your bosom, for the savage enemy is at hand. Haste now, royal Virgin, and carry your child to the land of Paraetonium (so the Father who rules the wide world is instructing you). There, Goddess, lies a safe home for you, and safe retreats.

But when with loving care you have lived through your Son's twelfth winter and twelfth summer, and many a problem, you will be bringing up from your heart's core deep lamentations, and assailing with unremitting prayer the glittering stars. For you will be frantically searching for your son, in vain (though often called through the city streets, often awaited for the pleasures of the daily meal) and you will
260 not see him seeking your cherished kisses, nor returning late at night. And three whole days will you bewail him in your grieving heart, and as many restless nights without the gift of sleep, searching everywhere, everywhere sounding your complaint, your hearts being stricken with cruel sorrow, both you and your aged husband. But at his fourth rising Lucifer (when he lifts his shining face from the tremulous sea) will bestow the one who is found, and bring him unbidden to those who are seeking him. O then what tears, what kisses then, what embraces (Mother) will you bestow, mingling your tears with your rejoicing! When with delight you will see your Son, seated before his Father's
270 shrines and altars, charming the old men with his speech and ravishing their spirits, while the whole congregation admires these marvelous first-fruits of a lad, no idle sign of a judicious heart and an intellect born to great things.

But why are you rushing to arms, you wicked soldiery? Why am I seeing helmets and soldiers' swords and their glittering array? and armed bands far off in the dark of night, and lances reflecting many a torch? Is it a single head that is sought by so many spears? Alas man's madness, alas his blinded mind, always ready for horrible acts of hatred! And now they have surrounded the olive trees and the sacred mount,
280 about and above, and blocked off the grove with their extended circle. Whither am I being carried? See, they are dragging the innocent away, his hands tied behind his back, he at whom just now they were struck dumb and astonished as he performed those miracles through their proud towns, openly teaching his Father's precepts, and they had no hesitation amid the applauding throng to proclaim him king and God, the guide of man's life and source of his salvation. Ah villainy! Do they

threaten even death, and cruel torture? They uncase their pitiless rods against his wounds, and set themselves to interweaving spiny brambles with Christ-thorn, a mode of torture; and then press down on his head
290 the lacerating crown. See how they ply him with steady strokes of the rod, and redouble their insults with savage tongue!

In another quarter I see huge palms torn up from their very roots, palm trees that reach to the stars—a piteous work, that from them may hang that light and ornament of all mankind! Ah wretched and boding ill for this shaken earth, when dying he will display to his heavenly Father his livid arms, his hair begrimed by black death, and his face; his eyes closed, and forehead wet with blood, and his side laid open with a gaping wound.

But his Mother—no longer a mother but a hapless image, un-
300 childed and weeping, a strengthless and weakened shadow—remains in tears before the cross, her eyes cast down, her hair dishevelled, and waters his breast with her sad wailing. And (if it is right that I utter all that is known) as she looks on the dying eyes of her unconscious son, she cries that Earth is cruel, the heavens are cruel; repeatedly she calls her own self cruel that she can look upon such wounds. Then filling every corner with her doleful wailing, thus she begins with sobbing speech— begins, and while she imprints her kisses on the unfeeling wood, ex- claims:

"Who, my son, who has enwrapped my wretched self, brought
310 down from such a height, in sudden storms? O son, my life's blood and your Father's vital force, whence comes this sudden savage tempest? What wave has snatched you from me? What hand has soiled with blood your innocent face? Who has been allowed so much against the gods? Who is intending impious war upon heaven? Unsheltered after my many toils, unhappy after the many troubles of my life thus far, do I see you like this? Are you, your mother's only sunshine, her peace of mind and her last hope and haven, are you thus snatched away? Are you leav- ing me thus lifeless and alone? O my sorrow! Sisters ere now have en- treated you for their dead brother, parents again and again for their chil-
320 dren. But I for my son, for you both Lord and God, whom (wretched woman!) shall I entreat? where turn my sorrowing heart? to whom shall I complain? Destroy me too, o cruel hands: strike me down instead (if there is any goodness in you) with your inhuman weapons; pour out on me all the malice of your heart.

"Or you, my son (if this be what mankind is worth), rescue the mother who is imploring you, and take her with you to the Stygian shades. I shall follow you through rugged lands, and realms intolerant of living creatures. Let it be granted me to watch you breaking down the gates of bronze, to dry with my maternal hand the destroyer of Erebus

330 wet with honest sweat." These lamentations and many more will she pour forth from her heart.

But as soon as the sun from his Eastern waves shall discover the crime, he will strive to turn backward his indignant team; and when he has vainly struggled with their reins, he will do what he can in the end, staining his golden locks with a lurid hue, and long will show to the earth a gloomy face that sheds no light, like one who still mourns his King and Maker dead. Yes, Cynthia too, made fearful by her brother's glooming countenance and by such state alarmed, will wrap her features in a dark veil, avert her eyes, and shed forth tears in vain. But Earth,
340 being shaken with a dread-resounding quake, will groan and mutter, and send forth specters roused from their shattered tombs. Why, ye noble spirits, why are you making ready to depart? This choice is not granted to all: few are allowed to revisit the light of day. But time is to come when the martial trump with its loud summons will shake the frame of heaven, and when all bodies everywhere through all the earth will suddenly arise.

For now, however, it is enough if the King break open the Tartarean tyrant's gates, and expose his shadowy courts: if, at the entrance of the light, the dread-faced Eumenides flee, their snakes hanging
350 down along their backs—they whom scarcely even Phlegethon's blasted grove can receive in her black mud and hide within her smoking sedge: if then many a pestilence and horrid monster seek out the depths of Dis: if the crowds of Briareuses be alarmed, the Cerastes, half-bestial Centaurs, gloomy Gorgons, Scyllas and Sphinxes, Chimaeras with flaming faces, and Hydras and Hounds, and terrorizing Harpies. Pluto himself will be led despairing in chains through Tartarus, while about him with sad murmuring grieve the rivers of Hell with broken horns.

But we, our temples bound with virgin laurel, shall lift our victorious standards high through Heaven's broad fields, following our leader
360 with a joyful noise: *Io the victor, Io the warrior, you bind the realms of the abyss, Erebus and his shades and fleeting powers, and govern Death beneath your sway.* Seated on a lofty chariot[1] he will loose the reins for his swift steeds, and manage with countenance serene his flying team, not descended from the seed of horny-hoofed horses, nor such as graze in their paddocks on ordinary herbage. For the first who bears the ivory yoke, supporting it with sinewy neck, is a bull, the guardian of the handsome herd, a bull starred with reddish hue, the horns of whose head are gilded, whose dewlaps bristle with golden hairs, and on whose hoofs cut gems shine forth new stars. The Bull's is a lowering visage, but there is none
370 other in heaven more fitting to begin the rainy season with his horns, or

[1] See Glossary, s.v. Quadriga Christi.

to challenge the stars with his loud bellowing. And yoked with him the terror of the woods and very king of the beasts, a lordly lion shines, whose shoulders are clothed with a flowing mane. The royal spirit waxes proud in his breast, not now that he should be savagely seeking struggle and death (his mouth is armed with teeth that mean no harm, and a gracious clemency smiles from his tranquil face)—but that he should be making his way through heaven and mounting to the lofty stars.

    After these comes the Queen of birds, with wings on her lovely limbs; the sacred feathers stand erect on her crest, and her head glitters 380 with a golden crown. Her own wings huge, like the huge thunderbolt she is borne above human dwellings, and mountains, and winged creatures, and assails the obstructive clouds encountered in her flight. The last who shares the task is a Youth with human face and winged back, whose golden cloak hangs down from his left shoulder, bedecked with Orient jewels. Interwoven in its purple a hundred kings variegate it in long array, an ancient race, and founding fathers of Jerusalem's people. Real faces can be recognized there: you would think the rivers and the mountains real, and true the golden Babylon shining in its lowest fringe.

    With such an equipage drawn through the starry heavens he will 390 arrive (bringing back his chariot hung with the spoils of the pallid kingdom) where the Milky Way opens out in a straight path and leads to the dwellings of shining Olympus.[1] There we shall marvel at the walls of the City of Gold, and the mansions decked with gold, and the roofs of precious stones, the pavements set with stars, and crystal rivers among lofty mountains. And there—whether we be allowed to dwell in the exalted inner courts of the mighty Thunderer, or in other dwellings, and under the roofs of lesser divinities—it shall be granted us to number the stars, and beneath our feet to view the rising and the setting sun, and to spend an eternity of days, prolonging our names through ages yet to come.

400

    When he had sung these things, the patriarchs standing thronged about received their prophetic poet with applause, and lifting him up from the river's embankment they bear him on their shoulders, and lead him rejoicing along untrodden ways. The dwellings of Erebus shook, and the gloomy gates of Dis. Sighing from the depths of her heart Megaera gives a groan, and gazes with vacant stare at her savage sisters. Then howling Cerberus tucked his black tail under his belly, and scared the shades of the sinners with his bawling. Black Cocytus shuddered within his stricken caves, and under the arms of Sisyphus the rolling 410 stones stuck fast.

[1] See Glossary, s.v. Galaxy.

BOOK TWO

Our queen, when she had felt those sudden motions in her inmost being and been blessed by the breath of majesty divine, arises without delay, being left in doubt at the departure of the winged messenger, and is intent on making her way in haste to the high hills far distant. That concern is the very first that occurs to her mind, to speak at once with the woman, weakened by age, whose womb had been unblessed—now (marvellous to relate!) in her unfruitful years grown fertile, and heavy with the weight of the sixth month—and to hear her speaking, and see with
10 her own eyes the pledge bestowed upon a sterile mother. Girt for the road therefore, she dresses heedless of preparations, not setting her heart on any ornament. Her veil covers her hair with its white scattering, as shines the star that makes the circuit of slow Arctos on a winter's night; or as Aurora rises in the morning, or the golden Sun when he is just come up out of Ocean. Wherever she steps the bountiful earth produces cinnamon there, and budding roses, and hyacinths no longer sad—crocus, narcissus, whatever the lovely spring breathes forth, whatever flowers nature disposes here and there among the grasses, commingling a variety of colors. Farther on, the running brooks stay their swift
20 currents; the hollow vales rejoice, and the low-lying hills; the pines surrounding her bow down their heads, and clusters of fruit break forth in the palmy groves. All things rejoice: Eurus and Notus grow still, fierce Boreas is stilled, while only the Zephyrs hold their sway over the flowering countryside, and blandish heaven with their warming breezes, greeting her passage with what voice is granted them.

As she arrives at the house, the aged wife of the righteous old man comes to meet her, with venerable countenance: and being that moment filled with the Spirit, and her womb disturbed with a sudden stirring, she clasps the new arrival in her embrace, and thus begins: "O woman,
30 our glory, the herald of our praise, who alone art found worthy to reconcile with Heaven the human race, and to lift up to the stars your fellow-women; thou whose womb is mantled by a blessed vine, that it may fill the earth with inexhaustible vintage: who among those above, who deems me worthy of such honor? And you, my Queen, have you come from afar to visit our humble dwelling? and are you here, most gracious

43

Mother of my King? Do you see how the child, being stirred within my womb, gave a leap just now, when the sound of your voice scarce first had struck my ears, doing reverence to his Lord as if he would be his herald? Blessed art thou, Virgin, blessed in thy spirit, whose faith alone
40 has granted you to deserve so much; for you will see fulfilled in you all that was told you by the winged and truthful messenger from mighty Olympus, descended on his secret course from the aethereal realm."

And she to this: "What voice is capable, Mother, of the marvellous deeds of the mighty Thunderer, to lift to Heaven their deserved praise? My heart rejoices with a pleasant movement toward the author of such works, who from his heaven has regarded me where I dwell in low estate, unworthy and unaspiring. For behold by his gift from hence forth I shall be called blessed by all generations, nor has my faith been vain, for he that is mighty has heaped me up gifts immeasurable with his im-
50 measurable hand, and holy is his name forever, whose mercy abounds that is spread abroad over all the earth, through which in every place at all times cherishing those who fear his commandments he never leaves them forsaken in any age.

"Therefore putting forth the might of his arm and the blazing of his hand, he has scattered afar their foolish rites and prideful minds, moreover he has cast them down: and putting down the mighty from their seats, he has brought them into great danger, and confined them to the abyss; and exalting those of low degree he has put them in their enemy's place, and banishing their poverty and hunger has filled with
60 his goods the needy and left those empty and naked who set no limit to piling up their wealth. Lastly his son (for he had no greater gift to give), his eternal Son, prior to all ages and equal with himself, the Father begot from the blood of his faithful servant (for this alone as yet was lacking from his multitude of praises), being not unmindful of his intention and his nature: for purposing this he had promised it long since to the faithful ancestors of our forefathers, and to the seed of their descendants."

The Virgin these. But the old man, who had lost the use of his voice, now does obeisance to the traveller's approach and to her virgin feet, kissing the earth they tread. Joyfully then he lifts both hands to
70 heaven, manifesting his pleasure as well as he can, with no more than a nod, and with his finger points out all those writings of the priests of old—things that each by the agency of God had once proclaimed when he was alive and left behind to be repeated by generations yet to come: such as rain shed forth from unseen clouds on a fleecy hide; as a budding sprung from the root of an ancient tree; as a bush unburnt in a crackling blaze, and from the ancient fathers a risen star.

While with grave countenance the virgin, aware of what is to be, reads over these matters again, in the depths of her heart she ponders

her strange conceiving, and the conception descended from Heaven in
80 the manner of rain, that being received on yielding fleece makes not a
sound or murmur. And she clearly recognizes and sees that she herself is
the bush and the branch and lastly the great star sent over the wide sea.
Yet she does not presume to speak these things, or to call herself worthy
of such a gift, but with a silent emotion she renders thanks to you, o
greatest of divinities, our Master, and lifts up her thought to the stars.

And now three times the moon had replenished her waning orb
with light, three times dark she had entered her wonted retreats, as is her
custom, when the Virgin prepares her return to her own village, since
she sees all is certain. The comforting speeches of her loving mother
90 come into her mind, and the house accustomed to sober conversation,
and the chamber that had heard the voice and the words of the messenger who had greeted her, and first received his winged flight—her chamber watched over by choirs of angels, and by heaven approved. So taking leave of her beloved kindred, she speeds the journey begun, and
retraces her way by the familiar landmarks. There is no delay, no resting
anywhere, nor does she turn her gaze aside (though surrounded by a
blessed band of angels) until she has arrived, a diligent traveller, at her
own dear threshold. And there (while she rehearses in her heart the joyful emotions now grown familiar to her) she sees approaching steadily
100 the time of her womb's full term. You may be sure that the might of
Divinity was a shield to her at this time: the Creator of the gods allows
her to feel no pain at all, nor in any respect to be wearied.

Meanwhile with peace established now on land and sea, Father
Augustus had closed up wicked war within the brazen portals and
bound it fettered with strong chains. And since as ruler he wished to
know about the wealth and strength of his powerful empire and about
its cities' exhaustion from civil strife, he issued orders that the whole
world be numbered, that the populace everywhere be written down,
110 and that there be brought to him a count of all the heads that the broad
earth sustains and Nereus encircles with his turbulent plain.

Therefore one law sets all in motion. They send in their names,
those who hold your mountains, Aurora, those realms of fertile Armenia,
who hold the valleys and towering cliffs of Niphates, a people widely
known for their painted quivers, a people not sluggish to ride their
boundaries, and with the bow to defend the fruitful plains where wandering Euphrates, where winding Araxes roll, and the spreading fields of fragrant amomum, granted them by God's gift. In every quarter Amanus's
native, Taurus's native is numbered; Cilicia's pirate, and he who tames the
120 fields of Isaurica, and your forests, Pamphylia; and he who breaks with the
curved plowshare the yellow earth of Lycia, and Lycaonia her fertile acres.

Then the Leleges, renowned in battle, and their neighboring regions execute the order: each tribe in its own way sends in its names. Those who defend Ceramus, and Gnidos lying between two seas, and the lofty walls where, ringed around with columns regularly disposed, the elaborate mass of the snow-white sepulcher lifts itself aloft,[1] which the barbarian queen erected for the husband taken from her. And the fields that are watered repeatedly by Maeander's wave in playful winding, then those that Cayster waters with his stream, while he feeds 130 the snowy swans on his grassy bank. And those that Pactolus encircles, flowing from caverns rich with ore, and Hermus no more sparing of his golden sands. The whole troop of Mysians, and Apollonian Celaenae, and Ida, and the Rhoetaean hills, and Pergamum celebrated by the Muses, and Sigeum's ridge, once Priam's realm famous for captains and their armies, now famous for the captains' graves—pointing to which the sailor says to his comrades, as he makes the passage of narrow Hellespont: "On this shore the weeping Nereids stood when with dishevelled hair the tearful Thetis was wont to make lament for her Achilles."

140 Bithynia adds her citizens to these, and Pontus's broad realm. Rocky Carambis complies; Halys is fervent, noble Sinope likewise is fervent with desire of complying; and Iris—which, swollen by boundless rivers from afar, divides the middle regions of the Cappadocians—the Thermodon and the Halybes, and the rocks worn smooth by Prometheus. Besides where the Thracians' martial land extends, and Rhodope runs into Haemus, bitter cold; where Axius in torrents rushes down over the cliffs of the Macedonians, and leafy banks overshadow Halyachmon. And where Pharsalia lies a reminder of grim war, and Philippi twice fatal with slaughter of Romans, the people vie in flocking 150 together, and obey the order.

You too joined to these your sons, you neighboring cities round about, with now deserted walls, anciently the cities of the Greeks, most excellent race, the moulder of our manners, famous for wits and daring deeds—whether you hold the mountains and the seaboard, or here and there rise up amid the waves. The coast of Epirus next, where the Acroceraunia, perilous to sailors, lift to high heaven their summits, presses on with the work. And now the palace of Alcinous yields its count, and the Illyrian bands, and the warlike Liburnians, and all the seashores beaten by the Ionian surge. Nor did you fail (o famous land, 160 whose warlike virtue and martial zeal has gained a far-flung dominion over land and sea) to number your families, o land unequalled for your arms and filled with triumphs, unequalled for your men, most powerful,

---

[1] See Glossary, s.v. Mausolus.

and heaven's rival, whom the cloud-capped Alps hedge in with their tortuous steeps, and father Apennine divides along your length, and twin seas thunder against with pounding surf.

These two (though not beneath a single sky) wrote down their native sons—on the one side Father Rhine, on the other Danube with his broader wave, who rolling through vast forest stretches never leaves off nourishing the people and gliding past the towns, until he has come with
170 swiftly flowing current to the long-anticipated isle of Peuce. Yes, and Gaul searches out her towering forests (Gaul made worthy of Latium through Caesar's triumphs), which Rhone, which Arar divides, which mighty Seine flows through, and Garonne washes with his fishy stream. Then Anas assembles the peoples that the rugged Pyrenees watch over, from their pine-forested cliffs clear to the pillars of Hercules; Duria, lovely along his either bank, assembles them, and Baetis fringed with the pale olive, and Tagus swirling golden sand beneath his waters, and Iberus who gives the land his name.[1]

On the other side, Africa summons her vast multitudes. The
180 chiefs of the Gaetulians and the Moors search out the groves of shady Atlas, and the huts scattered through his forests. Anyone met on the empty sands is written down too, whether shepherd or hunter girt with weapons, spying out savage lions in their desert haunts. Whoever inhabits the homes of the Massyli, whoever the secret groves of the Hesperides, and the fields walled in by mountains, shaking down from their branches their native gold; and the plowman who guides the bullocks that turn up huge slabs of stone where extended the citadels of defeated Carthage, whose fallen towers lie along that unlucky shore. What fear, what struggles that proud city made for Latium, and the
190 Laurentian fields! Now scarce preserving a relic here and there, scarcely her name, she lies buried, unrecognizable in her own ruins. And we, unhappy race, complain that human limbs decline with age, when it is clear that cities perish, and kingdoms.

Still the same zeal possesses the Macae; the Barcaeans came of their own will, from their fields the Nasamones came, who beside the shipwrecking Syrtes and all along those treacherous coasts are laden with the spoils of sorrowing men, and naked climb atop the towering dunes, turning another man's peril into their own plunder.

Lastly the Psylli, and those who inhabit the Garamantian fields
200 and with the plowshare turn Cyrene's soil and pick the fruits renowned for their surpassing flavor. And those by whom the palm groves of Jupiter are guarded,[2] and the secret haunts of the Asbiti, the spreading

[1] See Glossary, s.v. Ebro.
[2] See Glossary, s.v. Jupiter Ammon.

shores of Marmarica; the pastures of Egypt and of Meroe, flooded by holy Nile, Nilus who traces his origin from the aethereal heavens.

And likewise her aged protector went with the chaste Virgin, that he might duly record his name and his tribe in his native land, and not be sluggish in paying the tax decreed. Looking upon his former home and the fields once governed by his ancestors, he reviewed in order in his inner thoughts his royal lineage, and the famous deeds of its princes, 210 and from its beginning his noble family. And coming from afar he resolved to complete their number (although then poor, although unknown to those very kinsmen). Now having passed your borders, Galilee, and the deep vales of Carmel, and the fields which lofty Tabor shadows with his summit, and Samaria's plain dotted with palmy ridges, he had put behind him the heights of Jerusalem on his left, when from a little rise he saw ahead the walls and roofs of houses, and in that moment recognized the walls of his native land. At once he honors the town with welling tears, stretching forth his hands, and from the bottom of his heart he speaks:

220 "Ye towers of Bethlehem and kingdom not obscure of my forefathers, and Penates once great, all hail! And you, o city the mother of kings, who yet will see a King on whom the Sun and Earth's twin poles attend, all hail again! Jove's fabled cradle, Crete, will shudder at you, and fearfully put aside his worship: the walls of Thebes will tremble before you; and Ortygia herself be shamed to boast Latona's twins. These are small things I speak: suppliant, with her diadem brought low, will come that mistress of earth's realms and goods, illustrious Rome, bowing low her sevenfold hills to offer kisses." He spoke, and with his last words moved his steps. The old man quickens his pace and urges the 230 slow donkey, shaping his course to the shores that he has seen.

And now declining day was plunging into the western waves, leaving purple clouds and gold on the level sea. But behold, as they arrive they see before them, from the very threshold of the gate, a city filled with large numbers of people. A motley crowd, a huge throng, had run together from every quarter: you would think they had hasted there to purchase goods fetched from distant seas; or that fearful peasants were fleeing to safety from an enemy that was laying waste their fields. They could see that the winding ways and narrow passages all were filled with men and women in confused array: farmers intermingled with their flocks, some 240 hitching their wagons, some putting up curtains, others taking their meal in open doorways, every corner filled with noisy tumult, in various quarters the gleaming of lit fires. Marvelling at these things, while he surveys the particulars with quiet gaze, examining the doors and houses all around, and sees that there is no place left for shelter, the patriarch says: "We shall go where God and the holy oracles of our fathers are calling."

Beneath the walls of the little town is a cave, not large, whether formed by the hands of men or by the shaping spirit of mighty Nature, that it might offer these marvels to the earth and, long ago reserved against such uses, might receive divinity within its shelter. At its back lies a very large and rugged cliff, with overhanging rocks on every side and 250 broken stones surrounding its steep walls—a shelter not unwelcome for peasants who have finished their labors. When he had negotiated the tangle of the streets, hither at last with his blessed Consort her master came, being so advised through the guidance of God; and the old man repaired here in complete darkness. And first he kindles a fire from dry sticks and settles his companion on a bed of straw, spreading a robe over her weary limbs as she sleeps; then rubbing them down he ties up his animals, that follow him now willingly, not with reluctance now, as it chanced that there was a hay-loft there, supported by willow wickerwork, interwoven with palm withes.

260 *Now shall I tell of matters never heard in the caves of Castaly, or sung by the Muses' choir, or known to Phoebus: you hosts of heaven, show me the hidden paths through unfrequented places, show me (if I have so deserved) the haunts untrodden, now that I have arrived at the cradle and at Heaven's rejoicings, and the miraculous birth, and a roof resounding with a holy infant's cry. I am resolved to set foot where no tracks of earlier poets can be visible to our eyes.*

It was the hour when, drawn by slow-paced steeds, Night has not yet come to the mid point of spangled heaven and the stars are shining silently; when forest and town are still, when wearied from their work 270 the breasts of mortals welcome peaceful slumber. Not a beast, not a bird, not a snake with painted skin makes any sound. And now the last spark was stilled among the ashes, and his body being suffused with the late-night quiet the old man had laid down his head in the rocky cavern. When lo! a strange brilliance shines from on high, and where it comes it vanquishes every shadow of gloomy darkness. And choirs of angels are heard and heavenly bands, playing upon the curving lute and singing. The joyous Virgin recognized the sound and knew by no uncertain signs that the birth is near-approaching. At once she rises from the bed, reverently lifting her shining eyes to heaven, and speaking thus:

280 "Almighty Father, who rule the stars with your powerful command, and land and sea and the realms of air—is the time at hand when your Son shall show himself without spot in the clear light of day? when earth shall smile on me, and paint her meadows with fresh flowers? Lo, I return you the ripened fruits, the great gift entrusted: from your supreme height of heaven defend and care for me, lest any loss come to my upright modesty.

"Shall I then cradle you, dear Child, in my soft embrace with loving care as you nestle within my bosom, seeking the familiar breast?

Shall you smilingly give your mother tender kisses, twining your fingers
and childish arms about her neck, and finding there for your body wel-
290 come rest?"
    Thus she speaks, delighting in God and in the glittering array of
her attendants, and filling her soul with their heavenly harmonies. And
all the while for her the happy hour was drawing near whose star had
made its return.
    Who is whirling me away? Receive, Goddess—guide, Goddess, your poet.
I am borne aloft to the clouds on high: I see all heaven descending, aroused
with desire to observe. Grant that I may reveal the marvellous event, unsung,
uncommon, prodigious. Degenerate cares, begone, while holy things I sing.
    Joyous now about her labor, untouched by any fear, she stood
300 there, Queen of ages yet to come, with nothing in her heart of perishable things, thinking no mortal thought. About her stand the Father and
the Son and the Spirit that went in fire upon the dark waters, before the
Sun in heaven shone, before the Moon, and they calm her heart with
lofty meditations. Those things recur to her mind, moreover, that the
venerable priest had spoken: the months accomplished without weight,
and her chastity preserved. When forthwith from her unopened womb
(o night of joy for the angels, and for afflicted mortals!), even as was
written in the prophetic leaves, and supporting herself upon the resis-
tant straw, while heaven watches, while the stars all watch—she brought
310 forth her lading divine. As in the spring's mild warmth the star of morning silently sheds her dew, and rounded droplets sparkle everywhere
upon the grasses. The earth grows wet; the rustic traveller grows wet beneath his sprinkled cloak, and marvelling that he felt no touch of falling
rain treads the cool herbage with wet foot.
    Marvellous faith! Now had the child come forth into the heavenly
light of day; and laid without pillow on the rude straw he roused the
echoing cave with his first cries. His loving mother felt no disturbance
within her vitals, or any impact from the descending weight: her inner
organs remained steadfast, their walls unmoving. Not otherwise than
320 when glass panes receive the sun's bright rays: the light passes through
indeed, and flooding in dissolves all darkness, and dispels the shadows.
The glass itself remains unshattered, impervious to any wind or wet, but
for all that open to Phoebus's rays.
    Then the Mother wrapped the Child in a warm blanket, and when
she had taken him to her bosom and pressed him gently against her
breasts, she laid him in the manger. There the mild cattle warm him with
their breathing. O the hidden power in things! Straightway recognizing
his Lord the kneeling ox sinks to the ground, and without delay the ass
kneels too, bowing down his head, and makes his adoration with fearful
330 knee. Fortunate pair! That Cretan myth shall not be any stain to you, re-

tailing lies about that ancient theft, that you carried the Sidonian virgin over the midsea; nor yet shall drunken Cithaeron make the charge, while she is celebrating her monstrosities, that amid her infamous dances and liquorish rituals you sweated in the service of that wicked old man. For to you alone was it granted to recognize your god and Heaven's pledge, to you alone to watch by such a cradle. Therefore while Mother Earth shall stand, surrounded by the shifting sea; while the heavens shall turn with revolution swift; while in the temples of Rome the pious priest shall perform his rituals duly; your honors will al-
340 ways be spoken, your faithfulness always celebrated on my altars.

What then was your emotion, Mother, what pleasure in your blessed heart, when you see the mute attendants by your cradle and (bowing their knees to their mighty Lord) duly fulfilling his sacred rites, and drawing down Heaven, moved by the marvellous sight? O Father almighty, what consciousness has softened their rude senses? What fervor has roused such motions in their rough breasts, and made its way into the hearts of cattle? So that he who was rejected by so many cities and their rulers, by men whose sole charge it was to keep his altars and his rites, is welcomed now as master and creator by a slow-witted ox, a
350 sluggish ass?

Meanwhile the patriarch, awakened gradually by infant cries, had shaken off sleep and rubbed the dimness from his eyes, and now he sees the Child, and sees his Mother grown more commanding of aspect, and shining with a greater light, her face and eyes fixed motionless, raised from the ground, with a winged band of angels surrounding her.

Even as when she makes her way to our regions with brilliant wings the Phoenix glows, most radiant of birds, with a various band of winged creatures to accompany her journey. As she flies, her gold head challenges the sun for his native gold, and her resplendent tail is inter-
360 spersed with dots of roses. Her retinue is astounded, and through the clear sky an army of innumerable wings beats about her with resounding applause. The old man marvels at the strange light, he marvels at the angels' hymns of joy. Then, overcome and distraught, being stricken in spirit and unequal to such brilliance, he sank to the ground, burying his head in his folded arms; and remained a long time motionless, prostrated on the ground. The angels about him saw him lying there, the Holy Mother saw him, and did not suffer his old eyes to be long covered with shadows; she helps him to rise and support his trembling joints, and to proceed with wavering steps, and endure the faces of the
370 holy ones, and the brilliance of angelic fire, and their eyes that shoot forth heavenly flame. When by degrees he has recovered his strength and spirit, leaning on a knotty staff, first he greets in proper fashion the choiring bands, and their Queen. Then next approaching the manger

itself, and seeing laid on rushes from the marsh the Lord of land and sea (O reverence, o piety of mind!) he hesitates, not presuming to touch with his hand the infant limbs. Then drawing breath—the unlooked-for breath of one speaking with mouth divine—carried away with a sudden influx of divinity and inspired by God, thus finally he begins in a quiet voice, and fills his eyes with welling tears:

[*The Song of Joseph*]

380   "O child divine, no courts elaborate with Pharian columns, no fleeces variegated with Phrygian weave receive you (you lie with no gold to make you remarkable)—but see, your makeshift bed is barely provided by a narrow stable, a room scarce adequate, and by fragile reeds, and rushes plucked from the marsh. Let princes be received by fretted ceilings, and tapestries with royal ornament: your Father has made you rich, with the eternal honor of the angels. The golden mansion of starry heaven receives you with applause, and Nature is readying triumphs that will never fade.

390   "And yet this room will be sought out by kings, this cave by crowds of men from every quarter—some sent by sea-green Calpe from the distant Western shore, and from the swart Indians by the rising sun; and some by Boreas and burning Auster sent, contending between themselves from either pole. You our shepherd sent to call back your sheep wide-scattered through the fields, and to oppose your breast to dangers (ah too much prodigal of your life!) past weapons, past enemies, breaking in upon the shadowy wood—you will restrain the wolf's devouring maw, and to its fold return the full-fed flock.

400   "O my assured hope of heaven, o glory added unto Earth, born unto God, thyself God, o light from the Eternal Light—I myself, and your Mother, and these your joyous ministers, together we join in harmony about you, and are the first who sing your praises, proclaiming your long-enduring mysteries in our perpetual prayers."

BOOK THREE

Meanwhile the Father, the unassailable power over all, has ascended the golden dome of double-doored Olympus, treasuring the good tidings in his secret heart. Then he orders all the angels to be summoned to him—both those who pay service to his court from afar, and those who stand ready in his inner chambers, as well as those whom Aurora views on her rising in the East, and those whom Hesperus views, nigher the Western shore. For they say that of old when the King of the gods established his just laws, and hung the world on its mighty axis, he estab-
10 lished separate domains and separate lodgings for the angels, and assigned each order holdings befitting its merits. They inhabit the palaces assigned, and affix their arms and names on the brazen doors.

There can be no delay. Those commanded make haste. The whole host of angels flies throughout heaven, part all aglow with a wavering flame, part decked with starry crowns. Enthroned he settles about his gleaming shoulders a huge mantle, covering heaven and earth alike, which long ago (they say) Nature herself wove for her Thunderer, working night and day, and added marvellous ornament from her sacred loom, interweaving in its midst and on its outer fringes huge emeralds
20 and immortal gold. For there the wise Mother with skilled variety had depicted the world and its elements, with their conventional signs, both the outward appearance of things and their inner spirit, and all that the Father lavishes forth from the depths of his intellect. The formless dust, the beginnings of our race, could be seen there; one time you could see the birds with rapid wing borne through the fluid air; again you would think that beasts were roving the woods, the sea overflowing with fishes, and foaming with an actual wave. Here (when their glittering seats have received his winged bands) from his lofty throne the Father thus begins:
30   "Princes of heaven (for not unknown to you is the infamous attempt, and direful raging of embattled armies beyond the stars) if you please to consider with me those ancient broils from their beginning, and likewise call to mind your struggles now long past (since that victory has brought you praise)—turn hither your hearts, hither your minds grown calm. You, when all heaven blazed with slavish arms, and an impious

madness strove to ascend to the Northern pole and transfer the seat of power to the frozen Triones—you remained with me, a faithful band, and when at length you had tested their uttermost you bore your standards victorious through heaven and hung an eternal trophy on its lofty
40 citadel. I have bestowed on you a signal gift befitting the victory, and have received you as sharers in my sovereignty and in my works, and have held you in special regard, the chosen ministers for my commands—so far extends my unshakeable gratitude for that service past.

"And likewise have you often heard my lamentations and seen the fierce storms of my wrathful heart, when that original folly drove the new race to pluck the heavenly fruits of the golden-foliaged tree—fruits that were to grieve with bitter taste their latter-day descendants. Indeed, you drove them forth, unworthy the gift of the gods and the spreading shade of the sacred wood, and punished their wretchedness with un-
50 remitting labor and a shortened span of life.

"Why should I reiterate the sentence imposed for that ancient crime? the dread exile, and the deep shades of Erebus? These things along with me you have watched in silence, and you yourselves grieved in sorrow for Earth's bitter fate. Or why too should I tell how, after so long a time, Mercy at last has subdued the fierce anger of my heart? And how a secret power, descended imperceptibly through the gentle air, has filled the fertile womb of an untouched virgin? Do you think this done by caprice, or for no reason? Verily, thus have I seen fit to establish my enduring law, by which the heavens and the earth, man and angel alike,
60 shall abide in an eternal covenant, and by such pledge preserve a love that is mindful of their kindred origins.

"Come, therefore, and understand now man's fate. And first beneath the ragged rocks of a little cave, surround his bed of straw; surround his blessed room with its humble reeds; and all submissive make your approach to the new cradle, while the gentle Mother is warming her Son in her soft embrace, all through the night indulgently offering her milky breasts to the tender lips of the Child. Not far off on the straw with lowly hearts lie the mute cattle, and licking their Master's feet they keep their watch, while the flute pours forth its lengthy melody. Here
70 with your rapid flight through the empty air welcome the Child's auspicious birth, and his holy night, with praises resounding far and wide, and celebrate it with your applause, eagerly proclaiming blessed peace to all time yet to come, and the cradle of a world reborn, the serpent overcome and the serpent's deadly poison overcome. Such is my fixed decree, so to join to earth the alienated hosts of heaven, so to lift up mankind to the stars."

When he had said this, he inspires in the angels a new love, by which in a moment they may lay aside the ancient rancors in their

hearts, forgetful of sins; and following the Father's example be stirred
80 with concern for earthly things, and make mortal matters their care.
Without delay, he summons from among the angelic choirs
Joyfulness, who happens then to be at leisure—this angel tempers the
spirit and emotions of the mighty Thunderer, making serene his countenance, with every cloud dispelled—Joyfulness, who is always in waiting
about the dwellings of the heavenly host, a stranger who rarely seeks out
these lower regions; unmindful of cares, and a warrior-maid who finds
tears detestable, she roves free, and banishes grief from heaven's every
quarter. As she took her stand before the Father, and is ordered to visit
Earth, she adjusts the colorful wings on her nimble shoulders, and calls
90 up companions to cheer her on her journey. At once are gathered figures
joyous to behold: Song and Dance, and Rejoicing and Applause, and
Righteous Love burning with a chaste flame (whose progress is attended by two sisters like-minded in their admirable piety—by naked
Faith, and Hope that knows no sorrow). Then follow innocent
Pleasure, and Grace, and Harmony persuading to snow-white peace.
And when she approached the gate that in heaven is called the
Greatest, that radiantly gleams with the glittering signs of the eternal
stars (whereas the others shed clouds on hapless mortals and plague the
earth with fog), the ready Hours come up with hastening wings, the
100 wakeful Hours, for to these are entrusted the shining homes of the angels and the watch over mighty heaven. Straightway, bearing the weight
on their shoulders, they open the bronze portals by pushing back the
hinge with a noise and a mighty clamor that shakes the poles. Joyfulness
flies along the wind, shining through the dark of night. The stars rejoice
as she passes by; the Moon performs her festive dances. The Hyades
exult; Bootes rejoices for his wain transformed to gold, and with gold
his team of bullocks glittering. Then was Erigone seen to laugh, for the
first time since the death of her luckless father, and to put aside her ancient sorrow. And armed Orion sheathes his sword.
110 But when she set foot in the shadowy woods, she ascends to the
shepherds' rooftops and looking on every side with silent gaze she claps
her applausive wings; and while her colorful breast gleams through the
night, she smiled for joy and shone with undimmed radiance. The first
to sense her presence were the dogs; the young goats' mothers sensed
her as here and there they lay in their rude folds; the neighboring cliffs
and valleys echoed with bleating of sheep; and their masters lifted their
heads in astonishment. Then she says: "O guardians of your tiny flock,
o goodly men of the woods, a race dear to the gods, go now, blessed
shepherds, go deck the cave with fresh-plucked flowers. Now, even
120 now (be sure of it) the ruler of lofty Olympus is granting you to see
your Queen by the cradle, and your King laid in the straw. Make haste,

and bring your warming present of fresh milk, and give him honey stored within its cork; and with your reed accompany a song that is not familiar in the groves."

Saying no more she silently withdrew among the clouds and hid herself deep within night's ebon shade. They discuss it among themselves with various opinions—what the divine instructions might mean, what cradle, what king and queen they might be ordering them to seek, what cave to wreathe with branches. At once they bind their temples 130 with various sprays: the mastic is woven in, the wild strawberry taken from deep shade, rosemary and box and thick-fringed terebinth: and the whole troop is wreathed with a leafy crown. Next they seek through all the wood, lighting its remote ravines with flaming torches. From a distance you would think the fields afire and the whole mountain ablaze with light.

Worn out among the briar patches, they spy a cave beneath a hollow cliff, and hear the sound of a braying ass, and catch sight of him, and of an ox, and an old man, and the Mother standing watchful by the light, warming her Child in her arms' embrace. Thereupon swiftly, re- 140 joicing at this unexpected stroke of luck, they lift on their shoulders a full-grown laurel with spreading branches and a palm tree torn from the earth by its very roots; and singing at intervals, with applause and dancing and loud-resounding music, they stand them before the entrance and crown the whole place with foliage, fastening up great olive branches and leafy cedar, adorning the threshold with trailing garlands, and everywhere scattering Idalian myrtle with foxglove.

The good old man, coming forth from the cave, addresses them with friendly speech, and in his gentle voice he speaks these words: "Tell me, shepherds (for not without God, I warrant, have you held so 150 sure a course) for whom do you prepare such gifts? for whom are you weaving green shade with your leafy branches? or has some one of the angels, sent by the Father on high, instructed you of this dwelling, and told you to come to this place?" So speaking, he pleasantly greets his visitors.

And they: "Strange amid shadows (father), a strange semblance of light just now was seen shedding brightness in the midst of the woods, and diffusing joy into our minds. Whether a god come down from heaven, or perhaps a messenger from the gods, remains in doubt. We have seen the face and the dress of her who spoke, and have heard the 160 wings rustling in the night."

When they have said this, they clasp hands; then in a long line entering the cave they bring their rustic gifts in heaping baskets and as they enter they greet the Mother with joyous countenance. Then taking their stand before the Child are Lycidas and mighty Aegon—Aegon who has

170 a hundred pastures on the Gaetulian plains, a hundred flocks roving the fields of the Massyli; himself the principal man in many places, where Bagrada, where winding Triton wander, where roll the sands of the Cinyps; Aegon, a great man among the farmers, great among the shepherds: but Lycidas, scarce known in his own village, scarcely on the neighboring ridge, addressed his song to the waves of the sea. And yet these two, unequal in voice, unequal in their powers, amid the worshippers' dance and the angels' plaudits, attune their rustic song to the sevenfold reed:

[*The Song of Lycidas and Aegon*]

"It was for this, dear Child, that in his native grot our Tityrus rejected a rustic song for his polished reed, and sang woods worthy of a Roman consul. Now is come the last age of the Cumaean prophecy; the Magnus Annus[1] is reborn through its accomplished course. Clearly this is the Virgin, this is the reign of Saturn; this new birth has descended from heaven on high—a birth through which a golden race will arise 180 throughout the entire world, and the vine will flourish in mid-harvest. Under his rule the traces that yet remain of our sinfulness, being done away, will free the earth from her abiding fear, and the forbidden entrance to great Olympus will lie open. The serpent too shall perish who in the beginning, imbued with monstrous poisons, deceived our wretched parents. Are you to take on the life of the gods? and are you to see gods and heroes mingled, and yourself be seen by them? and are you to rule by your Father's virtues a world restored to peace? Behold the heavens, suffused with a joyous light, behold the fields and streams and the very grasses on the high hills—how all rejoice at the age that is to 190 come. Of themselves the goats will bring home their udders swollen with milk, and the herds will have no fear of the powerful lions, and the lamb will go in safety among the dangerous swords and twice-dyed will preserve the redness that overspreads it.

"Meanwhile these first gifts shall be yours, little Child, the ivy and ivy-berries intermingled. Your cradle will abound with lovely flowers and the durable oaks will drip down honey-dew. Oaks will yield honey: all Earth will bear all things. And after maturing age has made you man, and now your deeds are known through all the world, then will be another Tiphys, and another Argo to carry the chosen heroes: other wars 200 will be fought, and you will descend, a mighty Conqueror, upon the Stygian waves. Begin, dear Child, to acknowledge your mother with a smile, beloved Son of God, great scion of Heaven."

---

[1] See Glossary, s.v. Magnus Annus.

While such songs the shepherds sing, the pathless woods are echoing far away and the shaggy mountains toss their words to the stars. The very cliffs through their thickets, the very groves resound—"A god, he is a god, Menalcas." Here suddenly flights of angels are seen in the broad expanse of air, swift circlings and re-circlings swift; and voices are heard far off, and a sound of chariot wheels. In truth, a jubilant army was flying through the cloudless sky, with weapons that intend no harm:
210 troops in array were setting in motion a triple line of battle drawn up in threes, in semblance of war. Now might you see them piercing thrice the yielding clouds with their shields, thrice hurling their lances through the empty air, thrice shouting their leader's name; then rallying their scattered standards and presenting a single front with their joyous phalanx and traversing again the aery fields in military order; and others far off marching at a steady pace through the clouds and along the broad highways, and linking their arms in a chain, waving their wings with a perpetual motion and bearing in their hands the symbols of our salvation—the thorns, the nails, the scourges made of rough twigs, and the spear
220 that is to be fixed in his side, the cup flavored with gall, the cross erected and the cruel pillar. They went their way and soothed the air with their sweet singing.

Others are singing the Father's unbounded praises and his mighty works—how he laid the first foundations of the new world and divided the earth from the shifting waters; how throughout heaven he hung her various lights, both moon and stars; how he brought forth the light of the mighty sun when the shadows had fled from the farthest Orient.

[*The Song of the Angel Chorus*]

"O thou who art to be dreaded, you cast down the warring legions, you thrust them forth from heaven; you shatter with your thunderbolt their standards and their captain, and plunge them into gloomy
230 Avernus, decreeing that they dwell beside Cocytus and her melancholy waters. Thee the twin poles sang, thee the earth most mighty, and thee in thy victory Ocean sang with his immeasurable surge. Mankind's betrayals have not escaped you, nor his unspeakable crimes, but you look upon mortal affairs with countenance serene, and comfort with your divinity an earth deemed worthy. Hail, great architect of Heaven, most mighty king of the gods, salvation of the earth and of mankind, thou whom the stars fear and the sun, the monarchs of the nether world and mighty Tartarus, thou whom mankind everywhere serves, who alone art
240 ruler over all, and lovest all alike. Thine are a thousand names, a thousand princely honors, a thousand royal. Hail, creator; hail, lord of unbounded Olympus; abide in peace with us and with the fallen earth. Let

the clouds redouble our salutation and our voice be borne through the air to every quarter, and heaven's dome resound."

Then it came to pass that on his grassy couch in a wave-resounding cavern Jordan, the sea-blue king, the source of cooling waters, was revolving in his secret heart the things that were fated yet to come. With radiant
250 visages were gathered about him an attendant troop, his daughters:[1] loveliest Glauce, Doto, Proto, Galena and Lamprothoe, their shoulders bare, the garments falling ungirdled from their naked breasts; Callirhoe, Bryos, Pherusa, Dynamene, and Asphaltis whose custom is to float on the buoyant waves; and Anthis bedewed with fragrant liquids, Anthis, than whom is none more skilled in arranging fresh flowers or in adorning her head with colorful garlands; then Hyale and Thoe and Crene with radiant features, Gongiste, Rhoe and fair Limnoria, and Dryope and Botane, her abundant locks flowing unbound. All lovely in feature, all in white garments, all with their ankles bound in crimson sandals.
260 Reclining against an overset urn in the midst of his cavern, he pours forth his waters. Adorned with strange designs, the urn is a glittering thing, shining and transparent, being made of crystal and unclouded glass, a splendid ornament and a marvellous gift from the gods. Here a wood was flourishing, with shadowy foliage and trees thick-set. All through it the stags and fugitive roes were seeking a midsummer coolness in the green shade. In the middle a river, its golden waters shining, was wandering through a meadow, and by its course dividing the fertile fields. There a youth, his body clad in tawny skins and standing on a jutting rock, was washing the king and lord of the gods in the
270 swirling waters in midstream. But on the green bank his chosen attendants await him, their garments tucked up decently; and with their hands reached out over the water they offer snow-white garments, heavenly linens. The Father himself from an unclouded heaven was sending far and wide his manifest signs, and dispatching to his Son through the empty air a swift dove, resplendent with radiance and a coruscating fire. Around him the astonished Nymphs are worshipping his divinity and the river is calling back to their source his fleeing waters.
While Father Jordan, ignorant of the Fates, is examining such things on the graven urn, and marvelling turns his eyes to exact details,
280 he sees an unusual volume of water burst forth to flood his spacious dwelling, and his hollow cave filled full of waves, and the water taking on a strange savor. And while he hesitates and at the same time fears, as he raises from the waves his mossy head, and the horns on his bull-like

---

[1] See Glossary, s.v. Hyale.

countenance, he sees the riverbank everywhere flowering in strange fashion, and running through the dense forest the brilliant light that puzzled the shepherds; and he hears the joyful singing rising to the stars and the heavenly voices, and divinities on every side bearing witness to the advent of God. Straightway he joyfully raised both hands to heaven, with these words:

[*The Song of Jordan*]

290   "O creator of sea and land, of gods and men, what bold spirit has brought hither from high heaven your inscrutable decree and buries it amid my waters? These things once (I remember) the sea-blue Proteus was wont to tell me while often he discussed such matters with me and gladly returned to them. Though Proteus were in other things a liar, yet in this prophecy he uttered no vain speech.

"Jordan (he said) there will come to you as the years go rolling on, there will come one, believe me (Heaven has given most certain indications, and its oracles are not deceiving me), who some day will extend your fame beyond the sources of sevenfold Nile, beyond Indus and
300   Ganges and the fountainhead of Ister with his double name; who will place you above the Tiber and the Po, and make your honors equal with the stars. Everywhere at his coming grievous diseases will begin to depart from men's bodies. The cruel scabies will yield forthwith, and abate its ugly scales and spots; and leprosy spread into deformed limbs will check the running sores in its bloody putrefaction. Yes, deadly fevers (marvellous to tell!) will flee when commanded, relinquishing the limbs that they possessed. And the wrath more violent than outraged Diana's will give way—the deadly wrath that lays bodies groaning on the ground, as if stricken by the ruinous thunderbolt, and one time with fire
310   and another time with water hastens to destroy (o piteous sight!). For armed with its Stygian poison it gains the mastery, and spurts from the mouth the swelling foam. And now no more as prolonged old age diminishes their vigor will infectious dropsy, stealthily creeping to the destruction of wretched men, make its way unopposed through their secret parts, destroying their organs swollen with various pains. Likewise repeatedly tongues that have been bound will break their silence; or eyes that have never seen the stars, never seen the blazing lamp of the mighty sun, will shake off time and again their night and their former shadows.

"I might indeed tell you many things, too much for belief, but
320   true, such as might hold fixed the very eyes of those who see them—but I hasten on. The coming age will stand amazed. It will see that the halt, who always dragged their ailing joints along, will suddenly rise and walk, their trembling gait made firm. Then limbs long tottering, with

ruined sinews (who could believe it, save that my Apollo sings me the truth?) made whole again, and acquiring strong vigor in robust health. And he who is ordered to take up his bed and arise will start up without delay and making his way to the temple with quickened pace will carry the burden himself on his own shoulders. There a loud clamor will begin, and around the sanctuary innumerable voices of people who saw

330 it and felt fear at the novelty of the thing. Another time you will see an arm completely withered and lacking all sensation brought back forthwith to its former powers. Moreover, a woman's issue of blood being checked by touching his garment; and bloodless limbs and pallid faces promptly glowing again, made warm where once the veins were obstructed. Yes, even the Furies, the dread Furies of Erebus, driven down to Tartarus: then relief brought to weary hearts and limbs racked with excruciating pains. Thereafter the empty air on every side filled with the cries of the Furies vainly lamenting, and quivering beneath the savage lash, and seeking to escape within the hollow clouds. I see life after

340 death restored to corpses already mourned; already the grieving procession is begun and the funereal trumpet goes before; then the mothers' unexpected joy and the fathers' weeping grown joyous, reversing the natural order, and the city crowded with a rejoicing populace.

"How often you will see the nodding mountains rise in reverence before him and (marvelous!) in strange wise their forests bow their tops. How often your custom will be to soothe him with your gentle murmurings as either he finds relief from summer's heat on your cool and grassy bank or takes soft slumber to his breast. All hail deservedly to your banks, hail to all your waters! To you the divinities will make haste

350 with the offered sacrifice; they will strip bare their sacred limbs and sing their harmonious songs when you will have the good fortune soon to receive in your holy water, divested of his garments, the Creator of things and Father of gods and men (such honor, such praise for your stream, o greatest king); and astonished at such a guest you will call to your solicitous Napaeans:

"Go now, make haste, my sea-blue followers; set out incense for burning on the pious altars: make ready the benches with green moss and hang up garlands on the crystal pillars. Blend together the purpling rose, blend hyacinth and lily and cover your king with a cloud of loveliness.

360 "Then will the high hills lift to the sky the name of Jordan, famous everywhere: Jordan the mighty plains of ocean, Jordan the streams and forests will resound. But that day (though it will be bringing aid, and an end to mankind's ruin, though its coming should be most welcome to the cities, and desired through all the world), yet for the rivers and for my ocean waves—if there be any credibility, any foreseeing of the truth in Proteus—more happily will display its rosy beginnings to the laughing

stars. For he, the power and glory of his Father, will seek not riches, not honors, after he has of his own free will taken on mortal limbs and perishable flesh: he will not invade the dominion of Cyrus, nor ravage the
370 Caspian realms: he will not destroy proud Babylon for her spoils, or mount the Capitol in his lofty chariot, with his soldiers about him and the cheering senate in his train. But scouring the stretches of the wave-resounding sea and the length of the curving shore, he will seek out his followers along the beaches; and will call to his Father's throne, and to his mansions, sailors scattered over the sea and naked fishermen, preparing to cast on the waters their billowing nets, or diligently mending their damaged gear. And upon them he will confer all his rights and healing power; they shall drive out diseases and blunt the viper's tooth; and the legions of Hell and her monsters shall flee before them.

380   "Yes, and he shall set them as guardians before the entrance of shining Olympus and command them to keep the approaches and the walls of gold. Whom the savage strength of the Eumenides shall have no power to harm, or the dead's harsh gates obstruct. Then he shall create thrones for his servants dispersed among twelve stars: the separated band shall duly follow their leader. They shall give laws and divine judgment to those who are called, with their comrades' applause and in a joyous company. Blest souls, who putting aside now skiff and oars will ascend to the lofty dome of the unclouded day.

    "Moreover (if our faith is to be certain, and not vain our joy) we
390 shall see what we know to be water turned into Bacchic draughts. These first mysteries, these first marks of recognition the king of the gods will manifest as signs of the authority he has received. Pure water will marvel at its augmentation, being made to foam as never before above the brim of the capacious bowls, and lavishly to pour forth a strange nectar, and to cheer the feast and the joyous marriage rites.

    "More than once, being rowed out onto the open sea, when he shall find that his comrades are returned after fruitless labor, he will enrich them with a huge catch, and will set out dripping piles of fish on the strewn seaweed. Moreover (rebuking them by his authority) he will re-
400 press the angry waves and raging winds that stir up swirling sand from the very bottom, and even now threaten to sink the ship in the encroaching sea. The waves' bold onslaught will slacken and you would think that the Euruses and Zephyrs, and Coruses exulting in the storm, had hearkened to his threatening commands.

    "What shall I say of how with two fishes he will feed a numerous company, and with a scant measure of grain a multitude of the poor—men and women alike scattered over the grass—so that the broken pieces fill twelve baskets? or how walking upon the deep on a stormy night he will plant his steps freely on the sea beneath him, and dry-shod

410 scarcely touch the waves? The lovely Nereids will swim beside him, everywhere the waters will grow calm. Then frightened Neptune from his lowest depth will acknowledge his Master and laying his trident aside will hasten with Phorcus and Glaucus and that half-bestial crew, anxiously offering to kiss his sacred feet.

"But why should I continue to record it all, being carried onto deep waters in my narrow shell? Not if the Muses should open to me their Parnassian caves and sacred avenues and their golden homes, could I suffice. Not if a hundred iron mouths should speak for me, and a hundred tongues froth forth in words from a brazen throat the Phoebus 420 that is agitating my breast, would I have strength to number over the famous deeds of the prince who is to come, and to treat their particulars in my further song."

"These matters once (when he by chance had stopped within my cave) old Proteus then foretold, prophesying from a joyous heart. Now it remains to await the signs of the coming event.

"But a brighter gleam has begun to shine from the roseate east, and rising Aurora (a scout sent forth ahead of morning's rays) is lifting herself aloft on the furthest edge of Ocean, and clad in scarlet robes in 430 advance of day is urging her golden-maned team against the bit. And now it is time for me to run my course, rolling within my accustomed banks and cutting with my current the fields and spreading pools. Do you not see how the impulse is moving my stream, and a murmur of swelling waters is calling Jordan?"

When he had spoken thus, he hastily gathers round his shoulders the special robes that the lovely Naiads wove for him in their moist caverns, spinning the thread from the pliant moss. And steeping the unfinished web in Sidonian dye, they embroidered golden stars scattered on its hem. And thus arrayed, with foaming splash he returned to its flow- 440 ing bosom and mingled with the spray his shifting waters.

Thus far, ye powers divine, let it suffice to have made my attempt on the holy nativity. Lovely Posilipo is calling me to her pleasant shade, Neptune's shores are calling me, and the dripping Tritons, and ancient Nereus, Panope, Ephyre and Melite, and (she who specially supplies my welcome leisure, and deep retreats for the Muses among her rocks) Mergellina, whose orange trees pour forth profusion of strange blossoms — orange trees whispering tales of the Persians' holy groves — and who from no ordinary leaf weaves me my crown.

A
LAMENTATION
ON THE
DEATH OF
CHRIST

Introductory Note

The *Lamentatio* appeared in *Pia et Emuncta Opuscula,* printed in Paris in 1513, ultimately through the agency of Fausto Andrelini, who presumably acquired a copy of the poem (along with some religious poetry by Pontano) during Sannazaro's visit to Andrelini in Paris, in 1504 conjecturally (for details, see Carlo Vecce, *Sannazaro in Francia,* pp. 46 ff.). 1513 is much the earliest date for any printed version of Sannazaro's Latin poetry, and it seems unlikely that in 1504 he had any intention of releasing the poem to Andrelini for publication. Other piracies of his work—whether in Latin or Italian—met with Sannazaro's vitriolic scorn. Quite possibly he never heard of this example.

The poem itself is an undistinguished performance, and one is tempted to think that its genesis lay as much in therapy as in poetic inspiration, assuming (as I do) that W. J. Kennedy is right in dating its composition "probably in 1502" (*Uses of Pastoral,* p. 180).

A LAMENTATION

Addressed to Mortal Men
On the Death of Christ Our Lord

 If you have any belief that there was One who established the Law that the mighty sun should rise from awesome Ocean and spread his burning rays through all the sky, and that in rivalry night-wandering Phoebe girdled with her golden horns should orbit the earth in her course, and that the stars' eternal fires and the glittering heavens should dazzle our eyes, and that the Father of men and things rules from the sky, whom sea, whom earth, whom the burning air obey, who by his nod governs all things: Look upon him now, you wretched mortals (if sorrow gains entrance to your hearts), his breast transfixed with the unyielding steel, his breast and hands defiled and his mouth oozing blood, and his head bloodied and locks torn: see him, and pour out plenteous streams of tears.

Alas the crime! alas the cruel impiety! the noble ruler of Olympus lies dead and the elements lifeless in our fallen leader. Yes, and empty heaven vacillates without the accustomed weight and the golden thrones are searching for their king, whose pitiable body and head unrecognized by his subjects is held by an earth far off, alienated by a savage crime, his bloodless limbs enclosed in her embrace, as quaking she mutters her heavy plaints. Lurking now within a cloud the sun bears witness of his sorrow, marking his brow with livid gloom. You too, o Moon, cover the sunken cheeks and pallid features, and give the last rites to your Thunderer, shaving the golden hair from your yellow crown and pouring forth warm tears in the humid night. And likewise it is reported that ghosts came forth from their opened graves and in strange shapes wandered through the streets, and disturbed spirits howled through the night in the city's midst and filled with their wailing the households they had known.

What then? has not the raging sea been seen to pile up dreadful waves and roll up mountains of water as if to cast down cities and swallow the land within the ocean deep? At which sea-blue Triton lifting his head from his wave-resounding caverns blew with his hoarse trumpet across the waters and with dread voice gave warning to sailors that Nature's Father, King, and God was dead. Did not these hands establish the working laws of this vast world? Was it not their work, whatever moves, whatever lies still, whatever is anywhere governed by Nature, Mother of all things—the fruitful earth, the sea aswarm with living creatures, the vital atmosphere and upper air with shining flames?

And now (ah villainy! how much sinners can do!) his wounds give passage to the driven nails and soil his pallid limbs with dismal filth. Alas that head, all undeserving its thorns, deserving to be revered in heaven, and repeatedly crowned in imperial triumphs with a brilliant crown of stars: alas that gaping breast, that beard plucked by a cruel hand, those bruised joints and cold limbs. And you, the feet that were wont to tread the sky and the wandering stars and the glittering homes of the gods, mansions sublime, did you spatter with your blood the earth and the unyielding stones, again and again enduring the cruel strokes of the savage spear?

Is not man's blind mentality disturbed? what hardness so extreme stands stiff in his stubborn heart? do you not see the gloomy realms of Tartarus deprived of so many trophies from mankind, and her mansions left abandoned in the night, and her domain left sorrowing? And the souls of the blest following behind their king, and singing a joyous paean as they enter upon their seats in the serenity of Heaven? What if he had not willingly undergone such labors, and purchased with his death mankind's salvation, that creator of all things and unshakeable mind of our Father on high, who with his nod controls the mighty reins of this world? So that in the end, untouched from the pitch-black waters of Phlegethon, he gave you the gift of eternal life after death and summoned you to a share of his works and his kingdom: so much is his love and glory for our race that is to be saved.

So come now, mortal men, if anything be yet left of that ancient stain, expel it from your hearts and drive away at last from the profaned altars the lying gods and detestable rites of the ancients. Let not the ox drench the ground with his blood poured forth nor the poor lamb of sacrifice, torn from his mother's udder, bleat beneath the insensate knife. Let the sheep live: let all things live that have been created under the sun. Prepare unto God your mind and heart, not incense or entrails. Offer him these gifts, these entrails of cattle—do you see how he turns away his bowed head? how he extends his pitying arms and summons the graceless nations to his wounds? and warns them to be mindful of what they have forgotten of the road abandoned—for surely he will not reject their friendly embraces? But in your ignorance, unfortunate race, you avert your dull ears and do not see the antic dance of savage death, and how many torments even now are hovering at your back.

The time will come when you will see him recording the deeds you have done and pronouncing punishments on the wicked, en-throned on a lofty cloud: and a trembling will oppress your quaking limbs. And none of you, conscious of your natures, will dare then to en-dure his shining eyes in the ardor of their flames or to contend against his features swollen with wrath. The guilty troop will depart into the flames and will pay with their bodies the punishments of their guilt, to inhabit forever the pale rivers and spreading pools of Cocytus and trem-ble before the gaping Furies; and they will rue it that they did not give heed to his warnings. Then will you understand the hateful sins of the life you have led, being cast out of heaven and into the utter darkness of space; and vainly will you desire the triple-forked flame upon your head and vainly hold up to heaven your out-stretched palms. The bands of an-gels and blessed troops of the righteous will scarcely be able to restrain their tears when they see you driven beneath the lashes of Envy and the avenging Furies.

Therefore, ye wretched, while yet you breathe the living air, while your minds are sound, while capable faculties, while time and reason permit, go ye all together: proceed in piety, ask pardon for your actions, go purge your souls: frustrate the savageries of Orcus and in the end convert your mind to heaven which is your home.

Thus that king of men, despoiler of empty Avernus, forgetful of your sins, moved by love for a kindred race, mindful of his promises, will enter into your reconciled souls, and your heart strings will do him worship in your neglected temples. And after the many exhaustions of life and sufferings of death, with that countenance that drives away the rains, that banishes the clouds, he will receive you cleansed of sin and place you in joy among the starry princes, and in his sacred senate, and will grant you to see beneath your feet the gleaming walls of Heaven.

THE
PISCATORIAL
ECLOGUES

Introductory Note

The common consensus of readers rightly regards these poems as Sannazaro's finest Latin poetry, apart from *De Partu Virginis*. The translation here is based on that in my *Arcadia & Piscatorial Eclogues* (Detroit, 1966), with numerous minor revisions throughout. The eclogues are left without introductory notes, which seemed to me less needed for these poems than for the elegies. Some readers may be able to consult through university libraries the extensive annotations in Sannazaro's *Piscatorial Eclogues*, ed. W. P. Mustard (Baltimore, 1914). Moreover, Professor Kennedy supplies an extended discussion of Sannazaro's methods of adapting these poems to their primary model, the eclogues of Virgil (*Uses of Pastoral*, pp. 149–80).

ECLOGUE 1 Phyllis

Lycidas

 I marvelled, Mycon—as recently I went drifting along the neighboring shores, waiting for the swift tunnies to begin their feeding—for what reason the raven should be calling after me more than his wont, and why the dripping wildfowl, huddled everywhere along the cliffs and in the caves, were filling the gloomy rocks with their mournful cries, while the arching dolphin no longer rolled out of the sea nor led his dance through the waves as is his custom. Behold, the day was at hand when we resigned to earth our beloved Phyllis, and wept her departed spirit over her grave—ah wretched men; and we do not after this abandon our sad lives, nor rude Pylemon hesitate to bring us solacings.

Mycon

Surely that was the reason that all night long—while I was coasting the whole side of Posilipo, and rounding fishy Nesis in my speedy craft, wandering here and there—the plaintive divedappers were wailing I know not what mournful cry. Phyllis was calling them to her rites, Phyllis (if we may believe it) was calling them to lamentation, Lycidas, and to the ceremonies of her tomb.

73

Lycidas

Alas, dear Mycon, what scenes of solemn ritual (I see them in memory now), what hands and what features have I noted with these eyes; with these eyes, I say, what funeral rites have I seen, to my misfortune; yet my violent sorrow drove me not onto the reefs, onto the rocks, nor did the force of the flames consume me in the same funeral pyre, nor any divinity drown me in the sea.

Mycon

O Lycidas, Lycidas, do you not think that this has turned out better for her than if she had gone into Lycotas's smoky cave or under the blanket of shaggy Amyntas, and even now (alas!) were angling for her meager fare, or patching torn weels with the pliant osier?

But you—if you have anything that may lament those fires of old, that may bear witness to her shade and long-loved ashes—begin, for now the beach spreads forth her level sands, and the raging waves have stilled their murmurous noise.

Lycidas

Rather shall I begin these hurried verses which only recently I was fashioning for her ashes, when I was surveying the curving shoreline from the harbor's end, and paying my reverence to the stones of her snow-white sepulcher. You strew on the tomb your cypress boughs with their cones, and cover the grave mound over with green myrtle.

Mycon

Behold, we bring you mosses from the dark blue sea, behold for you the purpled conchs, and coral clusters searched out in every deep and from the bottom-most rocks scarce wrenched away; now begin the song that is her due. Begin, while Baian Milcon lays out his nets to the sun, and coils in a circle his dripping lines.

Lycidas

What reefs now, Goddesses, what caves, daughters of Nereus, do you reveal to me? What herbs, father Glaucus, from a hidden shore, what grasses now with magic juices, Glaucus, will you display to me, through which (ah, wretch!) having left the land behind, and made a new inhabitant of the shifting sea, with transformed body I shall follow you in the mid-most waves and beat the foaming surface with forked tail.

For why should I, alas, in my wretchedness desire a life without Phyllis in these lonely regions? or what could I consider sweet when my light is taken away? what can I hope for here? why should I, hapless creature, delay any longer? perhaps that cast down prone on this vile kelp I may spy out the withered shrubs and desolate shores, wasting my words on an unresponsive tomb? Am I to celebrate these marriage rites, these happy hymeneals? Is it thus that Venus gives me the joys of the marriage I longed for? Thus does Lucina offer ambiguous fears?

Who took you from me, who stole you away, O sweetest Phyllis, O Phyllis once the comfort and only hope of my life, now the sorrow and endless grief of my inmost heart? It was not granted that I share with you my pleasant nights, nor that I enjoy the sweet gifts of our early youth or that we live our life together unto the final years. Now you (who can believe it?) are held by this stone and are to me no more; nowhere on earth is Phyllis, but shadows and fables mock my nights, made wretched by dreadful dreams.

Wretched as I am, where shall I seek you out at last, where follow you? For your sake once the land was pleasing to me and crowds and cheerful cities with their walls; now my pleasure is to wander the borders of the vasty deep and to roam freely over the stormy waves mingled with crowds of Tritons and amid the monsters of the rocks and rude-shaped seals with fearful forms, where I can never see land. Now, now farewell that land where I lived so many years, and the people and the towns, ye happy shores farewell; likewise kindest Phyllis fare ye well. Seven altars for you will we raise beside the wet sea-waves, and seven rough sea calves, deep-water monsters, will we sacrifice to you in yearly ritual, and oysters will hang for you in sevenfold wreaths, oysters varied with shells and white pebbles. Here for you Nisaea and Cymodoce with yellow hair unbound and gentle Palaemon with his virtuous mother and Panope and Galatea, protectress of the Sicilian deep, will weave their ritual dance and sing the songs that Proteus the seer once taught them, being divinely inspired, when he bewailed the death of great Achilles and comforted Thetis's bitter lamentations.

But you, whether you in felicity dwell in the high Aether, or now among the Elysian shades and venerable bands pursue the fishes through the liquescent streams of Lethe, or whether you pluck unwithering flowers with your lovely hand, narcissus and crocus and immortal amaranth, and blend the delicate seaweed with pale violets, look down on us and gently come to us; you shall be ever the godhead of the waters, ever a happy sign to fishermen. As to the Nymphs and to Nereus, and golden-haired Amphitrite, so to you the triumphant fishing boats will pour out their libations. Meanwhile receive for your tomb this final song, a song that while he ties the line to the slender rod, the fisherman may read, and utter a sigh from the lofty cliff:

PHYLLIS LIES IN THE BOSOM OF

THE BELOVED SIREN.

SWELL GENTLY, SEBETO, AROUND
THE DOUBLE TOMB.

Mycon

Sweet are the sounds of your singing, Lycidas; not rather would I hear the laments of the kingfishers or the sweet complaints of swans on the wet grass of the bank beside the stream. But you (so may neighboring Megaria always supply you readily with conchs, so may adjoining Mergellina yield to you oysters and sea-urchins from her rocky cliff), since night as yet withholds her glooming shades and the Sun has not yet fully traversed the sky, begin again and repeat your song to me; things repeated have savor.

Lycidas

Do not, Mycon, do not urge a wretched man; enough my eyes, enough already my pallid cheeks have rained down; sorrow (behold!) has stopped my dry throat and shaken with sighs my inmost breast, and my feeble voice abandons my gasping breath.

Yet these and many others as well shall I sing for you, and better perhaps, if the Muse will be with me as I sing. These too I shall some day inscribe to be seen by the sailing ships, whether at Procida or under the spreading cliff of Miseno, and shall trace in rust great letters which the passing sailor will scan from the open sea and say: "Lycidas, Lycidas made these songs."

But since your joyful comrades await you everywhere along the shore, and ask for your strength at the nets, come now, let us rise. I shall remain by this tomb; you pay your comrades a visit, for it is time to seek out your meal and now your empty weels are floating weightless.

ECLOGUE 2 Galatea

 It chanced that the weary fisherman Lycon had settled himself in an empty cave where from the clifftop loveliest Mergellina presents herself to view over the broad sea. And while with their fires nearby the others are lighting the familiar bays and fishy flats, or far away are drawing to shore the linen nets and their captive fishes, he is fashioning his song in the dark of night:

"Unrelenting Galatea, have then my gifts in no way moved you, in no way my pleadings? I have poured out to the winds my useless words, and driven against the cliffs my unavailing waves. Behold, all things are silent, sleep holds the orcs and the mighty whales, the seals are stretched out silent on the shores. The breath of Zephyrus makes no sound, its drowsiness makes mild the watery plains, the stars are winking in the slumbering sky. I alone (ah wretch!) while through the night I tell over my plaints in my sorrowful heart—I have utterly driven sleep from my thoughts. And yet no concern for my health touches you. Not so once did Praxinoe despise me, nor the daughter of Polybotas, nor the wife of rich Amyntas, for all her bosom's elegance, for all that her breasts were gleaming white. Nay, even from Ischia's noble isle (if you can believe it) am I often summoned; loveliest Hyale herself is wont to praise my songs, she whose blood is renowned for Spanish ancestry, whom so many lands, so many shores obey, she who might set Neptune ablaze even in the middle of his waves.

"But what good is all this to me, if to you alone (who could believe it, Galatea?), if to you alone in the end I am so displeasing? If you alone in your cruelty flee my song, and you alone contemn my love? A thousand oysters torn from the tumbled rocks of Miseno have I sent to you, as many again Posilipo yet holds in store under his vasty depth, as many Euploea beneath her glassy wave. Nesis holds in store for me many sea-urchins, which neither the mastic tree in early spring taints with its bitter leaves, nor the losses of the waning moon have caused to shrivel. Besides, my hand is skilled at plucking murexes from beneath the sea; I have learned to recognize the Tyrian dyes and how the shellfish grow hard with thickened shells.

"Why do you flee from me? A fleece is being readied to be dyed for you wherewith you may shine and surpass the other maidens, Galatea, a fleece that is softer than sea foam. This to me the shepherd himself once gave, this the shepherd Melisaeus gave, when the old man chanced to hear me singing from a lofty cliff, and said: 'Boy, let these be the rewards of your Muse, for you are the first in singing on our shores.' From that time I have kept it in my baskets, that I might be able to send it to you. But you (lest there should be any hope remaining, any arrangement yet to be, Galatea), hard-hearted, you have denied me your hand. This, this it is, that has ruined my wretched self. Go, my pastoral songs, go far away; Galatea has scoffed at our complaints.

"No doubt you look down on me because I am crewman of a little skiff, because I handle the slender hooks and the knotty fishing nets. Did not Glaucus do this also on his native shore, was not Glaucus a watcher of the sands beside the sea? And now he is even a divinity of the swelling waters. But do not let that story of Lyda move you (which, false though it be, is causing me far too much trouble), for all that she boasts to the girls of I know not what garlands that she has sent to me. Not a thing, Lyda has not beguiled me to a thing, as the sea is my witness, and all her Nereids. If I swear false, may I make trial of those Nereids as a shipwreck, drinking the bitter waters under sea.

"Alas, what shall I do? I have long since had a mind to seek out foreign lands across the sea, where never a sailor, never a fisherman comes; there perhaps I shall be permitted to lament my fate. Shall I seek out lost seas eternally white with ice, under the uttermost pole of Boreas, or the burning sands of Libya and the warm South, and shall I see the people black and the Sun near at hand? Unhappy man, what am I saying? Will not my sick mind follow me over rocks, through fires, wherever my feet shall lead me? Winds are avoidable, rains and heats are avoidable, love is not to be avoided; it needs must be buried with me. Now its madness bids me hurl myself headlong from that rock into the waves. O ye Nymphs, ye Nymphs of the wave-resounding sea, secure for me as I fall a not-too-painful death, and quench my savage fires.

"Some day it will surely be that while he is travelling through these regions, whether he come from the curving shore of Gaeta or the tall shipyards of Cumae, the hoarse-voiced captain exhorting his crew from the helm will say: 'Turn her to the right, my lads, turn her into the waters on the right; let us avoid the cliffs made infamous by the death of Lycon.' "

Such words the unhappy fisher lad uttered in vain to the deaf winds and cherished such fruitless desires, when finally rising from the farthest east the morning star shone forth and suffused the broad sea with her rosy light.

ECLOGUE 3 Mopsus

Celadon

 Tell me (for the storms at Bauli, if Aegon was telling the truth, held you prisoner, Mopsus, for twelve days) what you, what Chromis the while, what your Iolas did, while the South Wind lords it over the sea, while the wave murmurs: were there any games you played in your idling among the deserted caves?

Mopsus

What should our Muses do in the unwelcome leisure, O Celadon? For it was impossible then with safety to try for mussels among the rocks, or for the eight-footed crab. Now the stones were securing the fragile fishing skiff on dry ground and the thin nets were hanging over the long oars. At our feet our hooks and delicate baskets were lying, and fishing rods and weels and labyrinthi made of wicker work. Then said Chromis, looking toward Ischia: "From these shores our fleet set sail (ah harsh exile) when after the war our country's youth accompanying its king entrusted its life to the unknown waves of the sea. The band of youths (according to report) sailed boldly past the Ligurian rocks, past the high Stoechades and sailing by the river Rhone (for if I rightly remember, Amilcon spoke of Rhone) saw the sea-wet sands of tidal Ocean and the shore that looks across to the blue-dyed Britons far away. There (unless they tell idle tales) whenever the ocean tide recedes the natives capture the fish left stranded on the shore."

"Do not, Chromis," Iolas answered, "do not renew our sorrows. Enough of these things your Lycabas recently told us on the lake of Lucrine: how there he had seen the sun, forsooth, falling beyond the waves and beyond the clouds, not otherwise than if from our mountains he should see it borne far off behind the shores of Gaeta, and how he had heard no noise of a chariot falling from the sky. Moreover he described the customs of the people and their towns and public places and houses made of oak, with wooden roofs. And he added the various peoples (Oh the barbarous names!), the Bellovaci and the Morini and (who could pronounce them?) the Tarbelli; how the rivers wander through broad meadows and how he had sailed in covered boats upon I know not what river Loire.

"But now other cares demand my heart's attention for themselves. Do you now if you have any (and burning love of Chloris is tormenting you too) on this cliffside rehearse by turns with me. Mopsus will listen and will run the scales on the slender reed."

So they: and I said nothing against it, but took in my hands the vocal pipe that was hanging from my neck. I was trying of course to pick up the alternate verses on the reed, for each was preparing to speak in alternates. No delay: now Chromis uttered these, and Iolas those.

Chromis

Daughters of Nereus, sacred lineage of the sea, either bring me from your deeps the gifts with which I may pacify unyielding Chloris, or, if she is not to be persuaded with gifts, seek out in all your ocean what medicine will cure my fever.

Iolas

Ye Sirens, objects of my devotion, hear these final vows. Either let Nisa call back and not reject her Iolas, or let her see him dying. These stones tossed up by the ocean waves, this vile seaweed will give a grave to her wretched lover.

Chromis

Even like the skiff that is borne on the tranquil sea, when the crests of the waves are gently curled by Zephyr—as it flies along safe and the merry band of youths tell jokes along the rowing benches—such was my life when my Chloris was in love with me.

Iolas

Do you see how the angry storms beat against the rocks, the bottom-most sands are roiled by the stiff nor'wester? Now the wave rages against the cliffs, now earth trembles with the tumult. Am I wrong, or is this the very image of Nisa when she is angry?

Chromis

O Proteus, shepherd of the watery main, O father, O king (since you frown, ye divinities, on excessive pride), do you, to whom it is allowed, seek out Ischia and say to proud Hyale that once you pastured your monsters along the salty plain.

Iolas

That cliff holds, that cliff preserves my love which is nearer the mainland: swim to it, Glaucus, and that Nisa may not condemn the hands of a hardworking husband, tell her that you too drew the scaly prey to shore.

Chromis

Cyprus is most pleasing to Venus, Crete to the Thunderer, to Juno Samos, to Vulcan chiefest Lemnos; while pretty Hyale shall inhabit the ports of Ischia, neither Samos will surpass Ischia nor chiefest Lemnos.

Iolas

Gradivus boasts Rhodope and Mercury Cyllene, Phoebe Ortygia, Minerva Hymettus; Nisa inhabits Procida; if they knew the rewards of Procida, Phoebe would leave Ortygia, Minerva Hymettus.

Chromis

Here is a cave, here a cliff and osiers the very best for weaving weels, rushes and myrtles dense through pathless ways; if now Pholoe, or if only Chloris were with me, how well I could laugh to scorn the contentious winds.

Iolas

No places smile on me without you, the sea displeases, the land is dull, I hate the slender hooks along with the nets. But if you will be with me, Nisa, all things will please; gladly then will I live my life as a fisherman among the Libyan sands.

Chromis

Sinuessa yields flounders, the shores of Dicarchus crabs, the cliffs of Hercules the mullet, Amalfi the bream; proud Parthenope abounds in tender maidens: who now would persuade me to search out other shores?

Iolas

The mullet abides in the running stream, the sargus in the grass, the octopus on the rocks, the black-tail in mid-sea; I am always hovering, my Nisa, outside your chamber doors. What happier island would offer me such haven?

Mopsus

Thus far, O Celadon, have I called to mind how under the echoing cliffs these lads contended between themselves in various song, laughing at the savage rumblings of the windy sea. They bore off, too, praises and gifts worthy their songs, even such as Triton might not contemn: the latter, a shell adorned with purpling and with natural spots, which I swimming naked plucked from Circello's depths; the former, a knotty coral with trunk curved back upon itself.

TO FERDINAND OF ARAGON

Son of King Frederick
[and] Duke of Calabria

ECLOGUE 4 Proteus

Ye Nymphs of Crater, now first we run over familiar waters with a larger spread of sail, for love is persuading us to tell in due order the chief glories of our beloved homeland: ye sea-green daughters of great Crater, let us tell the chief glories of our beloved homeland, while the blazing sun is seething the mid-sea with his rays.

Now you, your country's youthful pride, descended from heaven, the hope of so great a nation—whether the stormy Pyrenees are holding you instead of sweet Latium, instead of our native fields, or whether wandering Ebro shut you within his spreading barrier—now break through delays, and let not Hispania allure you with her broad realms, nor yet the primal origins of your house and honor of your family, though Tagus fill them with his lavishings of gold and father Oceanus wash them with foaming wave. For time will come, for me the time will come when I myself shall sing the scepters restored to Parthenope and kings broken under your lance. Meanwhile do not scorn the seaside Muse which after the forests, after the rugged woods of Mount Lycaeus (if that be anything) I first have brought for you to the salty waves, daring to make trial of their dangers in my inexperienced skiff.

What waters have not known, what harbor does not know of Proteus? Him once Melanthius and Phrasidamus had sight and sound of from the helm, as they chanced to be returning from Capri in the murky night, by the rocks of Minerva pasturing his seals and soothing them with divine song. His dolphins too they saw, playing with erratic course, and heard the straits resound far off, being struck by the choirings of the Tritons. The god himself moreover in festive mood was singing to the idle air verses not fitly uttered in mortal speech: how once earth-born Typhoeus springing from his mother's womb challenged the gods to impious war; how as his brothers' leader armed with furies and with gaping hydras he led their swarming bands; how with huge effort he hurled against the lofty stars the fragments torn from the mountain, Ischia and Procida, and shook all heaven with the sudden

blow; then the Father hurling his thunderbolts with ready hand over-
threw their giant soldiery, decreeing that Baiae's warm and sulphurous
springs bear witness as a battlefield memorial, that a conquered race had
bathed its wounds in those clear waters.

Next he calls to mind the bulls of mighty Alcides and the sea
covered over with rubble, and the procession paraded past the towns.
To this he adds ancient Cumae (the familiar haunt of Phoebus), and
the groves of the venerable priestess, and Diana's secret retreats, the
Cimmerians' homes and pitch-dark caves among the valleys.

You also, Posilipo, captive to the love of beautiful Nesis, he re-
proaches with lamentations from the angry sea. Ah wretch, ah man of
little providence, why do you hasten on the death of your girl? She
longs to escape into the mid-most waves, unhappy creature, she longs to
put an end to the unaccustomed pain. But to you it is no matter that
Neptune's monsters surround her, nor that the sea devours her with tu-
multuous swirl. Ah wretch, ah man of little providence, why do you
stretch forth your arms any longer? Desist; she lies motionless, that
huntress accustomed to the high country's snows, whom a thousand
creatures feared as she followed them through the forest glades. Receive
her, Panope, and you, fair Drymo and Cymothoe, and Rhoe and
Dynamene, and ring her round as partner in your dances.

Then he sings the ancient seats and opulent kingdoms of the goldenhaired Siren, her noble tomb on the mountain, the Chalcidean gods
and their rituals, and the fleet drawn over the deep sea under great auspices to these very shores.

Then he leads the flowing waters beneath the hollow walls and
raises castles, making their rooftops level with the mountains, and
throws vast seawalls out into the seas, and enables the fearful sailors to
recognize Pharos and Euploea from afar; he adds the cliffs and rugged
rocks of the Teleboeans, and Sarno's stream and rich farmlands.

Then he sings how Melisaeus saw Corydon in the sacred cave and
boldly played upon those reeds with which once Corydon sang lovely
Alexis and declared the Muse of Damon and Alphesiboeus, by whose
grace (the goddess dictating) he brought us forth so many splendid
things, he so revealed the very bourne of heaven.

Why should I speak of Stabiae, or the rocks that are famed to have
held the passing ships for the singing maidens,[1] or how he lamented the
thunder and fire of terrifying Vesuvius, and towns laid desolate in every
quarter?

---

[1] See Glossary, s.v. Siren.

Finally he numbers in order the kings and the battles of kings, he tells the arts of war and its rewards. He adds the sorrowful fates, and you whose removal hapless Italy weeps (whether it come from the heavy wrath of the gods, or harsh necessity) he draws across the lofty Alps, then carries near to the shores of Ocean, and finally sets down by foaming Liger and shuts within a little urn.

Alas the lamentable lot, alas the inscrutable counsels of the future! Was this last little stretch of earth among strangers reserved for you, exhausted after so many trials by land and sea? Yet put away lamentation, and do not grieve for the memorials of your ancestors, nor yet for the burial rites you hoped in your own realms. Rest in the homeland is welcome, but Earth is a grave for us all.

These matters he relates and such tales of heroes handed down from earlier times as venerable antiquity scarce could hold in memory (the sea responding with an answering beat) while by degrees the moon spread forth her light and heaven's divinities made their progress to their shining thrones.

TO THE MOST EXCELLENT LADY
CASSANDRA MARCHESE

ECLOGUE **5** Herpylis the Sorceress

But let us now tell too the acknowledged loves that they proclaimed in equal contest under the pleasant shade of the hanging cliff—Dorylas on the one side, on the other Thelgon, the neighbor of the Teleboean sea—to which the curving shores and sea-girt Platamon echoed, and the holy cave of Serapis with its fountain and its sea nymphs.

Do you now for me—whether you be encompassing the learned arts of Pallas and surpassing the gold of Maeonia and Arachne's web, or whether you be travelling in company with the choirs of Dryads and Diana's band (in no way their inferior) and, girded about with ornamented quiver, weary Prochyte and your native realm with hunting, or whether where ocean dashes against the mole at Dicarchus you gaze upon the sportive Nereids—come now Cassandra (if there be any honor from the sea), look upon my sportings. I sing songs not without power to please and of my own will, from deep within, nor ever shall time to come make accusation that you are omitted from my pages. Only let Apollo show me ready favor and the Pierian maidens who have borne me over the ocean with easy oar, from whom comes length of days and fame for what we write. Meanwhile please you to listen to Dorylas singing here.

Dorylas

Herpylis walked down to the lapsing waves of Sebeto, Herpylis not least of the Euboides, whom father Alcon taught, Alcon known to the Muses and to Phoebus. Also her likeminded sister came to take her part in the joint labor and bore the needed vessel. Herpylis with hair unbound and left foot naked mutters low and long over her potions and thus she speaks:

"Set up the altar and draw fresh water from the stream, and pluck pale wormwood from the neighboring field. Him, him will I try to inflame with magic spells who left me wretched, robbed of all my heart. Now, now, my thread, revolve the spinning reel.

"Let the brazen reel be summoned to the arts of Haemony, that has the power to make the rain to cease, to drive the clouds from the sky, to draw up quivering fishes from the deep. Revolve, my thread, revolve the spinning reel.

"First this seaweed, spindrift of the swelling sea, is cast about for you, and, being dry, consumed by the swift flames: thus, Maeon, thus for me may you burn to the marrow. Now, now, my thread, revolve the spinning reel.

"Three times this moss, Clearista, three times burn this crab without a pincer, and say the while 'With these I burn the guts of Maeon.' Revolve, my thread, revolve the spinning reel.

"Now the sponge is moistened with my tears. Ah good sponge, born in the great sea, drink up my tears with a will, and even as you draw them up thirstily, so draw up all sensation from the breast of Maeon, of ungrateful Maeon. Now, now, my thread, revolve the spinning reel.

"Let him grow fat as the pumice stone is fat, let him rest like a wave of the open sea borne hither and thither, driven and battered by the winds. But why should I, alas, my bosom stricken with grievous sorrow, make imprecations and hurl out my insults to the empty winds? Shall I repay Maeon as many words as Maeon does me wrongs? Revolve, my thread, revolve the spinning reel.

"Hither, come hither, fierce stingaree, who purpose wounds with rigid tail, and you, echeneis, whose nature is to slow the sailing ships; strive you to hold back the swift feet of Maeon, and you to pierce his heart. Now, now, my thread, revolve the spinning reel.

"Pound together the liver and spume of the black torpedo. Tomorrow I shall send this deadly drink to him. May he drink and straightway his pallid limbs grow numb. Revolve, my thread, revolve the spinning reel.

"Rip up the sea-hare by hand; the venom of the sea-hare is penetrating. This one was born in the Eastern waves, Aegle brought it, learned Aegle, and bade me touch with it mine enemy's threshold. Run now, touch, smear as you touch; tomorrow that faithless fellow will pay me his penalties; Maeon will groan on his own threshold. Now, now, my thread, make cease the spinning reel.

"Pound me the halcyon's nest to bits; it is said to disperse the winds and to tame the savage storms of the open sea. Haply this will settle the storms of my heart. Make cease, my thread, make cease the spinning reel."

Thus far he; now hear what Thelgon thereupon added in his turn; not one and the same kind of sorrow vexes all lovers.

Thelgon

Under this cliff with me sat Galatea; I was looking out on Capri and the fields far off that keep the names of the Sirens; Vesuvius on the other side from her smoking summit was marking the ancient ruins of Hercules. Lift up out of the deep, Triton, your sea-god countenance.

You, Triton, you have power to carry my complaints to Neptune, sounding them over the sea with your curved conch shell, and to tell them to the cliffs and the wave-wandering whales. Lift up, father Triton, lift up your sea-god countenance.

Here she yielded her first embraces to my pleading, here in her beauty she proffered her snowy hand and (alas, why do I recall it?) fixed on me her silent eyes. Lift up out of the deep, Triton, your sea-god countenance.

Here for you the lovely poplar spreads forth its familiar shade; often I embrace it and print my kisses on its bark, often I seek the very traces of your feet and, if you have touched anything with your hands, I adorn it with flowers. Lift up out of the deep, Triton, your sea-god countenance.

Whom now do you prefer to me? If wooded ridges please you, if bushes and she-goats pasturing through the countryside, I too am not now learning for the first time to join the slender reeds; my songs fill the carven beeches and already my pipe is hanging in the woods of Maenalus. Lift up, father Triton, lift up your sea-god countenance.

But if these shores please you more, or the wealth of the ocean deeps, who has greater skill to gather in the scattered fishes or to cast the unerring harpoon? Lift up out of the deep, Triton, your sea-god countenance.

With you as judge I would not hesitate—not I—to match my swimming with dolphin or tunny, even in mid-sea. But why should I be boasting to you, when I scarcely have time to number my hooks, my cords, and nets weighted with lead, and my weels woven from Sinuessan wicker? Lift up, father Triton, lift up your sea-god countenance.

The stern cliffs of Liguria, the Gallic shores have known me; Varus and vast Arar alike have known my fishing, and the wild monsters of the British sea. Let sink under the deep, Triton, your sea-god countenance.

And after all this, alas, hard-hearted you flee; not foreign lands, not winds have stolen you from me. But take this offering, take it; no more, Galatea, will you look on me seated beside you. Go, in your happiness prepare new dances. Let sink, father Triton, let sink your sea-god countenance.

FRAGMENT

 Now, Euploea, search me out pleasant harbors where the fisherman may net his quivering prey and temper the heavy heat with breathing Zephyrs, if any love of the swift sailboat move his desire.

And come, O thou no little reward of my labors, granted to me by Phoebus, by the learned maidens my consorts, and while I drive the bark from shore let forth the billowing sails and run out over the open sea, O Pudericus, part of my soul, for Nereus from along his shallow flats, for Doris in rivalry from amid the waves is calling you, while far and wide re-echoes the whole stretch of dread-resounding waters.

All the populace of Ischia and Procida had gathered at the temple of Lucrine Venus. For Zephyraeus came, you know, from shady Ischia, Eutychus from noble Procida: both of them famed for the reed, and both for verses, each one skilled in the channels, each in fishing, Zephyraeus at managing the hooks, Eutychus at paying out nets in the deep sea. Then first Zephyraeus sang these:

Come, O ye arts of fishermen from every shore, search out the watery realms, turn over the lairs of the Tritons, explore the haunts of the Nereids. You will never quench my fires. Pholoe never, Chloris never will love me. Now, hollow shell, breathe forth your song with me.

Cymothoe be my witness, lovely Clotho my witness, how often I have longed to hurl this sick heart into the midst of the waves, how often I have assailed huge monsters in the swirling deep, that savage jaws might tear my wretched flesh. Now, hollow shell, breathe forth your song with me.

All manner of things have I tried—land, sea, the clouds, the sky, the homes of the winds, and the year's four seasons—but all alike are harmful. Go girls, go goddesses of the sea, fetch for my raging fever now these medicines, now those herbs of Melampus. Now, hollow shell, breathe forth your song with me.

I have not declined the magic incantations and the secret names of things and the unlike gods, Erebus and Chaos. Yes, I have even learned with my thread to revolve the Reels themselves, and piecemeal have drawn up my sea-urchins from the shore, moss from the rocks, waves from the ocean surges. Now, hollow shell, breathe forth your song with me.[1]

[1] The Latin text used for the translation of this fragment appears in the Cominian edition (Patavia, 1751), though slightly detached from the rest of the *Piscatoriae* (pp. 73–74). Professor Mustard in 1914 printed a somewhat different text (*Vat. Cod. Lat.* 3361), which was reprinted and translated in my *Arcadia & Piscatorial Ecloques* (Detroit, 1966). The two texts give a slight glimpse of Sannazaro's process in revision.

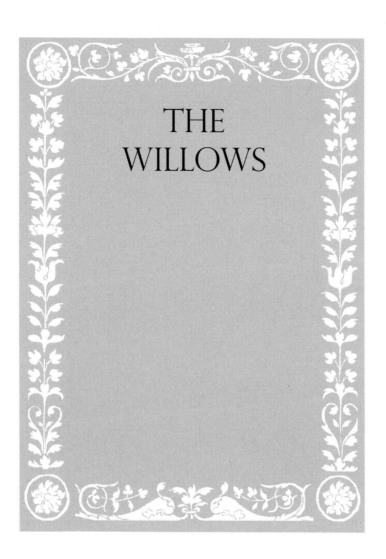

THE
WILLOWS

Introductory Note

This excellent imitation of Ovidian technique in mythological narrative has been deservedly praised recently by William Kennedy (*Sannazaro and the Uses of Pastoral*, pp. 90–95). A few remarks on the poem have been incorporated into the General Introduction (see pp. 24–25, above), but a word should be said here about the dedicatory heading.

Troiano Cavaniglia (b. 1479) was orphaned when his father died in 1481 in the liberation of Otranto from the Turks, under the leadership of the then Duke of Calabria, Alfonso. King Ferrante made special provision for the care and education of this son of a war-hero, as we say today, and he was probably admitted to the Pontanian Academy as early as possible, although his inclusion in the list of guests for Sannazaro's birthday feast (Elegy 2.2), along with Lucio Crasso (d. 1490), strikes one as poetic licence. Certainly he was old enough, by Renaissance standards, to be a reasonable choice for the dedication of this poem, if we assume a date of c. 1499 for it.

The dedicatory heading, however, calls him Lord of Troia and Montella. Troiano Cavaniglia could not be called Lord of Troia until 1521, when the DBI entry tells us he succeeded in purchasing that title—evidently thereby ruining his finances for ever after. 1521 is, however, an impossibly late date for this poem, with its language of "firstfruits" and the poet's "preparing his mind to greater things." Hence we need to make one of two assumptions: Sannazaro dedicated his poem to Cavaniglia as Lord of Montella and later updated the title to include Troia; or an editor either did the updating or provided the whole text of the dedicatory heading, as part of his editorial process. In short, these dedicatory headings can be useful clues, but their apparent testimony about date of composition needs to be consistent with other factors.

It may be useful also to comment here on Sannazaro's muted allusion to a secondary source for his poem. Obviously the emphasis on specifically woodland gods and their musical instruments is meant to remind the reader of Ovid's tale of Pan and Syrinx (*Met.* 1.689–712), and Syrinx is no doubt the "virgin of Nonacria" of Sannazaro's line 29. But the other admonitory tale, of the "Penean maid" (*Salices*, 28) is a mode of referring the reader to the even more famous myth of Apollo and Daphne, daughter of Peneus (*Met.* 1.452–567). Comparison of these two Ovidian tales with Sannazaro's poem will demonstrate that the vivid detail of lustful pursuit and metamorphic process appears much more extensively in Ovid's tale of Daphne than in the truncated tale of Pan and Syrinx.

TO TRAJAN CABANILIUS

Lord of Troia
and Montella

 If you are at leisure, and even now the goddess is fanning for you the alluring flame, she who is borne across the waves on her sea-green shell, the guardian deity of towered Paphos and rich Amathus: o Cabanilius, known to me by no uncertain fame (but esteemed far more for your capacities), accept a song sung briefly beside the river's flow. For the learned sisters have bound me so to you, they soothe my heart so with the pleasing-anxious care, that scarcely any of my leisure can I spend apart from you, scarcely by night enjoying quiet slumbers.

Come then, Trajan, forgive your poet who (even this moment preparing his mind to greater things) brings forward these firstfruits at your command, and do not scorn his slender Muse.

It chanced (if report be true), while the sun was wearying the shrill cicadas in the fields, that here and there the rustic divinities—goatfooted Satyrs and Pans, together with Faunuses and upland-roaming Sylvans—couched on the green broom plants were avoiding summer's heat, where shallow Sarnus waters the fertile fields and with gentle current seeks the sea. A pleasant peacefulness reigned throughout the woods, with trickling streams and Zephyrs whispering through the alder thickets.

And while they are shaping their slender reeds—while they explore their piping tones with the finger's pressure and seal up stops with pliant wax, modulating their song in varied melody—from behind a leafy oak catching sight of them, the goldenhaired Nymphs give voice in ringing peals of laughter, but are fearful of venturing close to them. For many times they had heard of your troubles (Penean maid), and with what fortune alas the hapless virgin of Nonacria—hapless virgin, for what did she not attempt?—from Cyllene's summit fearfully fleeing Pan (Pan the god of Arcady), most lovely though she were, the choicest of Diana's holy troop, long since transformed her lovely bosom into the knotty reed. The forest crew, licentious and unrestrained, creatures half-wild, as soon as they caught sight of the maidens afoot in the grassy meadows, lodged in their very marrow the hidden flame, and undertook to encourage the timid creatures with blandishing speech:

"Over here, pretty maidens, over here, ye gentle company: why stand so far away? Come rather to this riverbank and on the greensward weave your subtle dance as you are wont. For we are playing unresponsive pipes and to the deaf tree-trunks address our song in vain."

They made no objection, but kept their legs untrammelled, ready for swift flight, considering that they had a safe line of retreat, if by some chance God or their fates should decree that they break away over the rocks and escape to the high country. Then the youths shout, "Put away this fear, girls, put it far away. Free your minds of these idle apprehensions. Here are no snares, no ambushes in these clearings. Everything lies open; this place conceals no deceptions. And we, we are not sprung from Lerna's monsters, nor Chimaera's flame, or Scylla's wolves, or from yawning Charybdis, that we would tear your vitals with savage ravening. But we are children of the gods, who would go leaping across the towering rocks, in the swift chase always at your side."

Their minds being soothed by these speeches, their confident hearts cast away gloomy fear, and quickly tripping across the watery meadow they come near the riverbank and the lustful gods. Then joining hands they dance their festive dances over the grass: joyously they repeat now this return, now that; now they lift their bodies in suspended leaps, now toss their gleaming arms, their tender sides, and move their feet with stepping and alternate stepping. Hereupon the remorseless Satyrs (however much they rejoice at hearing the singers' voices, at seeing their snowy breasts, and drink in the flame through greedy eyes), yet the savage force of the raging fever so swells in their hearts, and headlong love and insane lust, that their reed-pipes one by one being cast aside, and the truce suddenly broken, rising up from the ground swifter than the wind they all spring forward: and scorning good faith or gentleness they fall upon the Nymphs (ah, filled with fear and frozen with sudden horror), as greedy as savage wolves who assail the merry lambs (unmindful of themselves in their playful frisking), seizing them here and carrying them off there, as they run across the greening meadow or down the deep canyon—and their unwitting guardians far away and the friendly support of the dogs.

So with these. Divided in mind the hapless Nymphs fill the leafy wood with tearful clamor and fly now here, now there, considering no place safe, not boulders nor passages overgrown with thick briars. Bewildered, they see on the one side the steep ridges of the jagged mountain, on the other the water spreading through flooded fields. No path to safety: and now all hope of flight is snatched away. Finally then the fugitives come to a halt beside the water, with tears and moans and wailing laments tearing their golden locks from their heads, and call upon Sarnus and his flowing sisters. As they call, the whole troop of Naiads hastily rises from the deepest depths, Sarnus rises in haste, the sea-blue monarch of the crystal wave, and blowing a hoarse blast calls up from the watery deep his inexhaustible host. But what can Sarnus do, or that host of swimming Naiads, where iron Fate stands opposed and frames her decrees inflexible in hardest adamant?

So, giving up on the gods' concern and protection, and hating Heaven and the very sun as well, the Nymphs elect that one last end that remains in direst straits. Resolved to plunge themselves into the flood, already they were bending their limbs and seeking the water with down-turned face, when of a sudden their feet grew stiff and a root spreading all through their extremities slows their flight, and fixes in the earth the soles of their feet. Thereupon the uncertain breath of life begins to perish in their veins and paleness overspreads their innocent features: bark begins to cover their palpitating breasts. There is no delay: you could see the branches growing in place of their fingers, and their golden hair turning white with silvered leaf: and now no part retains its living heat, their vitals grown cold yield inch by inch to the encroaching wood. But though their bodies' every limb be hardened, and their flanks surrounded by stocks and stubs on every side, and they are wholly Willows: yet still they are governed by one sole desire, to escape the woodland gods: and clinging to the margin of the riverbank to lean out over the middle of the stream.

THE
ELEGIES

BOOK 1

Elegy 1: Introductory Note

Lucio Crasso (c.1430–90) was Sannazaro's teacher and friend in the 1470s, along with Giuniano Maggio (see below, *Elegies* 2.7). In the dialogue *Asinus,* Pontano presents Sannazaro as paying tribute to his teacher: "This hill was fancied the Muses' Mount by our Crassus—or, if you will allow me, *my* Crassus: for this man taught me, he consecrated me to these studies, to him is owing whatever in me is worthy of praise, if any such there be" (*Dialoghi,* ed. Previtera, p. 298). Pontano's dialogue continues with praise of Crassus by Giovanni Pardo, the friend to whom Sannazaro addresses the elegy following this one. Thus his collection of elegies begins with poems addressed to his teacher Crassus, and to their mutual friend Pardus, relegating his royal patrons Alfonso and Frederick to the elegies opening Books Two and Three, respectively. This ordering does not necessarily reflect the poet's own decisions, since his will entrusted publication of his lesser Latin poems to his long-time friend Antonio Diaz Garlon (see Pércopo, p. 94). But the irregular division into three books (of eleven, ten, and three elegies) suggests that the mss. at least implied an ordering that Garlon thought he should follow. It is of some interest that in his elegies Sannazaro consistently expends far more effort in praising his friends than in glorifying men of social or political power.

Elegy 1.1, of peculiar structure, begins as an epistolary poem, like Elegy 1.5, and the third and tenth elegies in Book Two (which, though not precisely epistles, at least appear to be missives sent to a friend—the third elegy bearing New Year's greetings, and the tenth accompanying a gift of pomegranates). For some thirty lines the poem moves at a quiet pace, mildly envious of Lucius's freedom— he seems to be on summer holidays, sightseeing along the Latian Way—while the poet is bound to obey his mistress's every command, as the poet of pastoral love. All this is standard fare, with Sannazaro trading on his already-established persona as Sincero, the narrator in his *Arcadia.*

But suddenly the reader encounters a drastic change in tempo, subject, and even in the audience addressed: *At mihi te te avidis liceat vincire lacertis* (1.1.33). Six lines later, a feminine adjective assures us that Sannazaro is not addressing his former teacher in the language of passionate love by lamplight. Rather, he is sending him a sample of his current studies, in the form of a reworking of several passages from Tibullus, with of course some incidental echoing of words and phrases in Virgil, Horace, Propertius, and others. The approach is characteristically uncompromising, without "editorial" aids, leaving the reader to discover for himself, as best he may, that Crassus is the former teacher to whom his star pupil is sending this example of what he has learned under his tutelage.

The pleasant opening section (lines 1–32) employs Sannazaro's characteristic mosaic method of echoing phrases and lines from the Roman poets. The *monumenta viae* (line 8) are a signal that Tibullus is in the offing (Tib. 1.7.57), as is Love's singing "with slender throat," like the birds in Tibullus 1.3.60; and the shepherds' names are scrupulously selected from Virgil's eclogues. On the other hand, lines 17–32 rely on extensive elaboration of rural piety and funeral rites, much in the manner of *Arcadia* (tr. Nash, 42–45, 109–11, et al.), and on restatement of the standard *topos* of the pastoralist-elegist renunciation of heroic gravity and grandeur, so that the *imitatio* here is not merely allusive and incidental, but becomes pretty much the whole substance of this part of the poem.

Even more so, when with line 33 the elegy abruptly launches into Syncerus's prayer to his mistress, Lucio Crasso recedes into the background and the poem becomes a formal exercise in imitation of classical models. From Tibullus's first elegy, Sannazaro appropriates his stance as the impoverished poet descended from once wealthy ancestors (Tib. 1.1.19–20, 41–43) and held in bondage to a fair mistress (1.1.55–56), happy as long as she is lying in his bosom (1.1.45–48). From Tibullus's second elegy in Book One he takes the lover's scorn of the luxurious but empty bed (1.2.75–78), the magic practices of the love-sorceress (1.2.43 ff.), and the lover's fear of having offended the gods. The passage on the power of "song" is modelled on Tibullus 1.8.17–23, and in addition Tibullus seems the chief model for Sannazaro's version of the *topos* of Oriental wealth (Tib. 3.3.17–18, 29–30; 3.8.17–20), as rendered in this elegy and again in another early epistolary performance, the New Year's missive to Fuscus (2.3.13–16, below).

The fleece in the Ethiopian forest is a reminiscence of *Georgics* 2.120, as the hair bedewed with liquid odors is a reminiscence of Horace (*Odes* 1.5.1–3); and of course a theme such as scorn of the costly but loveless bed can be found elsewhere, as in Propertius 1.14.15–24. But essentially Syncerus's prayer is an exercise in imitating Tibullus.

Everything indicates that the first two elegies in Book One are early work. Lucio Crasso was dead by 1490, and the insistence on pastoral décor is much stronger in these poems than in most of the other elegies. Altamura (*Sannazaro*, 1951) suggests a date of 1475–78 for the Crasso elegy.

A verse translation appears on p. 163.

[Elegies 1.1]   ## TO LUCIUS CRASSUS

 You the fertile fields of rocky Petrine hold, fields once by my ancestors made proud. And you gaze upon the nymphs of Sinuessa, my delights, and the soil that smokes with sulphur ever anew. Now you survey the ancient ports along the shore, now see with what cool water the river Liris flows, and wander along with a pleasant diligence while you examine the monuments of the Latian Way.

But to me the country Muses dictate woodland songs (the which Love sings with slender throat); the faithful grove makes answer to my secret complaints, and its caves re-echo stricken with my notes. Not so much the crowds, not so much the cities do we fear as the harshness of a froward mistress. This mode of life, this study my fate allots; from this I desire that my ashes have their fame. Let the rout of shepherds in their shady grots approve me, while they invoke rural Pales with warm-foaming milk. Let rustic Thyrsis play my song on his artless reed, and praise me for having loved with such a constant faith. Then above my tomb and buried remains let Tityrus bring garlands woven from green ivy. Here Corydon will dance for me, and handsome Alexis, Damoetas will strew flowers with either hand. Iolas will train the shade over the sacred springs while Alphesiboeus drives the full-fed flocks.

Not for me (Lucius) is it any concern to surpass Homer, to surpass Maro: if I shall be known for love, it is enough. What profit shall Achilles bring to me, what prudent Ulysses? What the pious Aeneas, or the boy Ascanius? These songs let others sing, whose Muse surrounded by triumphal shouting shall carry their soaring name from the tomb to the stars.

[*Syncerus's Song to his Mistress*]

But let me bind you, you in my avid embraces, and drink up long kisses with a pleasing delay. And let me admire your body when the lamp is lit, and weave the special blandishments of night, calming my hands and my face in your arms, and often keeping you warm as you lie weary on my breast. But why am I (alas, poor wretch!) in vain conceit imagining empty dreams—things that perhaps no day will ever bring?

Happy the man who has had the skill to persuade his unyielding girl, and to attain the joys of the union he desired. Day and night he repeats his songs of love, recalling the sweet thefts stolen from his Venus. And with his hair bedewed with liquid odors, he still pursues her tender flesh through the joyous night, calling to mind in his mistress's bosom their former fires, which golden Love fans lightly with his wings. He wants no fleece that they sing in the Ethiope's forests, nor wool that blushes with Sidonian dye. All to himself he has whatever is fetched from the dusky Indians: all to himself he has your riverbanks, gold-laden Hermus, and whatever crops the Persian harvests from his fragrant fields, and the Arab burned by an unremitting sun.

Not for gold, not for jewels are we wretched lovers tormented; he who will have the skill to persuade his mistress, he will be rich. I shall be rich (my life) beyond the rest, if I may have you willingly with me, though I be poor and an exile, in unknown lands. What use are the plains of the sea made ruddy with glittering shells, or the many fields that the black Sabaean ploughs? What use is a couch spectacular with plume and purple, if my dear girl is not upon my bosom? if wretchedly I am forced to drag out the night amid my sighs, and to deny the existence of the eternal gods?

Has a wisewoman put a curse on me for neglected tombs? do herbs and magic songs interrupt my slumbers? Song draws down the acorns from the unreachable oak; song checks the howling of the dog by night. And song stains the pallid sun with ugly blood, and stops the horses of the travelling moon.

Why am I complaining, unhappy man? Would that only songs were injuring me, and that Love had no dwelling in my breast. Stronger is he than Aeaean Circe's charms, stronger than poisons sprung from Haemony's ridge.

Spare me, boy: no empty matters do I lament; you wax greater by my wound, and (savage creature) riot in my blood. But if you are over-borne by the sorrows of my life, I pray that the black day of death be not long in coming.

Elegy 2: Introductory Note

Giovanni Pardo, born in Saragossa, was a close friend of Sannazaro, although himself no poet, as he says (and demonstrates) in an answer-poem responding to this elegy (printed in *Sannazarii . . . Poemata*, ed. Cominus, Padua 1751, p. 179). Sannazaro's elegy perhaps tactfully acknowledges this truth by confining its praise to Pardo's scientific studies, and passing on quickly to elaborating Sannazaro's own persona of poet-shepherd, as in Elegy 1.1.

In the first section the imitation of classical models seems perfunctory: the "primal bodies joined with firm constancy" have a Lucretian ring, and a relatively obscure passage in Ovid speaks of Charybdis vomiting up her swallowed waters (*Pontine Epistles*, 4.10.28; cf. *Heroides* 12.125). But in general the listing of subjects for scientific inquiry does not seem tied very closely to particular passages in the Roman poets, although the following paraphrase of Virgil suggests that Sannazaro does have that passage in mind:

> Happy is he who has been able to learn the causes of things, and also happy is he who has come to know the rural gods, Pan and old Silvanus and the sisterhood of the Nymphs. . . . [Among the "causes of things" are] the roadways of the sky, the stars, the sun's eclipses and the moon's waxing and waning, earthquakes, the swelling and receding of the sea, the shortness of days in winter "or why night is so prolonged." (paraphrased from *Georgics* 2.458–95)

Pontano quotes this well-known passage in his dialogue *Aegidius* (Previtera, p. 248), in which Pardo is assigned a long speech on "scientific" matters (Previtera, pp. 273–79). A similar passage in Propertius (3.5.23–46) bears somewhat less resemblance to the Pardo elegy but would of course be familiar to Sannazaro, along with a yet fainter echo in Tibullus (4.1.18–23).

Quite properly, the poem's emphasis falls on the rejecting of such scientific matter in favor of the poet's own specialty, the pastoral scene—a rejection implied in the Virgilian passage paraphrased just above, and explicitly made by Tibullus in his panegyric to Messalla (4.1.18–27). As in Sannazaro's first elegy, there are reminiscences here of the *Arcadia,* in the passages on hunting and fowling (tr. Nash, 77–80) and the shepherds' athletic contests (ibid., 119–28), but Sannazaro turns also to Ovid and Tibullus for several details in the latter half of his poem. The country cakes set out for the rural gods appear as *rustica liba* in Ovid's *Fasti* (3.670) and the Pales carven with an unskilled blade is as clearly reminiscent of Tibullus (2.5.28) as is the lamb stricken to atone for a thousand sheep (1.1.21–24). A similar juxtaposition of Ovid and Tibullus appears in Sannazaro's account of the rituals of the Palilia (Ovid, *Fasti* 4.727; Tibullus, 2.5.90).

Thus when we stop to examine these first two elegies in some detail, as examples of humanist *imitatio,* their parallel nature becomes the more evident, and their selection as the opening exhibits in Sannazaro's collection seems thoroughly effective—whether the selecting was done by the poet himself, or by his executor, Garlon.

For their probable early date of composition (not later than 1490), see the Introductory Note to 1.1, above. Three letters from Pardo to Sannazaro have been printed in Mauro's *Opere Volgari di Jacopo Sannazaro* (Bari, 1961), pp. 387–99, dated by the editor as 1486(?), 1493, and 1498–1501(?).

A verse translation appears on p. 165.

[Elegies 1.2]   **TO IOANNIS PARDUS,**
OF SPAIN

 Pardus, the ornament of your fatherland; Pardus, the chiefest hope of your people, and rare glory of the land of Spain: whose pleasure it is to search out the reasons of this boundless world, and its primal bodies joined with firm constancy; whether broad heaven is revolved by an eternal power of divinity, or this huge work operates by its own weight; why the seas are salt, why Aetna boils with fire; why vast Charybdis vomits up her swallowed waters; whence is the shining of stars, why night grows greater or lesser; why the moon shines not with her own light. Happy are you who are permitted now to climb to the sees of heaven; there, after death, may your fate allow you to remain.

But we go driving our goats through the woods and muddy fields, while Phyllis orders us to love. And we carve upon the tender elms our fires, for the band of roving Hamadryads to read. And now we hunt the deer, and now wild asses, and at times deceive with art the savage beasts. Often it is our pleasure to catch with lime the colorful birds; and in our fowling we yield nothing to the Satyrs. But though I had power to call up again with delicate pipe the snow-white sheep of the Trinacrian shepherd, I shall be always a dweller in the fields. Farewell the people and the towns; the fields will present a theater pleasing to my eyes.

There I shall watch the wrestling on the grass (the wars of shepherds), and the prizes parcelled out for the swift of foot. And I shall not object to strive with staves of hazelwood, or to armor my breast with hollow cork. The bulls will fight, the he-goats will fight with their horns: the victors will bear their garlands over the soft turf. The fleece-clad shepherd will make the rounds of his crowded sheepfold, and set out country cakes for the rural gods. Goatfooted Fauns will stand with the strength of firs, and Pales carven with an unskilled blade. The stricken lamb will fall before their established altars, stricken that a single lamb may atone for countless sheep. Then one will measure out the millet, and the cups foaming with snowy milk, and repeat the votive prayers: three times the draught will leap across the crackling stalks, and three times also the rustic crowd with nimble foot.

Grant it, ye gods, that among the flocks and herds I cease from singing, and that the black day overwhelm me in the woods. That the shepherd weep for me with no artful reed, and that I be buried beneath the plane-tree's shade. Let pasturing she-goats venerate my bones, and not far from my tomb a white sheep bleat. Let other shades make their vaunt with Panchaean rite, and seek out marbles quarried from the

Parian ridges. For me it will be enough that Phyllis reflect upon our ancient loves and weave, before my tomb, her vernal roses.

Elegy 3: Introductory Note

The mistress should probably be considered wholly imaginary. Sannazaro in this elegy is further establishing his persona as poet-shepherd-lover, but now with little emphasis on pastoral décor, apart from the flocks and meadows and garlands of his vignette of life in the Elysian fields (1.3.37–48). The poem fits together several passages inspired by various segments of Tibullus, plus some details from Propertius, achieving a neatly organized celebration of Love, dying and undying.

The opening lines seem to reflect a possibly spurious elegy of Tibullus, in which the Roman poet says, "No other woman can steal me from your bed: our love from the first was pledged under this compact" (3.19 [4.13], 1–2). Sannazaro at once moves on to extend this commitment to a mutual pledge that their love will last to and beyond their dying day. If he survives his mistress, he will bear frankincense and wine as guardian-priest of her tomb, somewhat as Propertius imagines his mistress will do for him (3.16.21–24). But should he die first, as he would prefer, he dwells on the several details of his mistress's grief and her ministration of his funeral rites, drawing on three different Tibullan elegies: for his dying gaze and her weeping and cutting her hair, Tibullus 1.1.59–68; for her gathering of his bones, and libations before his tomb, Tibullus 3.2.17–26; and for the Elysian scene (the singing, the praising, the cinnamon groves and floral abundance), Tibullus 1.3.57–64. Then, to return the poem to the generally transient and secular ambience of the Roman elegists, Sannazaro reverts to Tibullus's first elegy—"now, while fate permits, let us be joined in love," and so on (Tib. 1.1.69–74).

Such an account is an over-simplification of the process—as Sannazaro's process, in turn, may be considered an over-simplification of "Love and Death in Tibullus and Propertius." Tibullus too tells Delia that they should be an *exemplum amoris* when they are both white-haired (1.6.85–86); Propertius too has a poem in which the lover says that his first mistress has always (i.e., for three years) been his love and none other can share his embraces (Propertius, 3.15.1–10). Propertius too presents Cynthia as his mourner (2.13), and in 2.28.25–34 sketches a scene of Cynthia being praised when she has gone on to the underworld. The general spirit of Sannazaro's elegy is neatly summarized in one Propertian line (*huius ero vivus, mortuus huius ero*—2.15.36), and indeed Sannazaro concludes his elegy with a "signature line" (see the General Introduction, pp. 15–18) directly lifted and elegantly modified, not from Tibullus but from Propertius:

Sann.: Candidus et pennis omina firmet Amor (1.3.58)

Prop.: Candidus argutum sternuit omen Amor
(2.3.24)
Bright Love sneezed a clear omen.

Rather jejune in its materials, the poem gains interest when viewed as a skillful exercise in humanist *imitatio*. By moving away from the stormy particulars of those young Roman aristocrats and their slave-girl mistresses—the Delias and Neaeras and Cynthias—to a celebration of the poet's lasting love for his unnamed and probably incorporeal mistress, Sannazaro actually makes some gains in unified effect, for all that he loses in color and authenticity. Central to this unity is the Elysian scene, with the strengthless dead flocking around to praise the deceased Sannazaro for his poetry, and his still-living mistress for her faithful honoring of his memory. Any such scene must carry overtones of Virgil's sketch of Anchises (and Musaeus) in the underworld (*Aen.* 6.637–78), which Sannazaro brilliantly adapts in his rendering of the Song of David in *De Partu Virginis,* 1.211–20 ff. When we add our perception that the poem is moving away from particular passions to an idealized portrait of love's power to transcend, we recognize that this selecting and weaving of Tibullan and Propertian themes is being done by a young poet saturated with the poetry of Dante and Petrarch. Thus the elegy becomes one more example of the ingenuity of Renaissance poets in adapting Graeco-Roman material to their own culture.

The poem is likely to be fairly early work. Altamura does not suggest a precise date, but says that Elegies 1.3 and 2.7 are "appartenenti alla giovinezza del poeta" (*Sannazaro,* 1951, p. 172).

A verse translation appears on p. 166.

[Elegies 1.3] **TO HIS MISTRESS**

 No woman will have power to surprise my senses, though Venus herself should abandon sky and stars. You were my first fire in boyhood, in my tender years; you will be the last flame for a trembling old man. Once for all long since the gods have sanctioned the bonds between us, bonds not to be put asunder even at the last funeral pyre. So that if my life were to last beyond your death (may the gods let the omen vanish in the wind), I should pay homage to your buried bones in their well-wrought tomb, bringing in my sorrowful hands the frankincense

and wine. The sacred guardian of your shade and priest of your tomb, I should sound my sad notes on the mournful lyre. None would tear me away from the urn I embrace; even as I die I should bestow my last kiss on your ashes.

But if (which I prefer) your fate permitted that with your lovely hand you close my eyes, then—when I still could gaze upon your beloved face and speak with you even as my spirit took its flight—you would invoke my shade in lamentation beside my tomb, and gather my fragmented bones within your bosom, and (tearfully cutting your long hair before my monument) call out my name as if on the verge of death. Then performing the proper rites for my ashes and my flame now stilled, you would bestow white lilies mixed with the blushing rose. There in your grief you would elect to spend your days, there to spend your nights, and no other love would make a conquest of you; but mindful still of your lover, with white hair venerable, you would bring your precious gifts with trembling hand.

O if such honors be bestowed upon my grave, let greedy Lachesis cut my slow-spun thread—not that my urn should drink the exotic liquids of Araby, and my burnt ashes breathe with Assyrian odor, or the clarion fame of my sepulcher be renowned, and its marble tip reach to the lofty stars; but rather that it should hear your long-drawn wails and wear its garlands watered with your tears. Then wandering on the banks of Lethe's shore—where a false day shines with weakened light, where the wave washes the groves of slender cinnamon and fresh ambrosia, and the blessed flocks—recalling the pleasant dreams of that life gone by, I shall display for the Elysian bands what gifts I have. And happier yet among those happy souls I shall receive new praises throughout the broad meadows, as some one among my companions, joyous and cheerful, scatters fresh flowers on the ground, bringing me garlands, and (not content with this) extols our faithful loves, telling the others of your piety.

But since the joyous days of our tender youth are blossoming now, and fate allows us to embrace, let us blend our sweet delights on the wanton couch: already death's companion, crooked old age, is hurrying near. Already deep wrinkles are hurrying near, and a graver age, and we will not be able to sport in the yielding bed. Meanwhile let us twine our necks with lustful arms: now let the final hour, whenever it will, dissolve us two.

Grant it, ye gods, that this hope stand fast throughout long years, and Love in his splendor confirm the omens with his wings.

Elegy 4: Introductory Note

Antonio Diaz Garlon, Count of Alife, was Sannazaro's lifelong friend, commissioned in the poet's will to oversee the posthumous publication of his minor Latin poems. The occasion of this elegy is the birth of Garlon's first-born son, presumably the Ferdinando who was the fourth (and last) Count of Alife. The DBI entry (s.v. Diaz Garlon, Maria) unfortunately gives no date of birth for either Antonio or Ferdinando. Altamura's "c. 1500" is clearly only a guess at the date of this elegy, but probably close enough.

As a celebration of a child's birth, the elegy invites overtones of Virgil's famous Eclogue Four, the so-called "Messianic" eclogue, extensively utilized in *De Partu* 3.163–202. Not much of Virgil appears in this elegy, however, other than the unmistakable "signature" allusion, in the closing lines, to the infant's learning to smile from the cradle at his mother.

With its appeal to the appropriate deity for relief from distress, the poem bears kinship with Tibullus 3.6 (a salute to Bacchus and the healing powers of his *annosum merum*—Tibullus, line 58; Sannazaro, line 15) and also with Tibullus 4.4 (an appeal to Phoebus as god of healing to restore health to Cerinthus's mistress, and thus by restoring one body to return two to health—Tibullus 4.4.19–20; cf. Sannazaro 1.4.7–10). Indeed, the whole structure of Tibullus 4.4 strongly resembles Sannazaro's elegy. In addition, there are slight echoes of Propertius (e.g., 4.6.5; 1.14.11–12), as Sannazaro weaves a tissue of borrowed and modified phrases and lines in the process of creating a poem for a very specific occasion in the life of very specific friends.

A verse translation appears on p. 167.

[Elegies 1.4]   TO LUCINA

upon Cornelia Piccolomini's being brought to bed, the wife of Antonius Garlonius, Lord of Alife

 Now bring your assistance, Lucina, to a tender maiden: she is worthy that you preserve her with your aid. She calls on you and sighs to you alone with tear-wet eyes, and pours out silent prayers from her rosy lips. Sick she is, indeed, and languishing with the unfamiliar pain, and scarcely able to bear the many evils of the long delay. But come, goddess, and bring with you ointments from a special casket, and any herb there may be that can avail. So will you be able to quell the young man's tears, bringing relief to two at a single cast.

The great goddess of light is near; suppress your fear now, Garlon. Not vainly has she been summoned by your tears. Set out costum and myrrh on the altar, and whatever spices the sailor carries over the ruddy waters from a distant world. Stretched out prone before her sacred altars, worship the goddess and for the Genius pour out once and again the well-aged wine.

Your anxious fears have ceased, your lamentations ceased. Now the maiden gives birth, touched by the goddess's advent. Now has she brought forth a son. Do you see how his eyes resemble his mother? What loveliness in his soft countenance!

Hail, little boy, on whom the golden age is smiling now, to whom Love willingly resigns his quiver. For whether you please to load your shoulders with the golden arrows, or shake the flaming torch; or rather in childish play to flourish agile wings, and to let your careless locks fall down your back: who will not think you born in the Paphian valleys, or the Idalian goddess's son?

Live on, I pray, grow skilled at charming your mother with your laughing eyes, and learn to play your pretty tricks.

Elegy 5: Introductory Note

The elegy purports to be an answer-poem (cf. the Introductory Note to 1.2, above), responding to an epistle from one Giulio of Siena, who has not been identified.

In itself a rather perfunctory performance, the poem opens in a manner resembling Catullus 68, *To Manlius,* although without direct imitation of words and phrases. Thereafter, Sannazaro seems to content himself with his own shaping of standard classical materials—Ovid as the poet in exile, Hercules ("the Tirynthian") as exemplar of heroic virtue, Orpheus as the poet controlling and transforming his world.

The Orpheus passage not only is notable as a very early example of that myth's fascination for the Renaissance, but also its half-dozen lines give us insight into Sannazaro's workshop, since they appear (with only four words changed) in the midst of forty lines of verse addressed *Ad Albinum* (Cod. Vindob., lat. 9477, ff. 114–15, printed by Altamura, without comment on the echo in this elegy, in *Jacopo Sannazaro,* Naples, 1951, Appendix Two, specimen V, pp. 142–43). This fugitive piece was doubtless addressed to Giovanni Albino, a member of the Pontanian Academy, who performed several important diplomatic missions for Alfonso II between 1478–95. The *Dizionario Biografico* notes that nothing more is heard of him after 1497. It is reasonable to speculate that Sannazaro (who includes Albino in Elegy 1.11, below) wrote his verses to Albino at some time before Albino's death (or departure from Naples) in 1497, and at some later date quarried from them the Orpheus passage as a suitable *amplificatio* for his epistle answering Giulio of Siena.

We need to identify Giulio and the date of his exile, inasmuch as Sannazaro's complaint about lack of poetic inspiration, and his "cannibalizing" of the Albino elegy, combine to suggest that this poem may have been written after his return to Naples in 1505. But in any event, this double use of the Orpheus passage reminds us that we need not concern ourselves much about "sincerity" in Renaissance poetry, even when the poet has adopted the name *Syncerus*.

A verse translation appears on p. 168.

[Elegies 1.5] # TO JULIUS OF SIENA, IN EXILE

 Though my sorrow make war on my weary eyes, yet am I forced to speak, with mournful voice.

Amid distressful sighs and sad complaints, arrived a letter sent from your own hands. I have read it, and recognized your Muses, my divinities, and the Pierian draughts and the Castalian grace. You ask that my verses should placate wrathful Apollo, and move the goddesses unyielding to your prayers. I have not wit, I have not eloquence for this—go, I pray thee, and quench your thirst at another stream. Long since has he denied me favorable hearing and forbidden me to touch the strings of the tuneful lyre. Nor for me now does Calliope pour forth draughts from the accustomed spring, nor lead the pleasant choral dances. Why do you seek from a burnt-out torch a flame that is quenched? Why (hapless man) do you look for aid from my misfortune?

Your song still flows indeed in happy vein, and your Muse transports you, an ornament to your country. When you are lamenting I fancy that Thalia herself is mourning, and Apollo complaining with melancholy voice. As once when bitterly Orpheus bewailed Eurydice, beside the Strymonian waves: who with his song on the icy cliffs of Ismarian Haemus astonished the oaks, astonished the wild beasts: and drew down the rocks from the Bistonian mountains, and stopped your current, Hebrus, with arrested waters.

Shall Fortune always strike the best poets then, and always cast them down from her fickle wheel? Now (lest he who lies an exile in Tomi's soil should be the only one banished to the furthest poles) you also are oppressed by the harshness of unyielding fate, and driven to dwell too far from your native home.

But unless fame be sought through mighty labors, all will be gone with the blazing funeral pyre. So honest Aeneas, so Ulysses son of Laertes, earned a greater glory after their deaths. So also the Tirynthian, when all the monsters had been destroyed, mounted to his paternal realms from the Oetaean pyre. You too (believe me), when you have endured all your bitter troubles, Virtue will lead along the lofty highroad to the stars.

Elegy 6: Introductory Note

This dramatic monologue is the sole example among the elegies of an entire poem assigned to a human speaker other than the poet himself. Sannazaro is seldom able to avoid a certain stridency in his depictions of grief, and Lucretia is no exception. Yet, as one might expect, the poem does achieve an effective contrast between the hot-blooded impulsiveness of Sarro Brancaccio's death, and the long death-in-life of Lucretia's future, cold in her cold bridal chamber with the cold ashes of her husband.

Laodamia was the wife of Protesilaus, the first man ashore when the Greeks landed at Troy and the first man killed (*Iliad* 2.698–702). Thus the reference seems appropriate, as Sarro's story is told here; but probably it is also an allusion to Catullus 68.73 ff., in which passage Catullus twice speaks of Laodamia as he laments his brother's death near the site of Troy, where like Brancaccio he died "a stranger on foreign shores"—*Troja infelice sepultum / Detinet extremo terra aliena solo* (68.99–100). Otherwise, the poem does not show much direct imitation. Evander's paternal reproach of Pallas's excessive boldness (*Aen.* 11. 152–55) might have encouraged some of Lucretia's emphasis on rashness and broken promises.

The date of composition is probably early. It is reasonable to guess that Brancaccio was a casualty in one of Alfonso's campaigns in the early 1480s.

A verse translation appears on p. 169.

[Elegies 1.6]   ## ON THE DEATH
OF SARRUS BRANCATIUS

Lucretia His Wife

Have then the hasty Parcae broken your thread, the thread so finely spun from their spinning wheel? Shall I then, married but lately to such a husband, complain now cold in my sorrowful marriage bed? And has he died a stranger on foreign shores, who should by rights have breathed out his life on these lips? O sisters most fortunate and blest,[1] who offer Sabaean incense on his eternal altars—would that I had never

---

[1]See Glossary, s.v. Sabaean.

known his embraces, never known his kisses: surely I would be some small part of your chorus.

Dear husband, too much trusting in your daring youth, and shade too much to be wept by my tears, who ordered you to hurl your body against the thronging foe? Was not one alone enough for combat? Wretched me, no care for your wife occurred to you, nor did the certain ruin of your hapless family. You were wont to swear to me by the sacred rites of marriage, by the bonds of our inviolable union, that you would never be unmindful of your dear wife, not though the waters of Lethe were closing over your face. Indeed I warned you myself, not to go running rashly into the midst of weapons; alas, rash man, where is it you are running? why are you being carried away? where has it gone, your concern for me? can it be that you have no memory of your beloved wife? Scarcely can I believe (although alas I am forced to believe) that I can have fallen so quickly from your heart. But I have fallen; so unjust fate has allowed; and no vows on my behalf have obliged the gods to my protection.

So wept his wife for Hector, so for Achilles; so the hapless Laodamia for her dead husband. Now my virginity, since it remained untouched, may be preserved for your ashes, inviolate.

Elegy 7: Introductory Note

Jacobus Picenus (1394–1476), born at Montebrandone in the March of Ancona (in Roman times called Picenum), is more commonly known today as St. James of the March. The *Acta Sanctorum* (Brussels, 1940, 70.553) and Butler's *Lives of the Saints* (ed. Thurston and Attwater, New York, 1963, vol. 4) stress his ascetic life and his preaching as a member of the Fratres Minores, but also his extensive work for his order as administrator and at times inquisitor. See also John Moorman, *A History of the Franciscan Order* (Oxford, 1968, pp. 473–78). Nothing is said in these sources of any hermit-like existence, such as might be inferred from Sannazaro's poem. He lived at Naples only in the last three years of his life, dying there on November 28, 1476. Jacobus was not numbered *inter beatos* until 1624, nor *inter sanctos* until 1726, but books and poems concerning his life and miracles were being published as early as 1490 (see *Acta Sanctorum,* cited above).

Sannazaro's poem looks like very early work for the following reasons: the pastoral décor, with its woods, hills, streams and rugged caves, does not seem to fit with other accounts of the saint's life; the suggestion (lines 9–12, 39–42) that Jacobus contemplated "the accidents of nature," visiting in the mind the seat that he now holds in heaven, is not visibly appropriate for Jacobus, but closely resembles the elegy addressed to Pardus (1.2.3–12, above); the twenty lines

(13–32) devoted to retelling the old old story, from creation to resurrection, bear little resemblance to any "huge undertaking" in the saint's life; the ensuing dozen lines of *somnium Scipionis* material can be applied to almost any of the virtuous dead; and the concluding sequence of rhetorical questions accomplishes very little.

All in all, the poem appears to be exceptionally early work, perhaps written within a year or two of the saint's death, when he was quite literally a "new inhabitant" of Heaven. Altamura, however, suggests a date of 1516, on the rather slender grounds that Leo X in that year offered papal indulgences in exchange for prayers for Jacobus Picenus. He assigns no other elegy from the first two books a date later than 1503 (see Introductory Note to 1.10, below).

[Elegies 1.7]   **TO THE BLESSED**
JACOBUS PICENUS

Blessed old man, whom not the taint of our original sin nor yet the times had sunk to the level of their viciousness, you who counted great triumphs as one with poverty, so much was your love of snowy simplicity: the woods were your home, your couch the greening turf, the river stream and its herbage filled your tables.

Such was once the life of early man, though to live so was to those men a burden. But for you it was pleasure to contemplate the divers accidents of nature, and to reveal the awesome presence of the gods; in spirit to explore a heaven far removed from our eyes, and to visit beforehand, in the mind, the seat you hold there now. To know besides the origins of all things, which is scarcely consonant with the human condition. Huge undertaking! how in the first beginnings of the emerging world all things were brought forth in six days; how the Father at last when the world was completed ordered his bands of artisans to rest in holy quiet; the pious observances and venerable rites, and all things sacred entrusted to the lawgiving leader; and what the pure Sybils sang to their generations, and what the holy spirit speaks through the mouths of priests; the birth divine and the pledge sent down from heaven, and the humble cradle and the bed of straw; long awaited on earth and by Heaven approved, very man and very God, in mind and in spirit; then the dreadful suffering and the shame of death, and the proud trophies borne from the Stygian domain; finally how he returned to his Father, with their people looking on, and reigns in the realms of light; and all the joys that await us in the promised life, and the glory that will be in time to come.

Shall we wonder at it, if the sanctuary of the unmoved Thunderer and the gleaming courts of boundless heaven lie open to you? since to merits such as these it is but little to mount to the highest heavens, where the Galaxy points out the ready way? Surely from there you are granted the vision of our low-lying lands, and the curving arms of the surrounding sea, and the burning rays of the sun and the moon's recurrences, and how the elements stand by firm compact. And no less how the stars shine with eternal fires, and day and night accomplish their successions. Happy are you who have been able to leave behind our cares, and from afar to despise the things that allure mankind; and happy the hills that saw you speaking and the grass that offered you your pleasant couch—the tree or cliff that held you protected under its blessed shade, and the urn that holds your ashes now. For though you lived your life in rugged caves, now the stars are made a pavement for your feet.

Yet tell me, o holy father, tell me, o glory added unto heaven, tell me, o fame and ornament of your fatherland, whether Wisdom is soothing you with her familiar pages where the soft breeze is stirring the Elysian grove? Or is it your pleasure while meditating songs on your golden reed to wreathe your white locks with the purpling rose? or more so, to sit watching over the virginal choirs, if what was your pleasure on earth be seemly in heaven? Or rather, with the gods' whole senate looking on, do you plead the case for our sins in the heavenly forum? In fine, whatever you are doing, o new inhabitant of shining heaven, you will be in our hearts no slight divinity.

Elegy 8: Introductory Note

This elegy, by far the most political in the collection, is addressed to Guy de Rochefort, who became chancellor on July 9, 1497, during the reign of Charles VIII, and continued in office under Louis XII, until his death on January 15, 1507. There was good reason to address such an elegy to de Rochefort, who showed a genuine interest in humanistic learning, as is testified by Erasmus's suggestion (ten years after de Rochefort's death) that he was the model for Erasmus's own patron (*Contemporaries of Erasmus*, 3.167).

The poem begins with a play on the chancellor's family name, Rochefort. I can find no reason for Sannazaro's failure to correct his mistake about the Christian name (if the dedication did come from Sannazaro himself, and not his posthumous editor). The chancellor may well have had a string of Christian names, including Pierre, but he is everywhere referred to as Guy de Rochefort. The eighteenth-century Benedictine monks, Edmond Martène and Ursin Durand, visited his tomb in the abbey of Citeaux, but unfortunately did not transcribe the text of whatever names and dates were carved on it (*Voyage Litteraire*, 1.205–6).

Sannazaro goes on to imagine Astraea, goddess of Justice, presenting the chancellor with her prayer for the restoration of justice at Naples. Astraea resides in the zodiacal house of Libra (the Scales). Autumn begins when the sun enters Libra (September 22) and continues through Scorpio and Sagittarius (to December 22). Hence the reference to "the house of Autumn and the Claws." Astraea's suggestion of a possible Crusade (lines 49–54) is less anachronistic than it may sound to modern readers. Charles VIII probably seriously contemplated such an enterprise, and kings such as Louis XII (as well as popes such as Alexander VI) at least found the concept politically useful. A similar suggestion by Sannazaro in 1493, in a less public kind of poem and addressed to Ferdinand and Isabella of Spain, is briefly discussed by Benedetto Croce (*La Spagna nella Vita Italiana*, Bari, 1949, p. 100). In this elegy, the triumph would be held along the banks of Arar (i.e., the Saône) because France would have led the Crusade.

Perhaps with a view to the audience being addressed, Sannazaro confines his humanist *imitatio* chiefly to Virgil, making allusion to Astraea's departure from the earth (*Eclogues* 4.6; *Georgics* 2.473–74) and in line 25 to probably the most famous line in the *Aeneid* (*parcere subiectis et debellare superbos*—6.853). Also a well-known Virgilian tag is "A race of men sprung from tree trunks and the rough oak tree" (*Aen.* 8.315), alluded to here in lines 39–40.

Interestingly, moreover, Astraea's prayer suggests also, in lines 17 and 27–28, a pair of less familiar passages, from the Old Testament book of Lamentations:

> I was a derision to all my people; and their song all the day (3:14)

> Our inheritance is turned to strangers, our house to aliens. We are orphans and fatherless, our mothers are as widows (5:2–3).

If these passages are reflected in the language of this elegy, we are witnessing a process of composition unusual in Sannazaro, whose poetry—excepting *De Partu Virginis*—may be said to contain a minimum of Scriptural allusion.

Altamura conjectures a date of 1495 (i.e., the conquest of Naples by Charles VIII), but the poem—which says nothing about which king the chancellor serves—was presumably written between July 9, 1497 and September 1505, when the treaty of Segovia made final disposition of the estates of some of the nobility to whose spoliation the poet refers (e.g., Andrea Matteo Acquaviva d'Aragona—cf. the Introductory Notes to 2.10 and 3.1). It may well be, indeed, that this poem is rather more concerned with the particular than with the general, for it seems entirely probable that Guy de Rochefort is being addressed on the poet's own behalf. Pércopo (p. 66) tells us that the Royal Treasury at Naples, on Nov. 13, 1501, and thereafter, instituted proceedings to return to the Treasury Sannazaro's sulphur mine and other holdings at Agnano, and that Louis XII peremptorily counteracted these proceedings (see Pércopo's Document XXV, signed by Louis XII and dated from Blois May 7, 1502). This information gives special emphasis to such a line as *Adrogat iniustos dum sibi fiscus opes* (line 24), and strongly suggests that Sannazaro made his appeal by addressing Elegy 1.8 to Guy de Rochefort at some point between November 13, 1501, and May 7, 1502. For a more detailed chronology of these six months, see Carlo Vecce, *Francia,* pp. 179–80.

No doubt Sannazaro accompanied his king into exile out of love and loyalty, and no doubt the Aragonese disasters eventually caused him to fall into such deep depression that Apollo deserted him. But the dating conjectured here would present a rather different picture, as the poet creates an opportunity in the midst of troubles and griefs to win at least a temporary victory in his long struggle over that sulphur mine at Agnano.

[Elegies 1.8] **TO PIERRE DE ROCHEFORT**

Grand Chancellor to the King of France

[*Astraea speaks*]

Because your heart is strong, because the citadel of your heart is hard to storm; because you have a name befitting that strong heart; because its courts preserve the laws, under your protection; and because to your virtue every road is easy: I Astraea have left the house of Autumn and the Claws, and have come to your home, my pupil. With sedulous care I nourished you (if you know it not) in your cradle. You insinuated yourself (a pleasing burden) into my bosom. I myself moulded your manners, in mind and in body; I gave you quickness of wit, and judgment. Hence your consistent regard for me, and your enviable knowledge of affairs, hence so many claims on your protection. Therefore to you on bended knee I lift my clasped hands, distressed by my inordinate troubles:

[*Astraea's Prayer*]

Suffer not my strength to languish away in Italy: all my hope depends upon your aid. I am brought low, a laughing stock among bold ministers, and cannot lift up my free-born head to the stars. The realm that long since had its birth from virtue and from mighty armies, it is bondservant to filthy avarice. And it is no wonder if that land be far removed from your values, since it is so far distant from your sphere.

Who can believe it? the citizens are driven from their ancestral homes, while the state treasury arrogates to itself undeserved riches. The treasury gets riches from the wretched. Alas, is it this to "spare the conquered peoples"? Is it this to restore the law to Ausonian soil? An unhappy nobility, despoiled of its patrimony, is driven forth to wander along alien shores. Faith kept to a former master, unshaken by the perils of land or sea, becomes a crime. It is a crime, for sure, to despise cruel death—a crime, for sure, to love their rulers.

O rightly mindful of fortune, all those who have kept their prideful hands from conquered peoples. For though plunder may hold attractions for savage tyrants, glory alone rejoices magnanimous kings. Our merits are not blotted out by any stretch of years, and as far as reason allows they make us gods. But if a man despises the accolades of slow-growing fame, you can number him among the mountain oaks.

Therefore may you, who can soften a powerful king, grant prospering voyage to my desires. Bring it to pass, that to Justice her accustomed honors be restored (you are worthy the task, who are your nurse's protector), but also that our government be shared equally with our sister Mercy, without whom I may be called too harsh and obdurate. O thou ornament, o thou most constant hope of a fallen age, o thou who art stronger than thy fortune. So may it befall you to see a triumph over Jerusalem's populace, and their standards taken by our captains. So may you see the Rhone decree the laws to conquered Nile, and the grandest of triumphs make its procession along the banks of Arar. This do I, this does Phoebus along with me, and the learned sisters too, this do Piety, Justice, and Nobility request of you.

Elegy 9: Introductory Note

The elegy addressed to Giovanni Pontano (1429–1503) has the look of a poem originally intended as a companion piece to the Crasso elegy (1.1), concentrating much of its *imitatio* on Propertius—perhaps in compliment to Pontano, who edited a Propertian ms. discovered in a musty wine cellar (according to Alessandro Alessandri's *Dies Geniales*, 1591, p. 52). The first twenty lines, however, introduce motifs straight from Tibullus—the man of iron who can prefer warfare and plunder when he might have the lovely girl instead (Tib. 1.2.65–66); and, in another variation, the man of iron who can harshly separate youth from maid and maid from youth (Tib. 3.2.1–2). As usual, other Roman poets are visible in the background: possibly Statius (*Silvae* 2.2.12) for the weariness of the long road; certainly Virgil (*Aen.* 4.366–67) for Dido's famous charge that Aeneas was sprung from the cliffs of Caucasus and suckled by tigresses; and certainly also Ennius (through Cicero, *Tusculan Disputations* 1.15.34) for Sannazaro's hope that his fame will be "afloat on the lips of my countrymen."

Soon Tibullus is joined by Propertius in a segment (lines 15–32) that becomes the transition to a new subject—praise of Propertius's fellow-Umbrian, Giovanni Pontano. First comes merely the reminiscent phrasing of "that last funeral" (*extremi funeris atra dies,* Prop. 2.11.4), but then follows an unmistakable signature line:

> Prop.: Vt nostris tumefacta superbiat Vmbria libris
> That swelling Umbria may wax proud over my poems (4.1.63)
>
> Sann.: Et nostro celebrata superbiat umbra sepulcro
> (line 17)

The coincidence of sound can hardly be accidental, despite the different meanings of *Umbria* and *umbra:* for brevity here, comment on these lines has been relegated to the General Introduction (see p. 16). More reminiscences of Propertian language seem to appear in lines 29 and 32 (Prop. 1.6.21; 1.11.5), and perhaps Sannazaro is deliberately fusing Tibullus and Propertius in his *Ah pereat* at line 27:

> Sann.: Ah pereat, quicumque leves sectatur honores;
> Et sequitur famae nomina vana suae.
>
> Prop.: Ah pereat, quicumque rates et vela paravit
> Primus, et invito gurgite fecit iter (1.17.13–14)
>
> Perish the man who first readied ships and sails and made his journey across the unfriendly sea.
>
> Tib.: O quantum est auri potius pereatque smaragdi
> Quam fleat ob nostras ulla puella vias
> (1.1.51–52)
>
> O rather let all the gold and emerald perish than that any girl should weep because of my journeying.

At line 33, Sannazaro turns abruptly to Pontano, suggesting him as the active man, suitable for leading the fleet or Alfonso's troops, in contrast to the poet's pose as Propertian or Tibullan lover, unable to abandon his mistress for the pursuit of riches or empty honor. To this point, the poem sounds like a tribute to Pontano around 1481–86, when he was exceptionally busied with war and diplomacy. But at line 35 Sannazaro drops the motif of active life versus contemplative (or Politics vs. Love), and launches into a catalogue of Pontano's works in prose and poetry, alluding to works as late as the dialogue *Aegidius* (which alludes to the death of Gabriele Altilio in 1501 and to the scene of Sannazaro's departure into exile, in September of that year). We might speculate that Sannazaro in

France, having heard that Pontano was in ill health, is bringing his tribute to Pontano up to date, intending to send it off to the old friend whom he rightly expected never to see again. Some of the works alluded to, however, are even later than *Aegidius,* and probably not seen by Sannazaro until he was aiding Summonte in the publication of all Pontano's work, 1504–12.

In listing Pontano's works, without titles but with frequent allusion to names and details that appear in those works, Sannazaro probably has in mind the manner of Propertius's tribute to Virgil (2.34.59–84). Fortunately we now have in English a readily available account of the entire range of Pontano's poetry and prose, with extensive paraphrase and summary (Carol Kidwell, *Pontano: Poet & Prime Minister,* London, 1991). Pontano's mock-heroic poem about Sertorius and Pompey appears in the dialogue *Antonius;* the lullabies refer to the poems entitled *Naenia,* and Fannia and Cinnama appear in *Parthenopeus.* The reference to "our ventures" (line 77) is Sannazaro's modest acknowledgment of his own dominant role in the dialogue *Actius,* and the reference to the Asellus who scorns the waters poured over him is clarified by an amusing passage in the dialogue *Asinus* (Previtera, p. 304). The remaining allusions to Pontano's works will probably become clear if the reader is able to consult Kidwell's comprehensive account.[1]

Altamura proposes a date of 1501. As suggested by the foregoing, composition over two decades seems entirely likely.

[Elegies 1.9] CONCERNING HIS OWN
PURSUITS, AND THE WRITINGS
OF JOVIANUS PONTANUS

 That man who first could bear to abandon his native home, and suffer the weariness of the long road, and the sea, whom not his tearful household, not his parents could call back again, nor his lovely wife with her dishevelled hair—impious was he, and born from cliff rock or unyielding oak, and reared among tigers. No solid iron surrounds my heart, nor does the hard flint stand rigorous in my breast, that I could abandon my beloved Lares, and my mistress's threshold, to seek out a home in unknown lands. But I am driven to frequent the holy haunts of Phoebus, and the vocal wave and the Thespians' dance: that I may

---

[1]Carol Kidwell's *Sannazaro and Arcadia* (London, 1993) did not become available before this manuscript was completed and accepted for publication, although it is included in the bibliography of works cited. Her comments on Sannazaro's relation to the visual arts in his own time are exceptionally useful.

escape the luckless flames in that last funeral, afloat on the lips of my learned countrymen; and fame lift me up among the poets of renown, nor the black ash carry off my name, but my celebrated shade wax proud over my sepulcher, scorning the marble cut from Parian quarries—though not, however, that it should dare to rival the tomb of mighty Maro, or hope to have such glory.

But who will tear my neck from your snow-white arms? Who will forbid me to warm myself in your beloved bosom? Is Parnassus worth so much with its holy ravine, its shrines at every turn haunted by their goddesses, that you should bedim your shining eyes with tears, that you (dear girl) should weep for my departure? Ah perish the man who hunts after empty honors and pursues the hollow renown of his own fame! Shall I hesitate to dance the midnight dance with you, to invent delights with you, with roses strewn between? to besprinkle your delicate locks with light perfume? and to wear out the night with pleasures never grown stale?

Let Pontano, forsooth, dispose of the Turkish fleet on the high seas, and lead the mighty troops of Alfonso into battle. He who sings now the cradle of the nascent world and the golden stars established in their heavenly abode; how the rain falls and the hail, how fire leaps forth from the clouds, how the sea rolls her salty waters; the garden of the Hesperides, and the apples stolen from the dragon, and the rustic gifts sent to the noble marriage; and the song of shepherds sounding in turn on the clear reed-pipe your charms, o Lepidina; and how Sertorius shines in gilded armor and Pompey's chivalry makes trial of battle. Let none dare contend with him in elegant verse, for he can utter things worthy of eternal Maro.

Father Sebeto listens in his watery caves while you hurl your curses against his grudging doors. Then you call holy Hymen to the festive altars, repeating the vows of your long-awaited marriage, and how your wife first rising from your embraces sorrows for her virginity ravished away. Happy are you, being grown familiar with your wife's faithful ardors, to have seen the certain pledges of your children, and sung their simple lullabies, and their mother's loving kisses and crooning over their cradles. Happy the Fannia who tormented the polished poet and the Cinnama who stole the rule from her. Although they suffer the bitterness of parting, they will see their ashes become renowned.

But who can believe that thereafter by the river Po you have bound your white locks with the poplar leaf? and have sung your Stella, and expended your complaints, when just now she scarcely allowed her foot to be seen. And the bays of Baiae and the myrtle-groves familiar to her Nymphs, and the winding caves shut in among her sulphurous ridges. Then praise of the gods, and names inscribed on silent tombs, renewing their funeral pyres collapsed in ashes. Finally you have revived the Pindaric mode, the resounding plectra, and the strings of the Methymnaean lyre: the while you analyze as well the movements and marches of kings, and the wars of Campania's history.

Truly you engage the times with pungent jesting, as cunning Charon conducts his argument beside the Stygian river. And imitating the example of your Varro and Nigidius,[1] you do not scorn to begin your journey on the roads of grammar. Next you set forth the measures of poetry from our ventures, an old man deigning to repeat the words of a youth. What shall I say of how Aegidius drinks dry the holy streams of Marianus, while singing the true God? Or of how ungrateful conduct is reproached under an apt image by the Asellus who scorns the waters sprinkled over him? Young and old alike revere you as you transmit the precepts that Naples reads when Cicero is disdained; whatever Wisdom reveals from the inner sanctums of the gods, and the sound doctrine, Stagira, of your Old Man: what is proper for a man of courage; what are the arts of princes; what gifts it is best to give with lavish hand; what are the rules for attendance at court, and for conversation; how the skilled tongue delivers witty sallies; what fortune, what prudence can bestow on a man; how far violent passion can move the savage spirit; what are the parts, considered piece by piece, of the magnanimous man, whether he is living at peace or waging savage war. Nor do you shrink from opening up the hidden secrets of the stars, and the remote immutable laws of the Ptolemaic heavens.

Good health to you, blessed old man, whom rightly Delius has appointed father of poets in the land of Italy. The oblivion of Lethe's bank shall not consume you, nor wholly that envious day turn you to ashes. Your tomb will not be built on the public rubbish heap—it will surpass the Pyramids of Nile. Why, Umbria, are you hoping to have for yourself the palms of his victory? He has fetched them back to the walls of my native land. Long may he enjoy his studies, and his praises: let my pleasure be to have grown old in my mistress's bosom.

Elegy 10: Introductory Note

In his tentative chronological listing of the Latin poems, Altamura assigns this elegy (mislabeled *Epigrams* 1.10) to "1503–4, when he was very sick in France and entrusted his memorial to Giovanni di Sangro" (*Sannazaro*, Naples, 1951, p. 174). This sounds circumstantial, but needs verification, since the poem has in some ways the sound of a very early performance. One notes that Borghini suggests (p. 304, n.8) a date of 1478 (again, without an offer of supporting evidence).

The poet's imagining of his own death, and providing of a suitable epitaph, appears in Tibullus 1.3.47–56 and 3.2.29 (see

[1]See Glossary, s.v. Varro.

Introductory Note to 2.7, below), and also in Propertius, 2.1.75–78 (see the Introductory Note to 2.1, below). More direct allusiveness, however, appears in the Virgilian commonplace of the fledglings stolen from the nest (*Georgics* 4.511–13) and the Horatian votive tablets (*Odes* 1.5.13–16)—both these being very standard fare.

I have rendered Syncerus's phrase about living *patriis . . . in oris* as "on my father's estates" because the context also refers to the death of his mother (1475), and Sannazaro's early work is filled with consciousness of his position as an impoverished orphan. But the phrase may simply mean "on my paternal shores" (i.e., at Naples), and thus fit well enough with a poem written during his voluntary exile.

Pércopo (p. 94) lists Giovanni di Sangro as one of the executors named in Sannazaro's will. This fact has no necessary connection with date of composition, except to make possible a very late date indeed.

[Elegies 1.10]   TO JOANNES SANGRIUS

Patrician of Naples
Upon the Poet's Own Untimely Death

 If fierce Love had allowed me to live on my father's estates, or at least to die with my mother watching beside me, so that those projects might have been developed stage by stage, that now are huddled into barely a single volume, I could have scorned perhaps the inexorable Fates, and the sad thread spun from their gloomy spindle, and Libitina would not be carrying me off to a common grave, or the black ashes stealing away my fame.

Now am I compelled to abandon the sweet springs and the pleasant meadows and the holy ring-dance of the Pierian maidens, and cannot submit to your refining judgment that which my Muse poured forth in my early years. So (alas!) is the tender grain cut down in the furrows, so fledgling birds are stolen from the nest. Ah ye gods, shall Syncerus vanish into thin air? and will he be unable to triumph over the doom of the black funeral pyre?

But you, most worthy Sangrius (since Nemesis commands, and over the goddess man is not permitted to prevail), receive these votive tablets and shields from a stricken vessel, gathering up the relics from my shipwreck; invoke my spirit wandering on whatever shore, and carve upon my tomb such verses as these:

HERE I LIE, ACTIUS. HOPE LIES EXTINCT WITH ME.
AFTER OUR DEATH NOTHING REMAINS BUT LOVE.

Elegy 11: Introductory Note

Its closing couplet acknowledges this poem's unique place in Sannazaro's *corpus*. Only in his epigrams does he occasionally approach its scathing rebukes of enemies and indignant defenses of friends.

The story of Scuccha's punishment eludes me. Pardo's double tongue is a reference to the bilingual abilities of that native of Saragossa. For the founding of Cumae, see Elegy 2.9, below.

Largely confined to enumerating the literary strengths of Sannazaro's circle, the poem does not lend itself to the *imitatio* with which these introductory notes are principally concerned. One should, however, compare the manner of Sannazaro's couplets of praise with the last ten lines of Propertius 2.34 (cited above in the Introductory Note to Elegy 1.9). The praises themselves are in most instances reasonably clear from their context, or can be clarified by consulting where possible the DBI, or works such as Altamura's *L'umanesimo nel mezzogiorno d'Italia* (Firenze, 1941), or Mario Cosenza, *A Biographical and Bibliographical Dictionary of the Italian Humanists* (Boston, 1962, 6 vols.).

The circumstances that provoked this outburst are unknown. Altamura suggests a date of 1492–93, Giuniano Maggio having died in 1493 (cf. Introductory Note to Elegy 2.7 below).

[Elegies 1.11]   AGAINST FOUL-MOUTHED
DETRACTORS

 Presumptuous crowd, why are you falling upon divine poets, and making your savage assaults with slashing fang? Stop spreading your slanders with sacrilegious tongue, stop it! The god himself is standing up for his people. What strange resentment is provoking you into fury? Begone, profane, begone! pollute no more the innocent muses. Does not Scuccha give warning of this, neck-deep in the Stygian waters, while weeping he shrinks from the Furies' coiling lash? Time was he took pleasure in his arrows painted with poison: now the wretch is paying the full penalty of his crime. Cease to outrage the shades of my dear mother, with your whoring and dicing and drinking above her grave.

Let every man take pleasure in his own art: it is not for you to make the approach to Helicon, not for you to pollute the water of a virgin stream. But truly the buskined Muse of Jovian may drink of it, and utter things worthy of mighty Maro. In whose company Altilius, haunting the secret places of the sacred wood, may pour forth song from his learned breast. And likewise may Compater, repeating the productions of his jocund Muse, deliver his witty jests. And Elysius, his locks adorned with glistening ivy, sing melodies few but fitting for the Aonian choirs. And Acquavivus extend his ancestral glory through feats of arms, teaching the camp to recognize our goddesses. Cabanilius himself may restore the lofty walls of his Troy, and your ancient households, o realms of Appulia. And Corvinus, like a new branch rising from a tender tree, may sing things to be approved by any ear. Albinus too, not last to wake the echoes in the Pierian caves, may recount his prince's deeds.

You too, why refrain from bewailing with your learned complaints, o cultured Marullus, the ruin of your native land? And Maius—he who shapes and nourishes with his own birth struggle so many brave spirits and famous wits—Maius may weave his utterance into an honored crown, calling his rod so gentle his royal scepter. And Cariteus for certain may offer his Genius the honors that are his due, singing before the festive banquets. Moreover Aelius, trusting in the sweetness of a charming tongue, may wear away whole days with his eloquent art. And you, clear-spoken Scala, need not be modest today in offering the flowers of your eloquence to the age that is to come. The Socratic dialogues may be rivalled by the writings of Zeno, to whose mouth the bee has carried the honey of spring. But you, o Carbo, not to be disowned by the Castalian choirs, sing now the regions of your Castaly. You also, Pardus, whom Wisdom blesses with a double tongue, may make it your pleasure to wear out the night with your studies. And others, whose fame travels through learned ears, may prepare to transcend death on that last day.

We too, if mighty Apollo does not refuse, may sing the nymphs, and the goatfooted gods. For well have we come to know (though envy be listening) the Thespian waves, and have trod their caverns with auspicious foot. But be it yours to prepare poison for your unsuspecting cronies, and to plague with your thefts the houses of the poor. And be it yours in the manner of Oedipus to foul your fathers' marriage beds, if indeed common opinion allows that you have any certain father. Alarm the city with treacherous murders by night, and disturb the peace in her streets and public squares. These are the studies, these the arts that you have learned from your earliest years—not how to pluck the strings of the Aganippean lyre. For neither Calliope nor skillful Apollo has presented you with Permessus's holy stream; but dreadful Alecto accompanied by her twin has brought you draughts from muddy Phlegethon. Surely it is from this that your lives and writings are so stained with black pollution, and envy sits on your filthy mouth.

Am I deceived, or has overburdened Aetna sent down on us these Cyclopses? And do you feel this pestilence too, my gentle motherland? Alas, my Parthenope, what plagues are vexing you? It is not like you to bring forth such monsters. Gods of our fathers, through whose oracles the Wanderer brought here his fleet and founded Cumae, avert such pestilence from our shores, if you have founded these walls under happy auspices. And you, o innocent shades, whom their deadly poison has driven before your time to the Stygian waters, bring hither avenging torches and with pursuing smoke bring terror to the authors of your slaughter. And you, o Muses, most faithful divinities of the poets, divinities not to be profaned by my verses, pardon if now for the first time we have offended your ears: we have taken up the weapons of righteousness in our exasperated hand.

BOOK 2

Elegy 1: Introductory Note

For an informed and sensitive account of Sannazaro's stance toward Alfonso in this elegy, see William J. Kennedy, *Jacopo Sannazaro and the Uses of Pastoral* (Hanover-London, 1983, pp. 85–87).

Lines 1–24 present the elegist's standard disclaimer of heroic verse and subject-matter, naming the chief Roman writers in elegiac meter—Ovid, Horace, Propertius, Catullus, and Tibullus. Sannazaro claims that, were he to attempt the heroic, he would choose to sing of Alfonso in preference to the subject-matter of Achilles Tatius (*Argonautica*), Homer, Virgil, or Statius (*Thebaid*).

After sketching Alfonso's two predecessors as King of Sicily, the poet moves on to Alfonso's early campaigns along the Adriatic coast (2.1.49–70), in a passage studded with geographical names (or allusions) from Book Three of the *Aeneid*: Buthrotum (*Aen*. 3.293), Locri (399), the city of Meliboea (401), Caulon and Lucinia ("the holy temples on [Caulon's] ridge"—552,553), and the Ceraunian steeps (506). In Elegy 3.1, addressed to Alfonso's brother Frederick, we encounter a similar choice of place-names with Virgilian associations (lines 37–58), and both passages are probably to be taken as examples of the humanist device of glorifying contemporary leaders through association with the heroic Roman past. The place-names and allusions in the passage on Alfonso's later campaigns in Tuscany and Rome (2.1.71–104) are noticeably less literary, perhaps because Sannazaro is writing from direct experience, having actually accompanied Alfonso on his forays against Rome (see Kennedy, cited above).

In closing his eulogy, Sannazaro reverts to his posture as elegiac lover (2.1.109–18), as he has done in the first, second, and ninth elegies of Book One, concluding with a remarkably mature and skillful imitation of Propertius (Prop. 2.1.75–78), discussed at some length in the General Introduction (see above, pp. 18–19).

Altamura's date of 1494 is, in effect, the only year in which Alfonso could have been addressed as King of Sicily.

[Elegies 2.1]   **TO ALFONSO**

Son of Ferdinand of Aragon [and] King of Sicily

 Alfonso, thou glory to be added to your invincible father, no slight name among your Hesperian ancestors, why are you sending me to the honored springs of Parnassus? My thirsting is overwhelmed in a mighty river. It is Virgil's glory to sing of chariots and armies: it is Naso's fate to die in the full flow of love. The Muse of skilled Propertius follows the path of Callimachus: Flaccus's ear divides Pindaric measures. Catullus sings with broken voice the obsequies of a sparrow: you praise your Nemesis, o elegant Tibullus. Not all chariots make their exertions on a single course: our steed runs in a narrow circuit. If Phoebus had taught me in the shade of Castaly, and sprinkled my brow with the Gorgonian water, or if the Muse had granted me the Aeschylaean buskin, and there were to be a deeper timbre in my voice, I would not sing the struggles of the Colchian youth (a stretch of sea left undisturbed by the untried bark), not the princes sworn to overthrow Pergamum, not the gods fled from Troy after two lusters, nor the battle around Thebes, and the savage wars of brothers, and the fierce corpses stolen from the double pyre:[1] you and yours would I celebrate in my song, nor with reward so pleasant would the sweet burden lie heavy on me.

For I should sing of generals defeated, and Spanish realms, and dreadful battles won by your ancestors, and a race of kings descended from ancient origins; and all the deeds that are told of your magnanimous grandfather, while he is despoiling the Libyan regions, and Carthage's ancient hold, and the fertile fields of the Lotos-eaters; then at the queen's invitation he pursues Italian kingdoms, and enters into Parthenope and the Chalcidean strongholds. But since the hearts of women reverse their unstable minds, he leaves those suspect dwellings and seeks out the fields of his homeland; and without long delay leads back again his avenging gods in arms; and with his attendant Nymphs makes his entry into the besieged city, where the wandering water glides through hidden channels. Under that king they say the golden age truly was come again. Happy those whose merit reaped its fruits!

What shall I say of your father's invincible armies, of the stirring of trumpets throughout thy fields, o land of Daunia: and their leaders scattered, their camps destroyed, no royal battles more famed in any age! O if Fate should grant me my closing years, how much will I sing! how much applause (my voice) there will be! Then might I dare to

---

[1]See Glossary, s.v. Eteocles.

invade the Maeonian springs, and with dreadful trumpet to thunder savage wars.

And (to pass over the rest in silence) I shall sing your mighty deeds, and your many achievements will exalt my spirits: how as a lad you travelled over the furthest confines of your kingdom, bringing back trophies from the shores you traversed, and quieted tumults not settled until you drove the enemy from your native land. First of your honors, to have preserved with your powerful army the Locrians, and thy walls, o city of Meliboea; and come like Mars to the loftiest heights of Caulon, and into the holy temples on its ridge, temples of the goddess who rules over all the vast ocean, at once Jove's faithful consort and his sister.[1] Chratis will be witness, the waters of Sybaris will be witness, and the shores that look out over the Ionian surge. Moreover, how you filled the Etruscan fields with your army's march, and Arno flowed for you with captive waters: and you rendered up many a quivered band, the Turkish troops,[2] as sacrifices from Ausonian hands, thank-offering to the gods of Italy. The Ceraunian steeps have feared our menacing, and Butrinto's hold; and we have seen their leader captive and their weapons broken, that your fleet bore hither over subjugated waters.

Next the passions of the Ligurians, and quarrels put down by the sword, and the French towns split into two factions. I shall sing what I myself have seen: the land of Tusculum knows it, and Anio's stream that falls from its highest ridges. For under your leadership, while you were subduing by the sword the Latian fields, I spent the first years of my military service. Twice we have seen the castles of Nomentum, twice the strongholds of powerful Tivoli lay down their arms before our feet, when almost half Subura was in alarm, and vows offered up to Capitolian Jove. And not once only (as I may bear witness) have we broken and repulsed the armed leaders before the threshold of the Colline gate. Yet pardon me, o venerable mother, if I have followed righteous banners under Alfonso: he was my king.

Unlucky Lanuvium, o land contrary to our fates; you are able to change the pattern of our fortune. For that Victory inclined to the enemy's side, was more the work of Fortune than of skill. But he, unbroken, carrying the struggle to the noble banks of the Po, visits the realms of his dear sister: and when his base was established he spread over all Insubria, and led his army through the Euganean hills. Cry *Io,* ye peoples: you have seen the cheering throngs, and treaties established by his victorious hands. And let not Farfar fail to tell how he laughed at the enemy yielding the day and at their leader, stripped bare, turning his back in flight. Ah, where are they now (Robert), your threatening words, when you were seeking the gov-

[1]See Glossary, s.v. Juno.
[2]See Glossary, s.v. Otranto.

ernance of Campania for yourself alone? You were ready just now to overthrow our princes, to overturn everything: now look how clearly your flight displays your craven fears. And you encourage your troops to abandon their standards—ah, shame!—and the booty of their long campaign. Yet good Alfonso took care of them, though they followed another, and blessed them with his gentle aid.

Hail, honored protector of mankind, hail, most honored of kings, you are the Sun of Italy, you are her only father. Why should I relate your arts in peace and labors in war, and the perpetual glory of your genius through all time? But me the commands of my lovely mistress deter, that I not spend my pains upon such song: and harsh Love forbids my scorning his sweet sorrow, making me bow my neck to his hateful yoke. Nor do my tears avail, nor my prayers for death: still he continues to shake his torches against me. Wherefore if Fame shall come to you as the messenger of my death, let your triumphal wheels come to a stand nearby, and as you shed a tear say to my buried ashes:

Lie quiet, poet, taken from us by the harshness of your mistress.

Elegy 2: Introductory Note

This elegy, like the eighth below, is an example of the *genethliacon*, or birthday-poem. Its structure may have been suggested by Propertius 3.10, which begins with the poet awakened by his Muses, continuing on through his mistress's birthday until poet and mistress retire to bed in the closing couplet. But Sannazaro handles this structural concept in his own way, and very obliquely.

After greeting the new-born day (that day which had greeted the new-born child before), the poet goes about his house making preparations: wreaths, and piles of roses and hyacinths, wine and incense to sprinkle on the hearth, and a glittering array for the table at which he will feast his friends. Then he sets out place-cards, so to speak, naming each honored guest and stating what each will contribute to the after-dinner conversation. Finally, the feast will close as Garlon plays his lyre and the moon looks down on the genial, civilized scene. It is an attractive performance, wholly typical of Sannazaro's poetry of friendship.

Altamura proposes a date of "1490 sgg.," with a terminal date of 1500. Perhaps this is his way of acknowledging the awkwardness of having Sannazaro's birthday feast attended by Crasso (d. 1490) in company with Cabanilius, or Troiano Cavaniglia (b. 1479). Apparently we need to adopt Sir Philip Sidney's view that poetry, unlike history, is not "tied to the truth of a foolish world."

A verse translation appears on p. 169.

[Elegies 2.2]   ## ON THE FEAST DAY

of the Blessed Martyr Nazarius
who is the poet's birthday Genius[1]

 Lo, now returns my day that I have awaited through the whole year: renew my garlands, Aonian goddesses. This day brought me forth new-born into the lifegiving air, and bade me lift up my head erect toward the stars. Now heap me the altar with purpling hyacinth, and wreathe my threshold with the woven rose. Fetch wine and incense for the flower-crowned hearth: for this is the way to reverence Genius and Lares. And you, my glittering table, soon to be welcoming poets garlanded with parsley, prepare the annual feast.

Here will Pontano's muse, with buskin of royal purple, begin to sing me her song when the wine is set out: and will proclaim the ways of Nature and the beginnings of the youthful world, and how all things are to die on the appointed day. And let Crassus, bound about with the lasting honor of his wreath, unlock his lips bedewed with Pierian measures, and tell me of ancient Linterno, and quiet Petrine, and my grandsire's fertile realms: realms not destined, alas, to come to his latter descendants, as hostile Fortune performs her various changes. And let Altilius, bringing the gods fresh honors, strike up his skillful song on the Pindaric lyre. Then let him sing the marriage of the houses of Sforza and Aragon, with which he may justly (o Homer) match your song. And the Muse of Spartan Marullus, a talented visitor to our feast, let her not weep for her exile, but recite the words and numbers of antique Lucretius, as with high praise he lavishes the gods.

Add to these (o Pudericus) your witty sallies: add the famed eloquence of your father: add those many gifts sprung from your genius. And add to the reckoning the jests of Panormita, and his writings, and the days of his friendship with Jovian. In the midst of these let Acquavivus returning from his well-deserving troops assert the benefits of honorable service, and as leader of the group set forth the doctrine and arguments of observant Plutarch, with their underlying principles. Cabanilius too—he need not hesitate in telling his own deeds or his mighty grandfather's, and approved no less by his Phoebus than by Mars let him bathe his comely locks in the Phocian stream.

You too, my dearest Garlon, youth whom I revere, begin now to play your lyre with skillful hand, and rouse for me your Allifae, while the wandering stars attend the moon on her silent journey through the

[1]See the Introductory Note to Elegies 2.8.

night. Under such auspices as these it is our pleasure to conduct our genial feast, making our celebration as Thespians should.

Elegy 3: Introductory Note

This shortest of the elegies makes a kind of epigrammatic play on Janus, the double-visaged god of doorways, as titular god of the month of January and also resident deity of the Roman temple of Janus, whose doors were open in time of war, closed in peace. Janus throws open the doors of his temple because Alfonso, Duke of Calabria, is launching his successful campaign to expel the Turks from Otranto. The reference to Otranto in line 19 makes clear that this is quite an early poem (1481), as one might also guess from the standard *topoi* of rivers with golden sand, and of Oriental wealth (cf. the passages from Tibullus cited above in the Introductory Note to Elegy 1.1).

Sannazaro's seventeenth-century editor Broekhuizen (Amsterdam, 1689, p. 203) cites a Thomas Fuscus included by Petrus Crinitus in his *Libri de poetis latinis* (Florence, 1505), and it seems virtually certain that this is "il giurista Tommaso Fusco" whom Crinitus knew in 1503 as a member of the Accademia Romana (see DBI, s.v. Del Riccio Baldi [Crinitus Petrus], 38.266). Symptomatic of Sannazaro's troubled times is a poem that Crinitus himself addressed "Ad Thomam Fuscum de malis & incommodis suae aetatis" (in a reprint of the volume cited above, Basle, 1532, p. 551). That poem, written evidently some time after 1497 and probably as late as 1503, when Crinitus met Fuscus at Rome, opens with a reference to ten years of warfare and strife just past, and closes with a prediction that the princes of Spain will be filling Italy with bloody war. Crinitus was a better prophet than Sannazaro.

A verse translation appears on p. 170.

[Elegies 2.3]   ON THE FIRST OF JANUARY

To Fuscus

 A genial day is dawning: the Sun discloses that golden head which so many times has cheered our forefathers. It dawns: behold, the beginning of a better year returns. Ye who approach, repeat your prayers with reverent voice. Let the holy temples' pediments be duly hung with garlands that the roving Naiad plucked from Sebeto's stream. Let Janus himself throw open the doors of his temple, his double brow dripping with odorous perfume. Let the sacred incense smoke on his spotless altars, while he stands above watching over their fires and announcing to you (Fuscus) new honors for your virtue. These promises now I

judge will warm your heart. Nor could you more desire the sands that the Lydian river rolls,[1] that the proud waters of golden Tagus roll. Nor more whatever the Persian gathers from his fertile acres, and the Arab burned by an assiduous sun.

Just things I pray: that the enemy should decamp from Latian shores, and foiled should straggle abroad with his horse in disarray. Let him be driven in defeat to abandon Otranto's territory, or collapse in his blood on our soil. That day will come (Fuscus), most hospitable to your prayers, when Peace will be granting our city welcome respite.

Elegy 4: Introductory Note

Sannazaro's success with Ovidian metamorphic narrative, in this elegy and in the hexameters of *Salices,* makes one wonder that he contented himself with only those two. Did he perhaps consider such inventions too easy—or perhaps too much a dead end? Such questions should give us pause before we simply discard humanist *imitatio* as the pallid production of cooks who dare not go beyond their recipe.

Virtually the whole of the *Elegies,* and much of the *Epigrams,* is composed of "occasional" poetry, more or less firmly attached to specific occasions, and often to specific friends. It is quite plausible that this elegy too is so attached. The locale of the poem is remarkably specific—eventually we discover that the song is sung beneath the shade of a white mulberry which is perched on a ledge of a sheer cliff bordering the sea, accessible only through a kind of natural bridge hollowed out of volcanic rock, in the general area of Vesuvius, and quite close to the *colles leucogaei* ("white hills") described by Pliny (*Nat. Sci.* 18, § 114; 31, § 12; 35, § 174) as "lying between Pozzuoli and Naples." The location, indeed, precisely fits the sulphur mine at Agnano, mid-way between Pozzuoli and Naples, concerning which Sannazaro was involved in much litigation between 1487 and 1505 (see Elegy 1.8, above). The eighteenth-century volume publishing the testimony in that litigation is entitled *Anecdoti istorici sulle miniere delli monti Leucogei, etc.* (Naples, 1790). One is tempted to speculate that Sannazaro and some companions had happened upon just such a tree, and that Elegy 2.4 is the poet's tribute to this tough survivor.

The Ovidian nature of the poem is evident throughout, but Sannazaro does supply a signature line (or phrase, at least) at line 73 (*niveis uberrima pomis;* cf. *Met.* 4.89).

Altamura does not speculate on a date for the poem, which may not have been given a final polishing. (Line 5 contains only a single word, although the lacuna might be an effect deliberately contrived.) Possibly this elegy, and the *Salices* (which seems closely akin to it), both belong to a period in the late 1490s when Sannazaro was casting about for a suitable enterprise—ultimately deciding on the

[1] See Glossary, s.v. Pactolus.

Piscatorial Eclogues (which he worked on while sharing Frederick's exile in France) as well as the *De Partu Virginis* (which is alluded to in the dedicatory lines introducing *Salices,* and which occupied him through fifteen years or so after his return to Naples in 1505).

[Elegies 2.4] **ON THE WHITE MULBERRY**

Now weave fresh ivy-berries, Erato, for my head: and tune the singing strings of the golden lyre. Let us call to mind the bitter misfortunes of a shading tree. This was a tale not known to our clime before. Let the tree herself listen, and cover the singers with her gentle shade.

Once upon a time there lived in the forests of Baiae a Naiad most lovely, an expert hunter of the wandering beasts. Often transparent Lucrine longed to be able to clasp her to his bosom in his hidden caverns, and not once only did the shepherd's pipe praise her quiver and bow in rustic song. Cumae be witness, the waves of Linterno be witness, and the Hamadryads, holy divinities of Gaurus, how she hated the Sylvans, and the double-horned Pans, and whatever gods are worshipped in forest and grove.

But what are the Fates preparing? From her accustomed mountain haunts Morinna was returning—that was her name, and the name an omen too—when a cloud covered over the sky with sudden darkness, and whitened the ground with a shower of hail. The head with garlands crowned now crowned with hail, here and there she ran through the fields in her flight from the storm. Near the sulphurous mountains was a valley barely passable, whose Greek name signifies "white ground." Beyond it hung a cavern formed by a rockfall, a well-known shelter for the peasants' shaggy flocks. Here it chanced that the half-god goat, the half-goat god had diligently driven his contentious he-goats. As the Nymph caught sight of him from afar, he pursues her with all his heart, uttering such words as these: "Where are you making such haste, ah hard-hearted girl, and scorning my complaints ungraciously? Nymph, do not flee my sight. With me you shall hunt the mountain goats, with me the fallow-deer. This heart will be all obedient to your commands. There is no reason you should flee: believe me, my new-made beechen cups will always be foaming with snowy milk. You will always be able to have from my purse gifts adorned with roses, gifts woven with privet-blossom."

He spoke: but she in her flight outstrips the driving winds, the hailstorm no way slowing her swift pace. And directing her flight now to the gloomy lake and the sterile marsh, and then to the uplands as well, planted with young trees, she sees far off at the mouth of a hollow cave a path almost concealed by the blinding dust of the storm. She hurls herself into it, as into a hiding-place—he follows her all the same, drawn by desire for his prey. Now in the open again she saw the sky, and the sun, and had left the hollow mountain behind her back. On her right was the sea, on her left the sheer cliffrock: and now the lover was pressing close upon the weary girl. All at once crying out, she said "Grant me your aid, Delia, and hearken to my last cry." The goddess brought aid to her Nymph and showed herself to the suppliant. Fallen of herself, she is lying on the ground—and suddenly she becomes a tree: Morus, the mulberry, our fathers called it; and of Morinna she has nothing but the name. Her feet grew into roots, her hair into leaves; and what is now bark was her dark garment. Her arms are branches; but what is now gleaming fruit was the hail that you, poor Nymph, so ill avoided.

Misenus wept, Avernus wept the changed maiden, and by the warm springs their deities mourned for her. Aye, Sebeto's Naiads wept indeed within their caverns and Parthenopea with dishevelled hair. But Faunus yet more than the rest poured out his tears in tribute, and adds these words to her sad obsequies: "O maiden not unknown to the sylvan sisterhood, now Morus, long may you live, gleaming whitely above your shaggy bark, and forever shelter our heads with your foliage, so that the needled pine herself gives way to your leaves. You will never be spotted with the blood of wretched Thisbe; ah, may you not seem unmindful of your fate. You will one day stand (and the fates do not deny it) full-leaved within these bounds, abundant with snowy fruits, and about you the lads will sing, and the graceful lasses, leading the festive dances in your rites."

Thus far sang the Muse to her famous lyre, and joyously taking wing revisits her Aonian springs.

Elegy 5: Introductory Note

This cheerful and confident poem is, strictly speaking, the only elegy addressed primarily to a pagan deity, although Juno appears significantly throughout Sannazaro's *genethliacon* for his mistress's birthday (2.8, below), and somewhat less prominently in the poem for Antonio Garlon's first-born (1.4, above).

Both Tibullus (3.6) and Propertius (3.17) wrote hymns to Bacchus, although they too, like Sannazaro, do not often address entire poems to a god. Tibullus supplies the most obvious signature lines:

Tib.: Candide Liber ades: sic sit tibi mystica vitis
semper, sic hedera tempora vincta feras
Come, fair Bacchus: so may the mystic vine be
yours forever;
so may your temples be always bound with ivy.
(3.6.1–2)

San.: Bacche bimater, ades: sic sint tibi nexa corymbis
cornua; sic nitidis pendeat uva comis.
(2.5.1–2)

And from quite another poem:

Tib.: Pomosisque ruber custos ponatur in hortis
terreat ut saeva falce Priapus aves
Let Priapus, a ruddy guardian, be set up in my
orchards
that he may scare the birds with his savage
blade. (1.1.17)

San.: At deus hortorum, cui vertice fixa rubenti
canna tremit, saevas falce repellat aves.
(2.5.17–18)

Yet Tibullus's "To Bacchus" is far less like Sannazaro's than those
opening lines would suggest, being essentially an amatory complaint, as the speaker Lygdamus resolves to get drunk in an effort to
forget how badly Neaera has treated him. Passing references to
Ariadne and Agave do little to focus our attention on Bacchus as
deity—Tibullus is writing about Tibullus (or Lygdamus).

Propertius's Elegy 3.17, on the other hand, shares much of the
décor of Sannazaro's poem—the wine-making, the bare feet tram-
pling the must, the vineyard slopes protected from birds and beasts,
cymbals, tympani, and the reeds of goat-footed Pans, as well as numerous references to the god's myths (the birth, the tales of Pentheus
and Lycurgus, the island of Naxos, the arching dolphins, the
yardarm flowering into a vine, and so on).

From both these elegists Sannazaro creates his own amal-
gam—less amatory, less centered on the dangers of wine's relaxing of
emotional control; in short, more decorous. As if to reinforce this
decorum, two passages from Virgil appear in the four lines closing
Sannazaro's poem: Dido's stately banquet for the visiting Trojans
(*Adsit laetitiae Bacchus dator—Aen.* 1.734); and the Salic priests' invocation (of Hercules, not Bacchus):

Aen. Salve, vera Jovis proles, decus addite divis,
Et nos et tua dexter adi pede sacra secunde

Hail, true seed of Jove, added glory to the courts
of heaven,

> graciously visit us and these thy rites with
> favorable feet.
>
> (*Aen.* 8.301–2, tr. Mackail)

San.: Salve, cara patri soboles . . . laetitiaeque
  parens . . .
Et me pacato numine dexter adi. (2.5.49–52)

The effect of all this is somewhat similar to other synthesizings of Tibullus and Propertius in Sannazaro (cf. 1.3, Introductory Note), in emphasizing a logical sequence implicit in materials coming from a variety of passages in those elegists. An opening section (1–22) explicitly renounces the heroic aspect of the Dionysus legend, emphasizing a generally pastoral (and Propertian) scene of vine-growing and wine-making, with a supporting cast of Dryads, Satyrs and Bassarids, reinforced by Silenus and the garden god, Priapus. Then a second section (23–34) promises that the poet will eventually dare to sing those heroic aspects of the legend renounced before (Ariadne, and the conquest of India). Indeed, Syncerus becomes so daring in his drink as to predict himself "a mighty poet-priest, as never Virgil was, nor ever Homer." This bold claim leads on to a third section (35–52), not quite so clearly focused, which seems partially centered on the Horatian theme that poets cannot be waterdrinkers, but must pray for poetic inspiration from their wine.

All in all, more Apollonian than Dionysian—but perhaps that is what Syncerus is acknowledging when he asks to have his Dionysus *pacato numine*, peacefully disposed.

[Elegies 2.5] **TO BACCHUS**

 Twin-mothered Bacchus, come: so may your horns be woven with the ivy-berry, so may the grape hang down from your shining hair: whether now Thebes, whether now shaggy Ismarus shelters you, or friendly Naxos on her shady ridges. Hither, haste hither, with bright-leafed thyrsus, o father; turn your steps hither instead, o Bacchus. But lay aside now the tragic robe, and painted buskin, and you too stain your tender feet with must. And let the divine Dryads and double-horned Satyrs come with you too, sounding their pipes and hollow trumpets, and the perilous troop of Bassarids, their hair unbound, shake their loud timbrels with lifted palms, whom slow Silenus follows after, pleading from afar that they stop and wait for him. Then let the old man bemoan to himself the death of his long-eared ass, until he can make his approach

with tottering staff. But let the garden god,[1] his reed crown rustling, fixed on his ruddy head, drive away with his scythe the greedy birds. Meanwhile let the largest of bowls with graven gold foam forth for all its inexhaustible wine, an offering from Lesbos, and round about let the hollow flute proclaim your praises due, celebrating the appointed feast.

I through the streets of the city and through every crossroad shall conduct the rites that are ever to be observed. I shall recount the famous deeds remembered from the triumph over the Giants, and dancers shouting "Euhoe," the joyous rites of Bacchus. Nor shall I keep silent about the swarthy troops, the realms of Ganges, and battles waged along the perfumed shores. Then your marriage chamber, Ariadne, the nuptial torches, and the shining crown fixed in the midst of heaven. Now, observing the sacred rituals and mysteries not to be spoken, shall I plant rods to be covered with the greening leaf. And I shall make my procession to your altars, a mighty poet-priest as never Virgil was, nor ever Homer.

Holy father, drive away my gnawing cares: clear my clouded breast with aged wine. Bring quiet slumbers to my breast, and enlighten my weary eyes with your inspiration. For we know what troubles you endured in your setting forth, what fears for the flaming thunderbolt. Unhappy Semele, why are you asking of your lover a display so harmful to you, and to your son? Ask of Jove in your prayers such gifts as are fitting; ask, and you shall have gifts befitting your prayers. Not for you a child from the common crowd of the forest-dwelling gods, but one with whom Phoebus and Mercury can be equals, one that Saturn need not disdain to acknowledge from the deep, that Jupiter can approve with gracious countenance. Hail, dear pledge of your father, most mellow of the gods; hail, mankind's recreation, the author of our joy. And (if I ask what is proper) provide me with responsive Muses, and visit me graciously, your divinity peacefully disposed.

Elegy 6: Introductory Note

In itself, this elegy is a standard exercise, playing on the surname Montalto and turning this play into a reasonably graceful compliment. The performance, satisfactory for what it is, gives little scope to the qualities that make Sannazaro a poet worth considering after five hundred years. Its major interest, indeed, derives from considerations of literary history, as one of Sannazaro's most evident examples of patronage poetry written probably for socio-political reasons.

The poem has the sound of having been written expressly to congratulate Montalto on his rise to the office of *Scrinii Magister*—

[1]See Glossary, s.v. Priapus.

an office for which Montalto is suited because he has from birth been accustomed to high places, and which he fills graciously, so that those who approach him seem to be in a flowering mountain meadow rather than hemmed in by harsh defiles and ragged rocks. But regrettably I have been quite unable to determine precisely what office this is. Borghini confidently refers to Montalto, without elaborating, as *tesoriere di Carlo V* (Borghini, p. 337, n. 47), but this is perhaps only an assumption based on references to Montalto's having been in his youth a fiscal advocate (e.g., Minieri-Riccio, p. 4). It is true that DuCange (s.v. *magister*) has some entries, from the time of Charlemagne, that suggest *scrinii magister*=treasurer, but a majority of the DuCange entries, chiefly from early Christian sources, suggest something resembling the late-medieval English office of *magister rotulorum*, Master of the Rolls, who had charge of the records of Chancery Court and of all patents and grants under the Great Seal (see *Encycl. Brit.*, ed. XI, 1910, 17.873). That might square with Luigi Volpicella's note that after Casalnuovo's death, in 1516, "fu disposto dal re" that the use of Casalnuovo's "casale di Striano" should be passed on to "Ludovico Montalto, reggente la regia cancelleria" (Volpicella, p. 313, s.v. Luise di Casalnuovo).

Montalto, who was apparently born about the same year as Sannazaro, became an important figure after the Spanish occupation of Naples, but scholars have only recently begun to show uneasiness that so little is known about him (e.g., Guido d'Agostino, *La Capitale ambigua. Napoli dal 1458 al 1580*, Naples, 1979, p. 273, n. 29). Altamura tells us (*Mezzogiorno*, p. 75) that by 1508 he was enough of an important figure that the Neapolitan poet DiJennaro dedicated to him a portion of a poem, in manuscript. And clearly he was a person with whom Sannazaro took pains to remain on good terms, as appears in this passage from a letter written by Sannazaro to Antonio Seripando on June 26, 1518:

> I had a long conversation the other day with the honorable Messer Lodovico di Montalto . . . and touched on many delicate questions, perhaps not without some useful result in the future. (*Opere Volgari*, ed. Mauro, p. 330)

A reference to "Messer Lodovico" on September 19, 1517, is probably also to Montalto (Mauro, p. 314).

If Elegy 2.6 can be correctly taken as a patronage poem, as late as 1516 or even 1520 (in which year Charles was crowned Emperor), congratulating a fellow-member of the Academy on his rise to an important office under the new regime, it becomes a significant part of our total picture of Sannazaro's career, however slight a performance it may be. But the dedicatory heading may not carry that much weight. We need first to know the dates of Montalto's service as *Scrinii magister:* and then we may decide whether it is probable that the dedication's *Caroli Caes.* indicates the actual date of composition, or is merely an updating of Montalto's status, as in the case of Troiano Cavaniglia's titles (see the Introductory Note to *The Willows*).

[Elegies 2.6]   TO LUDOVICUS MONTALTUS

of Syracuse
Scrinii magister for the Emperor Charles

 *Mons altus* is your famous name, whether Aetna fertile with snowy ridges bestowed it when you were born, or the cliffs of the Nebrodes haunted by the roving Napaeans, or Eryx renowned for Dione's divinity. Or because you learned to crawl on the crest of Olympus, and lovely Arethuse brought you to her quiet bosom, your noble name has derived from leafy Olympus, renewing the ancient rites of Elean Jove. Or rather (because as a boy you passed the lofty Alps, until Belgium's land could lie open to your merits, and you could seek out the British Ocean's unknown roar, showing no fear of the caves of hoary Tethys), your name has come to you from the soaring Alps, that it might proclaim the deeds accomplished at that age.

Whatever it is, and whatever mountain and sheer ascent of unattainable height is author of this name of yours, it has in view not manners, nor deeds, but the sharpness of a lofty mind, and the heraldic banners of your genius. Yet though your spirit rise above the clouds, and the stars, and all things are almost insignificant in your sight, it is not through harsh defiles or ragged rocks that we approach you, but by the flower-strewn path of a valley, a valley clothed by its stream with grasses ever green, and warmed by the breezes from its neighboring shore. This it is, this (believe me) to equal the gods in merit; this it is to hold the scepter of eternal Jove. Abandon the other vanities of mortal toil, and let your life pursue this work alone.

Elegy 7: Introductory Note

Since Maggio, who taught rhetoric at the University of Naples, died in 1493, this elegy is of necessity comparatively early work. Bearing distinct resemblance to Sannazaro's other tribute to one of his teachers, Lucio Crasso (1.1), this poem nonetheless differs sharply, by discarding the pastoral décor entirely (save for one folkloristic shepherd) while retaining from the *Arcadia* Sannazaro's self-characterization as the poet enslaved to Love. This familiar theme becomes the central focus of the poem. The classical oracles and auspices are rejected as no longer efficacious in remedying love, whereas Maggio is praised for his skilled interpretation of the lover's dreams. Much of the poem's *amplificatio* expands upon the rather bizarre claim that Italian history would have been spared many of its disasters had Maggio been available to interpret dreams and oracles for the antique world as he does for Syncerus and his mistress. Thus a long stretch of the poem (lines 21–52), written from the vantage point of the post-antique world, explicitly acknowledges the deadness of Graeco-Roman culture and religion, dwelling on accomplished facts of Roman history and leaving little room for the young poet to show his skill at imitating Roman elegists.

Consequently Sannazaro confines most of his *imitatio* to the very beginning and end of his poem. At the outset, as he is defining Maggio's geographical location with reference to his own (cf. the Crasso poem, Elegy 1.1), he utilizes Propertius in what is almost a signature line:

> Prop.: Qua jacet Herculeis semita litoribus (1.11.2)
> Where the path lies along the shores of Hercules

> Sann.: Qua vetus Herculeos perduxit semita tauros
> (2.7.3)

Propertius, however, gives way to Tibullus in this elegy—not only in the folklore about mixing meal with salt (2.7.41–42; cf. Tib. 3.4.9–10), but repeatedly in the last half-dozen lines, as Sannazaro rather awkwardly imports a scene based on Tibullus's sketch of punishments in Hades (1.3.73–80), and with better grace uses Tibullan language to introduce his own epitaph at the poem's close:

> Lygdamus hic situs est (Tib., 3.2.29)
> Actius hic situs est (2.7.71)

A bit too long, a bit awkward in its transitions, but on the whole an interesting performance, promising better things to come.

[Elegies 2.7]   **TO GIUNIANO MAIO**

His teacher

 While you are watching from the sea the nymphs of Baiae, and the sheltering waters along her neighboring shores, where the ancient footpath led on the bulls of Hercules (a breakwater long since torn from the excluded sea), and where the road lies between Bauli and the Sibylline grove, stretching straight on for Prochyte's ridge; I, as you know, in the city here am constrained to obey my harsh mistress, and to pass my time in tedious delays. Nor is it of any use to have fixed the mind on

rigorous studies or revered the holy goddesses. And though fate has granted me so many affectionate friends, there is none among them to bring me proper aid. Cruel Love is pressing me hard, sharpening his arrows on the whetstone, and my neck may not move from under his heavy yoke. And though my heart is consumed away with so many constant cares, I ask from where so many evils can come. Would that Lachesis would put an end to my unhappy years, closing off the harsh measure of my life, or that some god worthy of belief should sing to my ear what remedy there is for the cruel madness.

But now the oracles are departed from laurel-crowned Delphi, and the Cumaean virgin's silent caves are mute, and Pan returns no answer from under the Maenalian shade, though the shepherd by night make offering of the slain sheep's entrails. I have no hope of hearing the Chaonian doves; horned Jove is ashamed to utter oracles. And Greece has marvelled this long time that the oaks, forgetful how to speak, keep silence when the god is by.

But you (Maius) can tell of things to come, and take counsel of benign divinities. You make your discoveries not so much from altar smoke or warning lightning-flash, but from dreams sent up from the Stygian realms: dreams which often disturb our uneasy sleep, while the mind perpends ambiguous images. O how many times I recall when I put away vain fear because of you, and continued my days in happiness! O how many times, when fearfully I thought they should not be ignored, I have been apprehensive of ills to come upon my head! Often when I told you my dreams about my mistress, you have surely predicted things fearful and not far off. Often you bade her wash her dripping hair in the river, and dissolve meal mixed with salt. If fate of old had granted earth such a man as you, martial Rome would have scorned the Etruscan soldiery. For who better able than you to understand the smoking entrails, or to consult the birds of the air? She would even now be governing under her law the conquered earth, and not be almost buried in her own ashes. Nor would she have seen the sad slaughters of the fight at Cannae, or her legions so ill able to withstand the Parthian captains. The shades of the Scipios would reside in their ancestral seats, and Spanish soil would not conceal so many bones. Your guidance would have made clear the leaves of the true-spoken Sibyl, dangerous when the god is not understood. Blessed are you as God's interpreter, acknowledged by heaven, who have the right to expound divinity's plan. The shameless boy has not touched you with his deadly bow, though he entangles even the lordly gods. No sighs break in on your untroubled slumbers: you scorn the deceptive snares of Venus.

But I am tossed blindly on the shifting waves, and conduct my life with no prudence. And who would wish me a long life now, when he can see my many trials? The stones that are rolled with Sisyphaean labor do not exceed me, nor the wine jars carried to the infernal streams. And the hook-beaked vulture of Tityus yields to me, and the mocking fruits[1] hung from the trees of Lethe.

You then, my friends, who mourn me now in my defeat, carve my tomb thus with suitable inscription:

HERE. ACTIUS. LIES. REJOICE. YE. BURIED. ASHES.

NOW. AFTER. DEATH. HIS. WANDERING.

SHADE. IS. FREE. FROM. SORROW.

Elegy 8: Introductory Note

The subtitle addresses Juno, as in Tibullus 4.6, because she was considered the presiding Genius for women, and one's birthday was a festive day for one's personal Genius (for women, one's Juno). The address to the Natal Day itself (sometimes Englished as the Birth Spirit) was evidently a standard mode of closing the *genethliacon,* or birthday-poem (cf. Tibullus, 1.7.63–64; 2.2.21–22; 4.5.19–20).

In his *genethliacon* for himself (*Elegies* 2.2), Sannazaro followed the lead of Propertius (3.10) in structuring his poem around the successive events of the festive day, from dawn to midnight. In this elegy, however, emphasis falls entirely on the preparation of mistress and poet for the day to come, as they don proper festive attire, prepare the courtyard and the altars, fetch the poet's lyre, and so on. The elegy is distinctly an exercise, once more, in weaving various hints from Tibullus into a single coherent poem covering these preparations.

Even from Tibullus's rather grand birthday-poem for his patron Messala, Sannazaro takes one or two small details—the robe (yellow, however) flowing down over the feet (Tib. 1.7.46), the cakes sweetened with Sicilian honey (1.7.54). From the Cerinthus-Sulpicia sequence, more analogous for a poem entitled On His Mistress's Birthday, he adopts the language of serious religious ritual (Tib. 2.2.1–2—"Let us have good words only . . . whoever draws near, man or woman, keep silence"), and also the language of serious, long-lasting love. In the elegy just quoted, which some regard as a misplaced member of the Cerinthus-Sulpicia sequence, Tibullus says that Cerinthus [or Cornutus] is making a birthday wish for a wife, and "the bonds that will endure forever"—*vincula quae maneant semper* (2.2.19). Again, Sulpicia says to Cerinthus, "That day that gave me you, Cerinthus, will always be sacred to me, and numbered among the feast-days" (4.5.1–2). Sannazaro seizes upon this language of eternal love ("This day destined you for me (my light)

---

[1]See Glossary, s.v. Tantalus.

through all my life") and elaborates upon it for a half-dozen lines, making explicit the pretty conceit, perhaps implied in Tibullus, that his mistress is herself a great gift for him on her birthday. Thus we have here a performance rather parallel to Sannazaro's mistress-elegy in the first book (1.3), both poems showing more concern than we commonly find in Propertius and Tibullus for celebrating the love that persists into old age and death.

A verse translation appears on p. 171.

[Elegies 2.8] ON HIS MISTRESS'S BIRTHDAY

To Juno

 To Juno (Muse) make sacrifice, gather fresh garlands: now my mistress's joyous birthday is at hand. But first let her don her ritual robes, and wreathe my temples with the purpling rose. And that we may meditate something pleasing for the goddess's altars, bring hither the singing strings of the gilded lyre. You too (my life) bind up your hair with gold, and let your finest jewel sparkle on your snowy bosom. This day destined you for me (my light) through all my life, this day decreed that I keep you surely mine. How many joys first shone for me upon this day! how great reward came to me at this one time! O day deservedly to be marked with Erythraean stones! O to be counted among my dearest delights!

Whosoever draws near—good words, and sing a joyful song; and offer cakes made sweet with Sicilian honey. For me, let my garment be white, unstained by any dye, and let it flow down smoothly over both my feet. Before the altar let the Dryads, a rustic rout, for their lovely tresses weave sunshades from the greening oak. Let Phoebus cover the courts with fragrant laurel: but you (Cytherean) with myrtle the double doors. Let the daughters of Nisus serve up Arabian wares, and Father Lenaeus bring the Naxian wines. Let all things be performed in due order for the joyous rites, and let the sky resound with snow-white wings.

Great mother Juno, draw near, attended by a hundred maids, and show your favor (goddess) to my prayers. You too, ye Nymphs who sport through the empty air, encircle the highest clouds with your joyous choir. Let these be the omens of good fortune sure to come, this day the harbinger of abounding joy.

I shall join in your celebration with delighted applause, singing and playing in various modes. Yea verily I shall receive your divinities on the holy day with garlands and with altars steaming with incense. But you, O Natal Day, may you go on prosperous through many years, always unclouded, in honored splendor. And my wish (if we believe prayer can accomplish anything) is that you may surpass the countless olympiads of the Cumaean prophetess.

Elegy 9: Introductory Note

Cumae, some ten miles west of Naples, was founded by the first Greek colonists in Italy, who erected a magnificent temple to Phoebus Apollo, by whose oracle they had been directed there. According to Velleius Paterculus, "some say that this fleet's course was directed by the flight of a dove which went before it" (*Historiae Romae Libri Duo,* 1.4). Apollo's temple at Cumae, the residence of the Cumaean Sibyl, is described by Virgil (*Aeneid* 6.14–45), who says that Daedalus, fleeing from Minos, after he returned to earth built the temple and "dedicated the oarage of his wings" to Apollo. Presumably the temple itself, its conspicuous hill, and perhaps the dedicated wings, constitute the *conscia signa* in line 6.

Pércopo (p. 110) provides documentary evidence for Sannazaro's acknowledged competence as a guide to the antiquities around Naples, and we may legitimately take the description of the ruins as stemming from direct observation. But all things, for these humanists, have their literary aspect too. Even today, any reader of the Cumae elegy will profit his soul by reading also the splendors of Isaiah's prophecy against Idumaea:

> The cormorant and the bittern shall possess it; the owl also and the raven shall dwell in it; and he shall stretch out upon it the line of confusion, and the stones of emptiness. . . . And thorns shall come up in her palaces, nettles and brambles in the fortresses thereof: and it shall be an habitation of dragons, and a court for owls. (Isaiah 34:11–13; cf. 13:13–22)

Moreover, the general theme has a degree of kinship with passages in Propertius and Tibullus (and Virgil too), all of whom reverse the contrast by comparing the present glories of their contemporary Rome with the rustic simplicity of its beginnings (*Aeneid* 8.626–731; Propertius 4.1.1–36; Tibullus 2.5.23–38). The reversed contrast does not lend itself well to direct imitation through the actual language of the model, but even so, one coincidence of phrase is worth noting. As the Sibyl in Tibullus sings the song of the rustic origins of Rome, she tells the pasturing bulls to crop their grass while they can: *hic magnae iam locus urbis erit;* "this spot will be the site of a great city" (Tib. 2.5.56). So with Sannazaro's *durus arator,* looking backward rather than forward: *Urbs, dicet, haec quoque clara fuit;* "he will say *This too has been a famous city*" (2.9.30).

Surely the best-known and most-praised of Sannazaro's elegies, the Cumae poem is unique among them for its total concentration on a single scene observed by a speaker who then moralizes his song by generalizing the observed scene into a quasi-philosophical view of human history. Interestingly, the view arrived at is in the direction of Giambattista Vico—history is cyclical, and Venice, Rome, or even beloved Naples, cannot escape from the cycle.

A verse translation appears on p. 172.

[Elegies 2.9]   ON THE RUINS OF CUMAE

a most ancient city

 Here where rose the celebrated walls of famed Cumae, prime glory of the Tyrrhene sea, where often the traveller hasted from distant shores to consult your tripods (o mighty Delian), and the wandering sailor entered its ancient ports, seeking the known signs of that Daedalian flight—now (who could believe it before, while Nature's laws stood fast?) a towering forest gives cover to the woodland beasts. And where the mysteries of the prophetic Sibyl lay concealed, now the shepherd at evening bars up his full-fed ewes. The council hall that called together of old the venerable fathers is made the nest of birds and snakes. The courtyards filled with noble statues everywhere—they lie at last overthrown by their own weight. Thresholds once laden with sacred trophies are trampled down, and the grass covers the broken gods. All those ornaments, and artists' handiwork, all those famous graves and reverend ashes one common ruin drives down. And now, among deserted homes and rooftrees scattered everywhere, the stranger spears the bristling boar.

And yet not this the god foretold to the Grecian ships, and not for this was the dove sent on ahead, over the wide sea. And do we complain if the days allotted our life so quickly vanish? violent death seizes upon cities too. Ah, would that my oracles deceive me who am their priest, and I be counted vain by long posterity: you will not always live, who encompass your seven hills, nor you who rise up in rivalry amid the waves. And you (who can credit this?), my fostering nurse, the rough plowman will turn, and say "This too has been a famous city."

The fates bear men along: under fate's urging, cities and whatsoever thing you see, that day will destroy.

Elegy 10: Introductory Note

This is the only elegy, other than the Brancaccio poem (1.6), presented as a dramatic monologue—in this case, spoken by the pomegranates themselves (a concept that Sannazaro may be borrowing from Petrarch's sonnet spoken by his gift of doves—*Rime,* ed. Zingarelli, 1.8). Through its quasi-epistolary function the poem bears resemblance to Elegies 1.5 and 2.3 (see the note for 1.5), but essentially the poet's eye is on his desire to send his friend these pomegranates. In writing a poem to accompany them, he will use whatever imagination and memory supply. In other words, the poem is a mature performance by a poet who is accustomed to work with imitation of classical models, but does not feel bound to make that imitation more than incidental to his development of his material. How does he proceed?

He takes his start from the nature and appearance of the pomegranates. They are in some degree esoteric—*Mala Punica,* the title says, or Punic Apples—and they have lovely, jewel-like colors (topaz, ruby, amethyst). This introduces the *topos* of Oriental wealth (see notes to Elegies 1.1 and 2.3, above), with an admixture of the Tibullan theme of the foolhardiness of seafaring merchants (see 1.9, above). Except for a stray phrase from Propertius (*gemmiferi . . . maris,* the jewel-laden sea; cf. Prop. 3.4.2), most of the material seems without direct reminiscences in diction. The comparison to jewels then brings on remarks on the evils of avarice, with probable reminiscence of Ovid on the power of money to disrupt and distort natural human relations (*Met.* 1.144–50).

In a rather complex development, the gem-like natural beauty of the pomegranates is thereupon associated with peace and love ("we are the work of peace, and the gift of peaceful love"—line 29), whereas the jewels "that seek through art a beauty not their own" (20) are responsible for setting men in conflict (13). We are in familiar territory here—Nature versus Art, Love versus War. It is the material of pastoral, and so acknowledged by Sannazaro, as "the beloved Naiad accepts [us] from her Satyr" (30). After the almost obligatory reference to Proserpina's pomegranate (*Met.* 5.534–38) and another to Pomona, we come to the point of these juxtapositions of Nature and Art, war and peace, familial treacheries and banquets of love. Acquaviva is a man for all seasons, at home alike in the study or on the battlefield, political man or pastoral man—the pomegranates offer themselves to him, to refresh him from his labors in one world or the other.

Sannazaro may be following Virgil (*Georgics* 1.39) in making Proserpina reluctant to return from the underworld, but it seems to be his own clever twist to attribute that reluctance to the deliciousness of pomegranates. Otherwise, Elegy 2.10 seems a poem wholly content with standard materials, but able to shape those materials into a neat example of the poetry of friendship and/or patronage.

For the patron himself, see the Introductory Note to Elegy 3.1. The date of composition for this poem is indeterminate.

A verse translation appears on p. 173.

[Elegies 2.10]   **POMEGRANATES**

 Why, poor sailor, do you seek out foreign lands? and search for riches in seas so far away? Is it not wearing to undergo the perils of an unknown road, and the threats of the winds, the storms of the open sea? Look with how tender a skin we cover our gems: right here we offer you whatever the shores of the Red Sea hold, whether you look for sapphires brilliant with a rosy glow, or what you love is amethyst an enemy to Bacchus,[1] or those that resemble fires and burning brands, or rather topaz with its light diffused.

But rudely the common crowd extols vain riches, and does not bear in mind how many evils spring from them. Riches have brought fierce wars upon men, and death, for before they came earth flourished in abiding peace. For riches the father is slain by the son and the son by the father, and the sister who ought to be revered is slain by her beloved brother. And not alone do savage stepmothers deal in poison, but even the avaricious mother murders her own offspring. Jewels, moreover, are valued only for their glitter, and seek through art a beauty not their own. But nature has granted us both, to slow the gazing eye and to drive away thirst from the parching mouth. Our jewels do not set men to arms in battle, nor persuade them secretly to dishonor the mighty gods, but they visit only banquets spread on quiet tables, where the drinking-cups are filled with cheerful wine. There the youth hands us on to his tender maiden, and the true-loving maiden hands us to her desirous youth. We are the work of peace, and the gift of peaceful love, such as the beloved Naiad accepts from her Satyr. And not by mere chance was the daughter unwilling to return to her mother, once she had tasted us in the gardens of the nether world. Pomona too, when she wandered through the Libyan fields, marvelled at us blushing in her swelling bosom, and (admiring our rare beauty, admiring our savor), transported us into her country from our native soil. These then are the praise and glory of the Punic grove, rivalling the glittering gifts of the jewel-laden sea, driving heavy ills from the languid body, refreshing the feverish mouth with

[1]See Glossary, s.v. Bacchus.

Paeonian remedies. The shores of the Erythraean will not surpass us, nor India's region mighty in its wealth.

You then (Acquaviva) whose temples gleam with the double laurel, leader of armies and of the sacred choir, accept us, content with the brilliance of your reputation: despise the parades of hateful luxury, and whether you be wearied with poetry or with martial affairs, let these jewels poured out profusely quench your thirst.

BOOK 3

Elegy 1: Introductory Note

Altamura suggests that the elegies to Alfonso II and to Frederick I were intended for their coronations, in 1494 and 1497 respectively—although the last twenty lines of the present elegy were, of course, written after Frederick's death in exile. Composition for the most part as early as 1497 fits well with this elegy's continued interest in various modes of imitation, whereas the two other elegies in Book Three (both obviously written after Sannazaro's return from France) show markedly less of that interest. Propertius and Virgil are the chief models—Propertius being pertinent especially to the last twenty lines, and hence relegated here to the discussion of the poem's close.

As he magnifies his prince's achievements in an early portion of the elegy (lines 36–74), Sannazaro associates them with Virgil, at line 37, through the rather strained device of a welcoming address, pronounced "in Phrygian phrase" to Frederick as he enters the town of Gaeta "with favoring approach" (*Aen.* 8.302). The speaker is Caieta, Aeneas's nurse, and her theme is a version of Virgil's *Troia nova* theme. That is, as Aeneas founded a new Troy in Italy (see General Introduction, pp. 12–13), and as Caieta used to be reminded of the youthful Aeneas by the youthful Iulus, who laid the foundations for the rise of Rome (lines 45–54), so Caieta's hope for a renewed Troy is awakened again when the youthful Frederick, resembling another Iulus, enters her walls (lines 55–56).

The biography involved here is quite obscure. Comparison to Iulus implies that Frederick is very young, so that the passage fits with Volpicella's remark (p. 234) that Frederick was sent "in 1461 . . . to Gaeta," presumably as his father was consolidating his power over his turbulent barons. Hence the welcoming speech of Caieta, for whom Gaeta was named (*Aen.* 7.1–4).[1] Then within the next four lines, in recounting Frederick's surveying mission for King Ferrante, the poet establishes further Virgilian associations by alluding to the river Galaesus "with its Oebalian stream"—a detail which reflects Servius's gloss on *Georgics* 4.125–26, concerning a mythical

---

[1] See Glossary, s.v. Antiphates.

Oebalus, King of Tarentum. Possibly the line is meant to be allusive to Frederick's title of Prince of Taranto, second in line of succession to Ferrante's throne.

The remaining mid-portions of the elegy (lines 75–162) narrate Frederick's travels on various diplomatic, military, and personal missions: to Rome (75–82); to Milan in 1465 (85–92), to escort Ippolita Sforza from Milan to Naples, where she was married to Frederick's elder brother Alfonso; to Venice, with opportunity for Sannazaro's digression in praise of that republic (93–100); and in lines 101–8, to Mantua and Milan ("the walls that are fabled to derive from the skin of a fleecy sow"—cf. Claudian, *De Nupt. Hon.,* line 183). The prince's travels then take him across the Alps in 1474–76 (lines 109–32), in unsuccessful pursuit of a marriage to Maria, the only child of Charles the Bold, Duke of Burgundy, who is called Claudius in this elegy.

At this point the poem virtually abandons its chronological approach, probably because Sannazaro was perplexed about how to proceed. For some elucidation of the biographical relevance of lines 109–62, the reader is referred to Appendix A in this book, "The Chronology of Frederick's First Marriage." In this Introductory Note, however, our interest properly centers on Sannazaro's exploitation of several opportunities that arise as he develops his travelogue from line 109 to 162. As one examines what the poet does with these opportunities, one is impressed with his shrewd adaptation of the materials that biographical fact has offered him.

The most visible of these ingenuities is a parenthesis for reasons of patronage (lines 141–46), in the manner of Statius, praising Giulio Acquaviva d'Aragona—indeed, as Sannazaro puts it, refusing to pass over him in silence. As the poet was doubtless aware, King Ferrante had put Giulio in charge of the whole expedition to the Burgundian court—"como governatore," as the Duke of Monteleone phrases it in his *Diario* (Muratori, *Scriptores,* vol. 21, pt. 5, Appendix, pp. 208–9). Giulio was a competent and praiseworthy soldier and courtier. The object here, however, is not Giulio (who was killed in battle at Otranto in 1481, long before this elegy was written), but his son, Andrea Matteo, seventh Duke of Atri. Andrea Matteo, along with his brother Belisario, was one of Sannazaro's chief friends in the upper strata of Neapolitan society, and was in trouble all through the decade 1494–1504 because of his repeated backing of the French against the Spanish in their contest to seize the rule of Naples. By imitating Statius's digressions of praise, Sannazaro is creating an opportunity to show his support of the beleaguered duke.

In adapting the obscure myth of Oenomaus to the Burgundian episode (lines 121–32) Sannazaro is adopting the manner of the Roman elegists in using recherché material from mythology, but he is also working with the internal structure of his own poem. When Charles the Bold was killed in 1477, in a mid-winter battle outside

Nancy, his body lay for two days unrecognized in the mud of the battlefield. Sannazaro uses this vivid piece of biography partly as an illus-
tration of punishment for the unjust, but also as an *exemplum* of the
vicissitudes of royal fortune. To do this, he pretends that Charles the
Bold is left permanently without tomb or epitaph—"no stone to cover
his bones with carven characters." Thus the wicked Charles is con-
trasted with the virtuous Frederick whose marble slab will be unable
to "comprise your deeds within its narrow inscription" (line 31)—as
Tibullus tells his patron Messala that "the inscription beneath your
name will not comprise your deeds, but you shall have large volumes
of eternizing verse" (4.1.33–34).

Having established his contrast between the virtuous prince
whose memory calls for heroic verse and the tyrant whose corpse lies
without tomb or epitaph, Sannazaro is ready, at line 159, to proph-
esy of things to come. If the elegy was originally a coronation poem,
as suggested by Altamura (*Sannazaro,* 1951, p. 173), prophecy of a
long successful reign, along with acknowledgment of Frederick's second marriage and the four children issuing from it, would have been
a natural conclusion. But after Fate intervened in 1501–4—or
Fortune, or History, or Real-Politik, or whatever abstraction we prefer—Sannazaro was left in need of a far different prophecy. He solves
his problem like a craftsman, using the materials already at hand.
Since his elegy had been structured on a narrative of Frederick's
youthful travels, now his prophecy turns on the irony of Frederick's
repeated voyage, this time into exile and obscurity.

At line 166, the poet stands on the shoreline of the Riviera, in-
voking the gods of the Etruscan Sea:

Candida felici solvite vela noto
Shake out his shining sails with a favoring breeze.

Then he goes on to the prophecy of the repeated voyage (167–76).
Line 166 is clearly an echo of Propertius 1.17.26 (*Candida felici
solvite vela choro*). Is it an unconscious echo, or a signature line? As
noted in the General Introduction (see p. 17), the editor
Broekhuizen considered this an unconscious echo. So it may be—yet
there is reason to think that Sannazaro is intentionally reminding us
of Propertius. For when he wrote his elegy for Frederick's elder
brother, Alfonso II, he had produced one of his most skilled and sensitive imitations of Propertius, in presenting a picture of Alfonso's
triumphal chariot pausing a moment while the great prince reads the
poet's epitaph (see General Introduction, pp. 18–19).

Now, after sketching the geography of Frederick's sad final voyage, Sannazaro is preparing to utilize another of his poem's themes—
the great man's epitaph. Early in this elegy the poet had said that
Frederick's achievements will not be comprised within the narrow limits of an inscription on a marble slab, but will demand the scope of a
heroic poem (lines 31–32). Then in the mid-portions he had strained

the facts of history, to present a scornful picture of the faithless tyrant denied any marble slab at all. And now, at the poem's close, reversing the situation that had obtained in Alfonso's elegy, it is the poet himself who returns as an unknown stranger from Italy to stand by Frederick's grave on the banks of the Loire, pronouncing a quiet epitaph that suffices, after all, to comprise his prince's achievements:

> Here (Frederick) has the limit of your sufferings been set.
> This little urn contains our divinity.

[Elegies 3.1]   **TO FREDERICK**

son of Ferdinand of Aragon [and] King of Sicily

 Was I then only born to serve a deceitful mistress, and always to make my complaint against an unprospering love? And is Phoebus not to see me entering my songs among the rival singers in the Pierian shade, where Helicon spreads her dense ravines and greening hills, and where her waters bathe the caverns of the Muses, while on her heights in orderly array the maidens weave their garlands, and the hanging lyres re-echo in the rocky hollows? Now will I drink from springs untouched and wander the sacred wood where pathway there is none. Things arduous are to be attempted: look you now, my verses, take on new powers: Glory exerts herself along the difficult road. Now the task is to bind my locks with another leaf—mine no more with your garlands, merry Bacchus. Boldly I shall pluck my greening laurels on Parnassus peak, or in your forest groves, melodious Pindus. I shall hang from my shoulders as my rare reward a lyre not stricken with the finger's stroke. Now no more wantoning do I meditate soft loves, nor hurl against deaf chamber doors my pleasing songs. A larger impulse is raising me to the hero's buskins: and a greater god is speaking his utterance through my mouth.

Be thou propitious, Frederick: I shall recount your praises in due order: under your auspices is my fame to be sought. For though your house stands firmly founded on so many royal victories of old, and makes you its vaunt for such great ancestors, your glory does not lie quiet, propped by the titles of your fathers, nor does it exult in old ancestral statues; but virtue strives to overgo great forebears, and to acquire a lasting glory with true praise. Nor will some day the marble slab comprise your deeds within its narrow inscription: that will be the immeasurable task of a great poem—whether one who has admired you from your tender boyhood years recounts those early periods of your life, or sings the various chances of your affairs, and the harsh labors, and battles fought out under savage Mars.

Aeneas's nurse became aware of you when you were scarcely out of your cradle, and was suddenly roused by your advent: and thrice paying reverence to the gods, thrice raised her head from the urn, and at length her voice rolled forth in Phrygian phrase:

[*Caieta's Invocation*]

Behold again, great Sun, my hope arises, after the destruction of my Troy's Pergamum, after Rome's founding fathers. Often did I once see my Aeneas playing at such an age, among the meadows of wandering Scamander. Nor were you older, lovely Iulus, as after the death of Creusa you crept within my bosom, and sought with your tricks to wile away from me my old-woman's anxieties, tracing caressing hands across my countenance. Yet under these auspices the towers of Alba grew to the skies, and Rome most powerful, head of all the world. Therefrom we saw the Decii and the Fabii, therefrom the Catos hardy of heart, and your fasces, austere Brutus. And saw triumphs celebrated over many an enemy, and noble pedigrees enriched by the Julian Caesars. Continue your course, and in good fortune enter our walls with auspicious tread, and pay your homage to deities well-disposed. Continue; the powerful city of Antiphates does you service, and gates kept safe from the Laestrygonian fear.

Let Crete be mighty because of Jove; let Delphi be famous for Apollo; let the land of Taenaris laud the Amyclaean princes; let Thebes raise Alcides and Bacchus to the stars; our country is blessed by your first beginnings. For your great-minded father sent you into the hardships of war while he was fending from his borders the destructive foe. Under your protection our castles yield to no invasions, our shores to no threatenings. But all is well: our fears subside, our dangers subside, the barbarian turns his cavalry to his own domain. Now the mountain ridges, now the far-spread meadows everywhere revive; nor any trumpet sounds alarm for the sailing ships. Then in your hour of victory you will be summoned back for your country's marks of honor, seeking out Parthenope's maternal bosom. Next as surveyor you will travel the Salentine countryside, where Galaesus cuts across the farmland with his Oebalian stream. But where, gnawing envy, do you fail to intrude? Lo suddenly your fates command you to travel a long road far away, visiting the father at Rome and the holy see, chiefly to propitiate the mighty gods. There you view bridges and triumphal arches, temples, streets, and theaters built in the public squares. Meanwhile there in the

Vatican you are at leisure to take account of all those memorials, all those works of artists.

Thereupon, having passed among the Veii, and ancient Umbrians and stout Sabines, it remains to traverse the Adriatic shore, the Aemilian domain and snowy Apennine, and the principalities bordering on Phaeton's River Po. Who shall tell your costly displays, your public spectacles (Leonora, descended from Atestian princes)? Now (wealthy Ferrara) you surpass the ancient games, offering rich stakes for swift horses and erecting statues of the gods, and spectacular art works for their altars, and in various quarters stage machines raised high.

Who shall tell over again the marvels of the city of Venice, who is the only thing of price in all the great world beside? Sole queen of Italy, proud Rome's most lovely rival, who lord it over land and sea, you make your citizens your kings (o ornament, o light of Ausonia), through whom we are a free populace, through whom it is that the barbarian does not rule over us, and the rising sun shines the more brightly on our world.

Next-neighboring are the sights of your realm (Gonzaga), and the gifts prepared before for mighty princes. Among these Mantua, and Mincius welling up with generous countenance, daring to raise his foam-flecked head to the stars — Mincius, pleasant sanctuary of eternal Maro, before whose golden stream transparent Meles yields. Thereafter comes the privilege of viewing your peoples (Ticinus), and the walls that are fabled to derive from the skin of a fleecy sow,[1] and Turin and the lofty Alps, the Pennine castles, and Rhone, and your shores (mighty Leman). From there you journey through the vast extent of the broad plain where Jura spreads her sacred wood, and the fortunate Claudius has in his care the ancient holds, Claudius preparing foundations for an enduring power. Here you review his dreaded army, and its general himself, puffed up with long prosperity. While he is preparing war on his neighbors, he entrusts to you both men and arms, and gives you the authority of an important command, in his wisdom having come to admire your genius and your skills, and the many signs you have given of your capacity. Therefore in the midst of war he chooses you for his son-in-law, promising you his daughter's inheritance, and her bridal bed. And just as resulted from the horses of Oenomaus and his trickery, he will evade the terms of the marriage pact. But as his horses and his deceitfulness turned out badly for Oenomaus, so this barbarian will pay the penalties of his perfidy. Three times defeated, thrice driven from the field by his enemy, in the end he will fall before his wretched time. For thrown from his horse,

---

[1] See the Introductory Note to Elegies 3.1.

and found in a deep trench, he will stain the filthy ground with his base blood. And there will be none to attend his corpse to the final flames; no stone to cover his bones with carven characters.

Exalted, eminent, victorious, you receive the honor rendered you by all France, in recognition of the Lingonians twice subjected by your arms, and your standards borne quite through the twice-defeated Swiss, besides whatever peoples the Meuse encompasses, whatever is flooded by the Rhine's blue water. And such will be the strength of our troops, that all these may be considered to have surrendered in justified fear.

[Here I shall not keep silent about you and your praises (o most powerful Julius), and the battles waged under your mighty hand—you whom Acquaviva your native seat adorns with lustrous titles, placing you between mortal men and the demigods. And presently the weight of the whole campaign is entrusted to you, who draw the whole enterprise under your command.]

But for you (o loveliest of youths), the war being over, it was time to bear your offerings to your fathers' gods, and to leave behind the pride and insolence of the lying tyrant, along with the land that lately you defended. Come then, break off delays, leave the hateful camps behind, and enter the safe abode of the great-minded king whom so many coasts by Ocean's edge obey, and the Celtic lands acknowledge the authority of his scepter. He will make ready for you the joyous torches and the marriage contracts, and will add his guarded treasures. Liger will be witness, as flowing out from Arvernian caverns he cleaves his journey down through the open plains. Meanwhile revisit your father and the dwellings of Campania, and realms that are destined (ay me) for your command; destined, but soon thereafter to be yielded to malevolent fates, when a barbarous enemy shall usurp such great possessions.

Gods of the Etruscan sea, through whom Tiber and Arno and deep Magra are joined with the sea-green waters, while the youth laden with so many honors is making his return to his fatherland, shake out his shining sails with a favoring breeze; and you (swift ships) make haste over the obedient sea. The fates will decree that you repeat these travels, and not once only will you see these tracts and the shores of the Ligurians, or the luckless hospitality of the river Var, and the bays protected by their reefs, the Toroentian harbors, and the Stoechades scattered over the sea; and at last the Phocaean harbors, and the shore dug out again by Marius, and the walls of ancient Massilia, until his unlucky fate permits your captain to approach the fatal walls of the Turones. Ah Liger, ah overladen with my nation's tears, what tombs you will see beside your stream—tombs where mighty kings may lay their crowns, and the grateful earth make ritual offering with garlands due. And where some unknown stranger, come from the realm of Latium, may bring his gift to the rites of the honored dead, and say:

Here (Frederick) has the limit of your sufferings been set.
This little urn contains our divinity.

Elegy 2: Introductory Note

Beginning with an unusual focus on the poet's childhood years, far more detailed than any such material in Propertius, Tibullus, or Ovid, this elegy (along with the Sixth Prose of *Arcadia*) is our chief source for information about Sannazaro's early years. The first sixteen lines sketch an interlude (from about Sannazaro's tenth year to his fifteenth) during which his widowed mother economized by moving with her two sons from Naples back to her family's holdings in the rugged mountain regions around Salerno. It would be naive to assume that Sannazaro's lifelong interest in the pastoral mode could not have developed without this experience: but the poet does describe the terrain and its place-names with a sympathetic precision. Benedetto Croce told the Pontanian Academy that the streams around S. Cipriano Picentino were still known in 1894 as *Acqua vivola* and *Savoncola,* and that line 16 refers to a stream passing through a region still called The Hailstones (Pércopo, pp. 5 and 25).

Perplexingly, the language of lines 17–34 undeniably seems to suggest that the poet's early schooling took place in these surroundings: "the native deities," "woke the echoes," "those joyous fields," "wild creatures came and kept holiday in that atmosphere." Brognoligo, editing Pércopo's biographical study, acknowledges (p. 26, n.1) the difficulties of the language in this section, some of which seem insurmountable. I remain as puzzled as Brognoligo when Sannazaro calls his mother a *nupta novella* although she is already a widow. On the other hand, perhaps the *Huc* introducing lines 17–34 might be taken as "Hither [to Naples where I now live]," rather than "Hither [to the place I have just described]." We know that his schooling in rhetoric and poetry, under Giuniano Maggio and Lucio Crasso, was in Naples—but possibly Sannazaro's craftsmanship is suggesting how imperceptibly the child's delight in wooded ravines and mountain streams slides into the young classicist's early ventures into shepherds' song. A further peculiarity of the language in this section is almost certainly intentional. The diction suggests religious initiation: "[They] washed me with their sacred water," "the youth they had cleansed," "the gods themselves were there." This has the sound of a novitiate—and, although his education was secular, we can well believe that the poet intends to suggest a dedicated intensity in his classical studies rivalling that of a religious "calling."

The remainder of the elegy outlines Sannazaro's career as poet and courtier. The summary of his literary production offers this sequence: the *Arcadia* (lines 35–44); *De Partu Virginis* (45–52); *Piscatoriae* (53–58); *Elegies* (59–60); *Epigrams* (61–62); and finally the vernacular poetry collected in the *Rime* (63–64). This sequence, which cannot be strictly chronological, may well have been decisive for the ordering of the Latin poems in sixteenth-century editions of the *Opera*. Certainly it coincides with them. Sannazaro's career as courtier (65–86) is treated as an impediment to the writing of poetry, rather like his chronic ill health (mentioned parenthetically, lines 67–68). Sannazaro dwells chiefly on the rigors of his voluntary exile with Frederick (71–78) and the bitterness of his king's death in foreign lands (79–84).

The final quarter of the elegy (87–116) gains in pathos for the modern reader as he recognizes the symptoms of a deep psychological depression which Sannazaro can only define in his cultural terminology, as the sinfulness of sloth or a quasi-medical "narrowness" in his poetic "vein."

The closing lines, with their announcement of Cassandra's prospective role in the poet's final obsequies, suggest an extremely late date, at least for this portion of the poem—perhaps even after 1525.

[Elegies 3.2]   TO CASSANDRA MARCHESE

How He Spent His Childhood in the Picentians

 There lies in the hills of Picentia a valley most lovely: here a pious folk honor their household gods. Rising to heaven above it on the one side hangs the cliff of Cerretia, to which an oaken forest has given its name: on the other side the rocks of holy Tebenna make their answer, and the jutting crag that rejoices in the name of Merula. And far around on every side a forest lies in black shadow, where the abundant wave pours down from well-watered ridges, the forbidding home (if they sing the truth) of half-bestial Faunus, where hungering animals have their dens. Here the heifer receives on her back the handsome bull: the snub-nosed she-goat receives the rank-smelling male. A thousand couching-places of Dryads, a thousand retreats of Satyrs, and caves that are welcome shelters for the forest-haunting goddess. Vivula the name of the water, and Subuncula with its narrow channel, and that which chatters along, named for the frozen hail.

When my mother brought me here after my early years, a young wife leaving her beloved father, she brought with her gifts for the native deities, especially garlands of flowers for the learned flock. It was the flock of the Aonides, Calliope herself the leader of the dancing chorus, accompanied by the band of her sister Muses. The Delian joining in song with his clear-voiced pupils would turn their ready fingers to the lyre, and here those washed me with their sacred water whose primal care was my well-being. Then they set in the midst of their chorus the youth they had cleansed, and woke the echoes with the sounds poured forth. Finally they taught me, garlanded with ivy and virgin laurel, the pleasant modes of the lute.

Such harmony of birds there was in those joyous fields that you might say the gods themselves were there. All manner of flocks, all manner of wild creatures came and kept holiday in that atmosphere. Then did I first in the number of the shepherds attempt my rustic pipings on the unequal reed. When I sang my slender song in the stippled shade, I startled innumerable flocks across the broad meadows. And when I had attended Androgeo and Opico and their rustic rituals, soon I was moving the pitying rocks with my tears while I sang my dear mother's tomb and early death, while I sang your lamentations (Melisaeus). And when I had explored the hidden paths through secret places, I gazed upon caverns, and rivers sprung from divers sources.

Then greater divinities summon me: that the awesome mysteries of God on high should engage my genius—the mysteries of God, both king of men and lord of gods, the primal miracle of holy religion; that the winged messenger should come from the ethereal stars, bearing his gifts to the bosom of the chaste Virgin. What shall I say of the sheepfolds and the celebrations of the singing shepherds, and your kings (o realm of Arsaces)?[1] No less amid these concerns the ardent love of fishing led me to drop my nets into the bays of the sea, to enclose the deceitful bait within the empty weels, and to allure with my hook the wave-wandering flocks— for I was the first to go down to the salty waves, daring to utter my song in styles not tried before. Why should I speak of my tender Elegies, lamenting song, and praises rendered the gods, not without incense? In other numbers I dallied too, whilst now I treat of serious matters, now scatter various jests among my lines. Moreover many Etruscan things, pleasing to my beloved mistress, I adapted back again to antique modes.

Let me keep silent at present concerning so many years devoted to my kings, so much time given to service in time of war; let me keep silent too about my body vexed with grave disease, scarcely to be cured by the hand of Machaon. Also the grievous banishments of the populace, and ruins of outstanding men, and exiles imposed on hapless citizens. I myself with you (o Frederick) through dangers and hardships encountered

[1]See Glossary, s.v. Arsaces.

many a peril by land and by sea. Harried over the Tuscan fords, across the
Ligurian waves, at last I arrived beside Massilia's shore. Then we passed
over the Rhone, and through the fierce Volcae, and the Vocontian plains,
and your borders (o land of the Belgians). Twice did we cross the frosty
Alps in our journeying, twice did we view the shores of mighty Ocean.
And then at the end we wept for you (o best of kings) as much as ever
wept Hecuba for her sons, as much as Cassandra, her tresses shorn, for
her brothers, or Andromache while she gathered up her husband's bones.
O hapless fate! o faithless fortune! what did we there? O my vessel sunk
on a reef of sorrow! Since then neither in summer's heat nor winter's rain
would the Muse when summoned yield to my genius any kind of fruit.
And now do we marvel, if vanquished by long suffering my narrow vein
has lost its vigor? Homer himself, the celebrator of gods and men, would
have failed—to say nothing of his lyre, sluggish and inert. The father
himself and author of song Apollo would have failed, who alone holds
the rule of the Muses' holy springs.

Now since such have been the losses of my life, you may sorrow
(whoever you are) for my change: that I have not reached fulfillment in
my nature or my art; that my mind is almost sunk through long neglect;
that like a creeping plague or pestilence, my body being broken, sloth-
fulness has invaded my inmost marrow; nor is it possible now to call up
again the eagerness of my lost youth, since my nature's ruin is so extensive. May you at least (good folk of time to come) excuse the grief that
causes my fame to lie in a lonely place and myself to be robbed of the
Muses' blessings as well as of the glorious name of poet—and take my
word that I have had troubles more than these. Let my recompense be
to have kept the name of friendship holy all my life, and for my princes a
fidelity unshaken to the end.

And do you (o my companions) bear with the slow or slothful
friend to whom harsh nature has denied her gifts, as long as I am yet free
from ugly ambition, and sinful lust, and the crime of hateful avarice.
And you above the rest (Cassandra), the witness of my weary age, on
whom awaits every decision about my funeral, be not aggrieved to fulfill
the last rites for your poet, his bones and ashes laid out in the honored
tomb. Yet forebear (my life) to mourn me with tresses shorn, or—but
alas my sorrow forbids me to say more.

Elegy 3: Introductory Note

Typically for Sannazaro, the elegy is a series of instructions—in this
case for building his house upon his return from exile, as in earlier
elegies for celebrating birthdays and funerals, his own and others'.
The seventeenth-century editor Broekhuizen (p. 214) quotes an as-

sertion by Valentinus Odoricius, commenting on the third book of the *De Partu,* that the house was built in the city itself (not at Villa Mergellina), and was later inhabited by one Marius ab Alto Mari. Circumstantial though this sounds, it seems more probable that this is a house not built with hands, but an early example of a tradition widespread in Renaissance and post-Renaissance literature—the description of an ideal architecture (as, for example, Sidney's description of Kalander's house and gardens, in the first three chapters of the revised *Arcadia* 1 (ed. Feuillerat, pp. 15–18).

It is a happy invention. Sannazaro's scheme allows him to reestablish the old days of cheerful banquets presided over by Apollo and the Muses (lines 19–24); and his amphitheater with its wall paintings, or tapestries, allows a review of the kings under whom he has lived: Ferrante I (Fernandus), Alfonso II, Ferrante II, Frederick I, and lastly the young prince Ferdinand, son of Frederick, now held hostage in Spain (lines 27–36). The instructions close with a sequence emphasizing the variety beloved through all the Renaissance (lines 37–44), and a resolution to live out his life in a busy and studious tranquillity, such as Parthenope owes to her aging poet (45–52).

This cheerful note of Resolution and Independence, which must not have lasted long after the poet's return to Naples in 1505, makes a plangent counterpoint to the tortured depression of the immediately preceding elegy. That poem, written at least in part after Sannazaro had made his arrangements for Cassandra Marchese to oversee his obsequies, probably belongs last in the collection by right of chronology. But whoever arranged the ordering—whether Garlon or the poet himself—shows taste and judgment in closing the book with this poem, which shows Sannazaro at his best—cheerful, resilient, faithful to his friends, and loyal to his beloved Parthenope.

[Elegies 3.3] ### HE INVOKES
THE WOODLAND GODS

Upon the Occasion of His House Being to Be Built

 Hail, ye woodland gods: from the neighboring cliffs, from the highest walls of my fatherland, I look to you. I look, and venerate. Let me hear applause, ye deep ravines; let the garrulous breeze make echo from the mountain ridges near. And you, my fellow-citizens, speak by your hearthfires words of good omen: and through the streets bestrewn with fitting flowers, let the victims pass in review before the festive altars, and the troop whose hair is bound with the Palladian leaf.

Let the custom be renewed, from the earliest days of ancient Rome, that a bull in yoke with a pregnant cow should plow the boundary. And before we begin to encircle the house with a plowed furrow, propitiate with incense the righteous gods. May no clouds cross the darkened sky, and may a white bird sound the sacred omen. Let the walls rise that they may repel the wind and rain, that they may extend around, bright with abundant light. Let the columns in series be artfully disposed, with numerous windows adorning half the doors. At the front entrance let two-headed Janus, an affable porter, greet my merry guests. Just to the right let the sacred sisters my consorts encircle the first atrium with their virgin band. On the left, let the Cynthian himself (his lyre laid aside) look down upon Python vanquished by his gleaming arrows.

In the interior let the curve of a small amphitheater offer to view the histories of our kings. And first let Fernandus, truly fearsome on his swift steed, defend himself from the enemy drawn up in triple column. And Alfonsus force the quivered troops, an ominous array, to withdraw from the beaches at Otranto. Then let the youth, himself a king, and endowed with kingly offices, compel the captains of the Alpine armies to abandon their campaign. Finally let Frederick, successful in his ancestral post, destroy Dalmatia's power with his mighty fleet. And menaced by hostile gods and fearsome alliances, let him enjoin upon his son the wars that must be waged.

Then let a sequence well adapted to the variety of the rooms present the region's celebrated views. I would have halls, colonnades, a terrace, heated baths, summerhouses, and that which is adapted for private uses. And let some face to the west, some to the east, and some submit to Boreas, and others hold back Notus. Let the square be joined to the lengthy, the diagonal to the round: and let the most of the chambers hold couches in orderly array. O my leisure, you will be pleasing to my studies, to be enjoyed to Pierian strains in a thousand employments. Here I shall pass my time in a tranquil course until that hour comes more kindly than my fate.

I have lived among troubles, and the tearful ruin of kings: now it is fitting that I enjoy my native city. That what so many cares, so many sufferings have stolen away, Parthenope may restore to her poet.

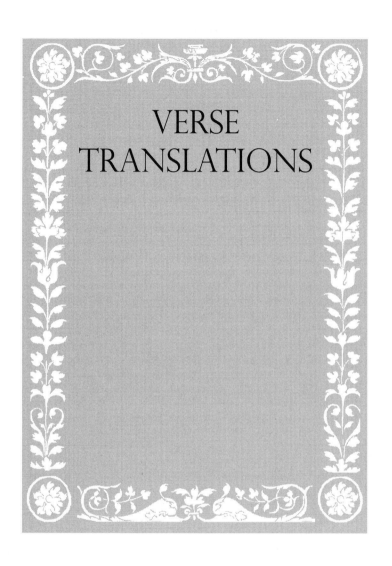

VERSE
TRANSLATIONS

Introductory Note

The versified elegies are, all in all, reasonably close translations, but comparison with the prose versions will show some compression here and omission there, usually to reduce mythological and antiquarian allusion. The epigrams, as one might expect, are virtually line for line (except for one labelled as a paraphrase).

The versifications were done for the best of reasons—that I enjoyed the labor and the result. But I have also had the hope that they might to some degree illustrate how a buried literature such as Neo-Latin poetry bears kinship with the manner and method of early English poets working in similar genres—Jonson, Herrick, Marvell, some of the Cavalier poets. Milton too, now and then.

And Spenser. The translation of Altilio's epithalamion is put into quasi-Spenserian stanzas partly to demonstrate that stanzaic division fits the structure of Altilio's poem surprisingly well. Any reader of Altilio's Latin will see that the first 55 lines divide into four sections of virtually identical length—perfectly adaptable to the *canzone* stanza that Spenser appropriated for *Prothalamion* and *Epithalamion*. Thereafter, the Catullan refrain marks off divisions of nine hexameters more often than any other number—segments of nine lines occurring six times, ten lines three times, as opposed to only five segments of other lengths (5, 7, 8, 31 and 45). Perhaps only accidental, these proportions do suggest some influence from the prevalently stanzaic mode of the native Italian tradition back onto the structural technique of at least this example of Neo-Latin poetry.

I have had also another motive in printing my version of Altilio's poem, which was written for the marriage of Isabella of Aragon and Giangaleazzo Sforza, in 1488. This splendid example of Renaissance patronage-poetry may well have owed much—perhaps a great deal—to suggestions or even phrasings from Sannazaro. If that is so, he was content to leave all the credit to his friend. There is no external evidence to suggest collaboration. But, to say the least, Altilio's epithalamion shares important poetic qualities that permeate most of Sannazaro's Latin verse. One such quality is its careful and effective attention to structural clarity, achieved partly through dividing some of the material (especially the succession of goddesses bringing gifts to the infant Isabella) into patterned recurrences, almost stanzaic but of variable length. Another is its vivid feeling for pictorial effect, as with the winding procession of rural divinities, or the landscape panorama of Naples, its populace lining the walls and its ruling family gathered around Isabella on the deck of the ship which is to bear her on her voyage. And indeed a third mark of kinship is the imagined voyage itself—a device repeatedly employed by Sannazaro.

One additional item is in itself of considerable interest—the undeniable evidence that Altilio's poem draws upon the eighteenth idyll of Theocritus, which purports to be a marriage hymn for Helen's marriage to Menelaus. There are numerous verbal echoes and structural parallels, but a single passage should illustrate sufficiently:

> But we, to-morrow early, will to the Course and flowery meads to gather fragrant garlands, filled with thoughts of thee, as tender lambs long for their mother's teat. We first for thee will twine a wreath of the low-growing trefoil and set it on a shady plane; we first will draw from the silver flask and let drip smooth oil beneath that shady plane. And on its bark shall be inscribed, that passers-by may read in Dorian wise, "Adore me; I am Helen's tree." (*Theocritus,* trans. A.S.F. Gow, vol. 1, p. 143)

Both Altilio and Sannazaro could presumably have had relatively easy access to one of the Theocritean mss. whose presence in Naples derived from the Greek studies of Lorenzo Valla in the time of Alfonso the Magnanimous, and which were indeed the source for the *editio princeps* printed at Milan c. 1480 (Gow, vol. 1, p. xliv). I see no way to prove that Sannazaro called the Theocritean epithalamion to Altilio's attention, rather than vice-versa, but the probability of that seems strong.

Some degree of collaboration is a possibility then, but it is probably more profitable for us to concentrate on noting the remarkable degree of kinship between these two poetic sensibilities. Perhaps we may take this as a benefit from Alfonso's immediate attempt, in the 1440s, to establish some degree of cultural as well as political stability, through his encouragement of what became the Pontanian Academy.

[Elegies 1.1]   **TO LUCIUS CRASSUS**

Now you the fields of rocky Petrine hold
(Lucius), the fields my fathers graced of old;
while Sinuessa's nymphs delight your view,
and plains whose sulphur bubbles ever-new;
whether among those ancient ports you go,
or watch the Lira's cooling waters flow,
or make your pleasant task to view today
the antique structures of the Latian Way.

Another Way, another life I use:
of woodland songs, sung by a country Muse;
of secret plaints Love sings with slender throat
(the woods and caves re-echoing every note).

Not crowds, not cities have I learned to fear,
but tremble at my mistress' frowning cheer.
This life, this study me the fates allot:
from this I pray my name be unforgot,
approved by shepherds, while the rural rout
for rustic Pales pour the warm milk out.
Thyrsis will modulate unlearned song,
praising my love, so faithful and so long;
then for my buried bones will Tityrus bring
(to deck my tomb) the woven ivy-ring;
others will dance; to cool my sacred glade
above the springs will Iolas train the shade
and (while Damoetas strewing flowers doth come)
Alphesiboeus drive the fed flocks home.

Not for me (Lucius) to aspire above
Homer and Maro: I'll be known for Love.
Prudent Ulysses promises me no joy,
nor Peleus, nor Aeneas and his boy.
Let others sing the heroes and their wars,
raising their names triumphant to the stars.
But let far differing fate be granted me
—this be my prayer:

                    that I may bind thee, thee
in close embrace, to drink throughout the day
long kisses made more pleasing with delay:
then gazing on your limbs the lamp I'll light,
weaving the special blandishments of night,

within your arms' embrace to take my rest,
or warm your weary body on my breast. . . .
but why should I dwell thus (deluded thing!)
on empty dreams no day will ever bring.

Happy the man, by joys of marriage blest,
whose love, persuaded, lies upon his breast;
all through the night he roves in amorous play
and celebrates his stolen sweets by day,
recalling with his mistress that first fire
which Love, with golden wing, now fans yet higher.
He needs no fleece from Ethiopian lands,
nor India's store, nor Hermus' golden sands;
he scorns the wealth by Persian laborers won,
or Arabs burnt by an assiduous sun.
Not for such toys are wretched lovers jaded:
he's rich whose mistress says "I am persuaded."

And I—I shall be rich beyond the rest
(though poor and exiled) if by you I'm blest.
An ocean strewn with pearls, what profit now?
or all the fields the black Sabaeans plough?
What use a bed spectacularly fair
with plume and purple, if my girl's not there?
if I drag out the wretched night with sighs,
deny the gods, and human life despise?

Sure I have been bewitched for ancient wrong,
my sleep destroyed through herbs and magic song.
   (Song silences the dogs throughout the town,
   from the unreachable oak draws acorns down;
   song stains the pallid sun with bloody rune
   and stops the horses of the travelling moon.)
Why speak of songs, and charms? Fool, you could rest
if Love removed his dwelling from your breast!

Stronger than Circe, potions twice as strong
as Haemony's poisons—boy, you do me wrong:
you deal me wounds that cannot be withstood
and (savage creature) riot in my blood.

Yet if my griefs should quench my love, I pray
let death's dark hour come without delay.

[Elegies 1.2] TO IOANNIS PARDUS, OF SPAIN

(Pardus) your country's ornament and grace,
(Pardus) chief glory of the Spanish race,
your pleasure is, and business, to inquire
the cause of things, through this vast world entire:
whether one godhead move the aggregate,
or the whole mass be moved of its own weight;
why seas are salt; why Aetna boils with fire;
why vast Charybdis vomits up entire
her swallowed waters; why the stars do shine;
why nights grow longer, and by what design
the days grow shorter; why the moon's made bright
not with her own, but with a borrowed light.
Happy are you, to climb to heaven now
—and after death remain, if fate allow.

We through the woods and muddy fields must move
our flocks, while Phyllis orders us to love,
carving our passions on the tender trees
(such tales the wandering Hamadryads please).
The colorful birds we catch with nets and limes,
asses and goats our arts deceive betimes;
in country pleasures always shall we dwell.
Farewell, ye crowds; ye crowded towns, farewell.

On holy-days I'll watch the rural scene:
the wars of shepherds, wrestling on the green;
their bouts at cudgelling with the hazel stave;
the prizes portioned to the swift, and brave.
Their bulls and he-goats when they match instead,
I'll weave a garland for the victor's head.

When fleece-clad shepherds, huddled 'gainst the cold,
libations make to purify their fold,
goatfooted Fauns like sturdy firs will stand,
and rustic Pales, carved with unskilled hand.
Beneath the knife the stricken lamb will fall,
stricken that one may expiate for all.
Then he who measures out the millet-seed
his foaming cups of milk (blest with due heed)

three times across the crackling stalks will throw,
three times the nimble rustic leap also.

Mid flocks and herds (I ask the gods one thing),
may it be there that I shall cease to sing;
there in the woodlands let the black day come,
let artless shepherds mourn my shaded tomb,
nearby a white sheep bleat auspicious tones,
and pasturing she-goats venerate my bones.

Let others vaunt them with Panchaean rite,
or marbles quarried from a Parian site.
For me, let Phyllis wandering through the grove
pensive reflect upon our ancient love,
and weave me for my tomb, before she goes,
a simple garland of the vernal rose.

[Elegies 1.3]   **TO HIS MISTRESS**

No woman can (I swear) my senses harm;
since I loved you, none else has power to charm:
and I have loved you from my earliest hour,
and shall, till black flames you, or me, devour.

If you die first (which saints forfend!) I shall
(your sacred priest) perform your funeral,
bringing for you sad frankincense, and wine,
and on my lute complaining. From your shrine
none shall remove me. Even as I expire,
I'll kiss the ashes left, of all that fire.

But (as I hope) if you my beadsman be,
gather my scattered bones and tearfully
cut short the hair that now luxuriant flows;
then mix the lily white, and blushing rose,
and with your offering call upon my name.
Such rites befit my tomb, and long-stilled flame.
And you—when old, and gray, by age o'er-set—
with wavering step, you shall perform them yet.

Then shall I wandering that Lethean night
(where but a false day shines, with weakened light)
amid the slender cinnamon, and the groves
ambrosial there, recount our faithful loves.

The listening shades will praise the songs I sing,
scatter fresh flowers, and woven garlands bring,
and each to other tell the tale again.
So shall our death, so shall our love be then.

But now our joyous days, and tender nights,
bid us together mingle our delights
whilst yet the fates our sportings will allow.
Too soon comes heavy age with wrinkled brow.
Twine, twine my neck with amorous embrace:
whilst thus we do, that hour may come apace.
Yet not so soon, but we may see all things
gathered by Love, under his splendid wings.

[Elegies 1.4]   **TO LUCINA**

> **upon Cornelia Piccolomini's being brought to bed,
> the wife of Antonius Garlonius, Lord of Alife**

Lucina, come: this maiden sighs
to you alone, with tear-wet eyes;
she scarce can bear nor make away
the evils of this long delay.

Come now, goddess, bring with you
ointments and herbs of special hue.
So may you quench this young man's grief,
so with one stroke bring two relief.

Garlon, now suppress your fear.
The goddess of the light is near.
Not vainly have you summoned her.
Scatter the costum plant, and myrrh,
with far-fet cinnamon, and consign
freely your cups of well-aged wine.

Now cease complaints, now quavering fear
relinquish. Lo, your son is here.
He's born, and in his infant face
his mother's beauty you may trace.
Hail, child! to you will Love resign
quiver and arrow all made thine,
the flaming torch, the golden bow,
the agile wings—accoutred so,

who would not think you Paphian-bred,
or from the Idalian goddess fled?

Live, child, and while on either hand
your parents round your cradle stand
smile then, and for them both devise
your pretty tricks, with laughing eyes.

[Elegies 1.5]   **TO JULIUS OF SIENA,**

IN EXILE

What though my sorrowing eyes be stunned with grief,
yet shall I strive in speech to find relief.

Amid complaints and sighs your letter came:
I recognized the Muse, and guessed the name.
You ask my song to soothe Apollo's ire,
to make the goddesses hearken to your lyre.
This task my spirit, my speech does not beseem
—go, quench your thirsting at some other stream.
Long since denied to touch the delicate strings,
I draw no water from the accustomed springs:
why look for aid where Fortune does but frown?
My flame is quenched, its torch long since died down.

But you, I hear in your abundant vein
Thalia mourn, Apollo's voice complain,
as when the blameless Orpheus by her grave
bewailed Eurydice to the Strymonian wave
—there by the icy cliffs, the Ismarian wood,
the beasts, the very oaks astonished stood,
heard how his music pulled down rocks headlong
and stopped your current, Hebrus, with his song.

'Tis always thus. Best poets always feel
the strokes of Fortune, and her fickle wheel;
your fate has equalled you with him who lies
exiled beneath the Tomitanian skies.
Yet if we seek not strenuous after fame,
the fires consume our ashes and our name.
Laertes' son, Aeneas—their renown
gives to great labors an eternal crown:
so the Tirynthian, born of heavenly sire,
homeward he mounted from the Oetaean pyre.

So you (I swear) your bitter troubles past,
Virtue herself will lead to Heaven at last.

[Elegies 1.6]   ON THE DEATH OF
SARRUS BRANCATIUS

Lucretia His Wife

Have then the Parcae slit the thin-spun thread,
and shall I then, to you but lately wed,
cold in my bridal chamber you deplore,
a venturer perished on a foreign shore?

Audacious youth! Who ordered you to throw
your single body 'gainst the thronging foe,
where one was peril enough? Ah misery,
you took no thought—and took no thought of me.

You swore to keep me ever in your mind
(swearing by all the sacred ties that bind
our married love), to hold my memory true
though Lethe's flood were closing over you.

And now so quickly fallen (can I believe?)
so quickly fallen from your heart I grieve;
yet, I am fallen. My fates bear wicked sway
and for my safety none is left to pray.

So wept Andromache on the Trojan plain,
so Laodamia for her husband slain.
Now my virginity may my bride-couch hold,
untouched forever, for your ashes cold.

[Elegies 2.2]   [ON HIS OWN BIRTHDAY]

Aonian Muses, make my garlands new!
Lo, for this day I watch the whole year through,
that summoned forth the babe and bade him rise,
lifting his countenance to the starry skies.

See that with hyacinth my altar glows:
and wreathe my threshold with the woven rose.

The hearth is crowned. Fetch wine and incense here.
Genius and Lares thus shall we revere.

And you, my glittering board, provide the feast
garlands of parsley, for each welcome guest.

Buskined with royal purple (like the wine)
Pontano's Muse here sings her song divine,
songs of the world's first birth, of Nature's ways,
and of the whole frame's death, in those last days.
Let Crassus next, with lasting ivy crowned,
tell me the tale of my ancestral ground,
Petrine, and old Linterno's fertile fields,
sequestered now, till hostile Fortune yields.
Altilius shall perform in Pindar's style;
Marullus' Muse forget her sad exile;
Pudericus too his witty jests supply;
and we'll recall, and one with other vie,
remembering Beccadelli's golden day
when he with Jovian reigned in friendly sway.

And lastly you (Garlon) to me most dear,
(Garlon) of all, the youth I most revere,
begin to play your skilful soft guitar,
waking for me the vales of Allifar
till the moon greets the stars and by their light
pursues her journey, silent through the night.

Such joys we'll share, each guest with honored guest:
And Thespians all, we'll celebrate my feast.

[Elegies 2.3]   **ON THE FIRST DAY
OF JANUARY**

To Fuscus

It dawns: and dawn brings in today
(Fuscus) that year for which we pray.

The sun that cheered our fathers dead
rears in the East his radiant head
for us as well, and brings us here
his promise of a happier year.

With reverence now your prayers address,
while Naias shall the altars dress
with garlands plucked from Sebeto.

Let Father Janus open throw
his temple doors, his double brow
bathed with an odorous liquid now.
Let him above the smoke, and flame,
of spotless altars call your name
(Fuscus) announcing honors new.
Such promises I pledge to you.

Not more could you desire the gold
sands in the Lydian river rolled,
nor (Tagus) more your golden hoard,
or Persian treasures richly stored,
or what's by Arabian labors won,
lab'ring beneath the insistent sun.

For those our foes just things I pray
—that foot and horse in disarray
shall flee; and he that does not fly
collapsed in bloody carnage lie.

That day draws near (Fuscus) when Peace
shall grant our sorrowing land surcease.

[Elegies 2.8] ON HIS MISTRESS'S BIRTHDAY

To Juno

Let Chloris on her birth-day bring
to Juno these, for offering.

First (Chloris) on that holy-day
fitly yourself you shall array
in solemn dress, and then enclose
my temples with the purpling rose.
Inviolate of any dye
must be my garments' purity,
but let them flow down, chaste and neat,
smoothly over both my feet.
See that your neck, and snowy breast,
be by your costliest gems caressed;
next, bind your hair with golden wire.
This done, fetch forth my sounding lyre

that on it I may celebrate
the great gift given me on this date.

Shepherds may come, whoe'er they be,
singing with joyous minstrelsy
their praises; then their offerings make
of the Sicilian honey-cake.

The Dryads too, with flowing hair,
each shall her green-oak sunshade wear.
Let Venus myrtle spread, and you,
(Phoebus) the courts with laurel strew.
Each god his gift; and (Bacchus) thine
be it to bring the Naxian wine.

So shall we celebrate for you
(Chloris) your day in order due.

[Elegies 2.9] **ON THE RUINS OF CUMAE**

Here once the walls of Cumae held their sway,
the primal glory of the Tyrrhene bay;
from alien shores the traveller hasted here
to seek the tripods of the Delian seer,
and wandering sailors, making port at night,
read the clear signs of that Daedalian flight,
where now the towering forest holds concealed
within its shades the beasts of wood and field.

Where once the Sybil's leaves the fates unrolled,
the shepherd now shuts in his evening fold;
the council halls of reverend fathers grave
are now the dragon's nest and serpent's cave.
The courtyards once with noble statues graced
—headlong they lie, by their own weight defaced;
thresholds once hung with monuments divine
—the grass o'ergrows the deity and his shrine.
Adornments, arts, of chamber and of hall,
ashes and graves—one ruin drives down all.
And where was once a home (now home no more)
the roving hunter spears the bristling boar.

And yet not this Apollo's voice divine
sang to the Grecian ships from his own shrine;

not this was meant by that great mystery,
the dove sent winging over open sea.

You ask if soon our time will pass, like these?
Cities and towns a violent death will seize.
(O to be false in my prophetic strain,
by long posterity to be counted vain!)
You will not always live where Tiber swells,
the mistress of your seven citadels;
nor you whose walls the Adriatic laves
rise up forever proud amid the waves;
and you, the nourishing mother of my youth,
you too (for who disputes the fateful truth?)
the rough rude peasant turning with his plough
will say "This was a famous place ere now."

The fates bear men along: that fateful day,
all cities and all things will bear away.

[Elegies 2.10]   **POMEGRANATES**

Why seek out strangers, sailor, and (from these)
riches far distant, over turbulent seas?
by paths uncharted, perilous, unknown,
menaced by storms, by wind and tempest blown?
As lustrous gems our tender skins enclose
as any that the Red Sea margin owes,
whether of hyacinth's rose-purple shine,
or amethyst, that hates the god of wine,
or ruby's flame, like torches blazing bright,
or topaz gentle with diffused light.

Rudely vain wealth the common crowd extols,
nor think what ills they purchase for their souls.
Fierce wars, and death, have sprung from wealth's increase
where earlier flourished an abiding peace.
Mother is slain by son, and son by mother,
the sister slain by her beloved brother:
some by the noose, others by poison fall
—fathers, stepmothers, avaricious all.

Gems that are prized for outward shine alone,
and take from art a beauty not their own,

lack the twin gifts that nature us supplies,
to quench men's thirst and slow their gazing eyes.
Not ours to shake the state with battle's din,
or shame the mighty gods with secret sin,
but ours the peace at quiet tables found,
their flowing cups with cheerful vintage crowned,
where youths and maids (whom mutual ardors burn)
handing us on, we're handed back in turn.
We are such gifts of peace and love, as those
the satyr on his woodland nymph bestows.

If Ceres' child had not our savours tasted,
homeward at once the willing maid had hasted.
Pomona on her dusty Libyan road
marvelled how we within her bosom glowed
when from the Punic groves, our native soil,
she fetched us home to be her proudest spoil,
our savour such, and beauty, as to be
the rivals of the jewel-laden sea,
whether by fabled Erythraean shores
or India's regions rich with treasure stores.

You (Acquavive) with double laurel crowned
—alike for arms and poetry renowned—
receive our gift; and wearied with the strain
(whether of study or the long campaign)
quenching your thirst with us, profusely poured,
refresh your vigor at the festive board.

[Epigrams 1.3]   **THE CALENDS OF MAY**

That time is here, the first of May.
Boy, bring me garlands for the day.
(So teaches sage antiquity,
the ancient fathers so decree.)

Let violets be with ivy joined,
the privet with the myrtle twined;
the lily white, and blushing rose,
in one harmonious blend compose.
Drained of her hues, let India's shore
her unexhausted odors pour;

drenched with Assyrian perfumes, all
my hair in floating wavelets fall.
Let foam from massive goblets burst
for the befuddl'd wine-god's thirst
and let his flower-crown laid by
amongst my cups, and tankards lie.

With death there'll be no drinking more,
nor vineyards set on Lethe's shore.
Alas, you race of mortals vain,
why from your joys will you refrain?
Deceive the day: black death will come
too soon t'invade your banquet-room.

[Epigrams 1.6]   **TO NINA**

Give me kisses thirty score
(Nina), neither less nor more.
And none of such as chill desire,
of daughter duteous to her sire,
of sister chaste her brother greeting
— not these, but such as bear repeating,
such as the willing bride bestows,
or maid to lover. Give me those.

Yet be not over-hasty; stay.
Kissing should be with long delay.
And (Nina) mark; remember this;
no silent marble would I kiss,
nor painted face of goddess cold,
but all your active tongue I'd hold
between my moistened lips thrust in
sucking and biting, to begin
our games, our little games of love,
billing and cooing like the dove.

Ah sweeter than Hyblaean mead,
or liquid of Sicilian reed,
or cups of Jove ambrosial!
Which to my lot if they befall
or if my straying hand (perhaps)
arrive upon your swelling paps

who will suppose I'd ask for gold,
or all that royal coffers hold?

I would not rather have my rest
by Venus or Aurora blest,
not Hebe's self would sooner please
though she abandoned Hercules,
and offered, too, that final bliss.
Yet would I not exchange for this.

[Epigrams 1.10] ### ON THE TOMB
OF THE MAIDEN LAURA

If gods could weep, the gods would weep for you
(Laura), and Cupid break his arrows too.

Venus would quench her torches with her tears:
but more than they, I weep your tender years.

Happy the souls who with your shadow roam
in that Elysian grove, your new-made home.

[Epigrams 1.12] ### TO KING FREDERICK

But now (great king) when you set forth your word
that none in private quarrel dare draw his blade,
you were the first to put away your sword
and publicly your naked side displayed.

What (Frederick) can we hope, what greater thing?
Our foes suppressed, in peace the city thrives:
and now, that we may prosper, this our king
doth teach, by example, how to live our lives.

*That commonwealth most just, and firmest, stands
whose king obeys the law himself commands.*

[Epigrams 1.18] ### ON ENDYMION
AND THE MOON

The radiant queen whose chariot rules the night
rejected Pan, his goatherd trade disprized.

But, when Pan brought her gifts of fleeces white,
Endymion's famous sheep she then despised.

Laid on their couch for one last time, said he:
"Death—this will be death, not sleep, for me."[1]

[Epigrams 1.20]

ON POGGIO
OF FLORENCE,
THE HISTORIAN

Poggio praises Florence all he can.
A patriot, true—but no historian.

[Epigrams 1.25]

TO QUINTIUS

My epigrams show brilliancy, you say?
Reason enough: I wrote them at mid-day.

Not all like you (my murky friend) must write,
hunched, without candles, in the dead of night.

[Epigrams 1.29]

ON FABIAN

You are a wise man (Fabian), in your eyes:
but to me (Fabian), neither man nor wise.

[Epigrams 1.31]

WRITING-INK

My pen-point boils in foaming stink
of acid rust, that men call ink.

Is this the Muses' method, then,
"to float upon the lips of men"?

Shall I from filth acquire a name,
and, out of this putrescence, Fame?

---

[1] Broekhuizen in his note quotes Junius Philargyrius: "When Pan burned with love for the Moon, in order that he might seem to her more handsome, he clothed himself in snowy fleeces and so allured her to the act of love." Broekhuizen adds: "The authority for this opinion is Nicander—it couldn't be anybody but a Greek."

From rust and acid, Ile (of these)
construct my tomb's *Pyramides*.

[Epigrams 1.34] **THE TOMB OF MAXIMILLA**

Stay thy steps here (traveller), here, I pray thee.
Enclosed beneath this stone with Maximilla
lie chaste Loves, and Venuses, and Graces.
This is her home, poor girl, prepared by Clotho,
this is her marriage bed. Mother and father
receive from fate this gift of tears and wailing
in stead of applause, and the dances of the maidens.

What do you think stands firm, or lasting (traveller)?
If she for the young men constantly a pleasure,
if she the constant ornament of the maidens,
now alas lo here lies Maximilla,
for the young men a sorrow everlasting,
a source of tears eternal for the maidens.

[Epigrams 1.52]   **ON CAECILIAN**

By the whole Pantheon you see fit to swear
—the brains of Minerva, Venus's golden hair;
"by Phoebe's horns" (or "by this light" instead);
"by Father Jupiter's shanks"—or by his head.

Why then (Caecilian), in the Spanish mode,
bawl in my ear "God's guts!" and "belly of God!"?
Can shameful matters wake no shame in you?
Or do you really think, "God has them too"?

[Epigrams 1.55]   **TO THE SAME
            [i.e., CESARE BORGIA]**

Caesar wants it all. . . . and Caesar wins!

It slips away. . . . Caesar's nothingness begins.

[Epigrams 1.59]   **TO VESBIA**

Look (Vesbia) how by varied passions torn
my tears survive the flame with which I burn.

Aetna and Nile together share my name.
Flame, dry my tears: o tears, put out my flame.

[Epigrams 2.12   **ON VENUS AND PRIAPUS:**
(cf.1.17)]   **A PARAPHRASE**

Venus scratched her hand one day,
toying with Mars's sword in play.

Then Priapus, with a suitable leer:
"This weapon fits *your* hands, my dear."

[Epigrams 2.15]   **[FRAGMENT]**

I climbed a cliff on Belgium's stormy coast,
where restless Ocean beats on either hand:
and, while below the raging channel tossed,
atop its highest crag I took my stand
and mastered there my grief—nor mine alone,
but all men's sorrows, all life's universal moan.

[Epigrams 2.18]   **ON A CHILD'S TOMB**

Child of our love (for whom we grieve)
what we can offer, now receive:

a tomb (alas!) inscribed to say
"Death's ill-timed envy stole you away."

[Epigrams 2.22]   **ON JOVE AND CUPID**

Dictynna once to Jupiter protested
"Cupid's too quick to want his arrows tested."

Showing his thunderbolt, the Father said
"Fierce child, these bolts will knock your arrows dead."

Shrugging his wings, the wanton boy replied
"When you're a swan, you'll lay those bolts aside."

[Epigrams 2.27] ON HIMSELF

The marvel is (with weeping so)
I've not become a riverflow.

Or dwindled into shimmering heat,
so fierce these fires my poor heart eat.

Save (that he might prolong his game)
Love tempers with my tears his flame.

[Epigrams 2.46] IN PRAISE OF CATO

The sand that covers Cato,
who died when Liberty died,
covers as well (great Caesar)
your monumental pride.

[Epigrams 2.52] ON THE RUNAWAY CUPID

The Cyprian seeks her son in wood and field
—who in my very heart's core lies concealed.

They have great claim on me, both one and the other:
the savage Cupid and his savage mother.
If I protect him, how my bones will burn!
Betrayed, how fierce an enemy will he turn!
And she—no schoolboy whipping has she planned:
these are blood matters that she takes in hand.

O runaway Love, lie hidden in your lair
—yet burn more softly, thus more safely there.

[Epigrams 2.55] ON MORINNA

Her breath is sweet, her hair is fine:
her body's every inch divine.
With Aphrodite's charm she vies
and like Athena she is wise.

All this is true, perhaps: but still
I have my freedom and my will.
Earlier on, I burned, I cried:
but never say for this I died.

EPITHALAMION

for Isabella of Aragon and Giangaleazzo Sforza
by Gabriele Altilio

Now joyous dawn new ris'n from Tithon's bed,
baring her bosom to the glorious East,
across the seas her tremulous light had sped.
This day the groom, his longings all surceas'd,
will learn the pleasures of the bridal pair,
the answer to his prayer.
For Aragon's maid, her plighted troth to keep,
this day must be bestow'd on Sforza's heir
(though for her friends and family she weep,
the walls and castles nevermore to see
of her Parthenope).
Neptune himself, the surface seas to scan,
flew in his chariot swift above the wave
and proclamation everywhere he gave
to calm the surge and stormy threats to ban
of fickle Ocean.
Never more quiet shed from heaven's serene,
nor wind more soft nor gentler wave was ever seen.

The chosen band of eager rowers fret
(their hair with garlands crown'd of myrtle green)
and make their brags, along the benches set,
bending their brawny arms in contest keen
that from their noise the hollow shores around
with joyous echo sound.
The maiden weeps against her father's chest,
and grandsire too. Her brothers her surround,
and as she clings and is by them caress'd,
caress'd in turn, they have not yet their fill
but keep her with them still.
And all this while the city sick with woe
repines, and turns her people out of door.

From the high walls, from all along the shore,
matrons and men in long and ordered row
watch her departure slow.
They watch, and follow her with tears and wails,
yet pray her voyage pleasant, and auspicious gales.

Beyond the town where gentle Sebeto
his crystal channel cuts the meadow land,
a variegated troop is come also,
three hundred singing nymphs, a virgin band.
Campania nurs'd them on her neighboring hills,
with them her caves she fills.
A hundred come from Gaurus' summit cool,
an equal number from her tumbling rills
Posilipo sends, and Baiae's steaming pool.
These come from Lira, from Linterno these,
thick-chok'd with mastic trees;
the vineyards of Vesuvius others send.
Volturno and Sarno from their lovely waters,
and Ischia sends her ocean-dwelling daughters.
Three hundred nymphs in long procession wend,
as it would never end.
Then from the midst of their wide-compass'd ring
twelve sisters of surpassing beauty rise to sing.

To Sebeto Parthenope them bore
—sea-born Parthenope, the Muses' pride,
and skill'd in song. They learn'd the Muse's lore
in modes and numbers that the Muse envied.
One came with garlands of that heavenly plant,
immortal amarant
—parsley, narcissus, hyacinth others wore.
For with those flowers ever as they chant
and dance their dance their vigors they restore
and ever so their brilliance they renew,
kept fresh with morning dew.
So joining hands, the graceful virgin throng
in artful patterning then their measure mould,
bidding the figure of their dance unfold,
now with the turns that to their dance belong,
now with their vocal song:
song that within the hollow vale rebounds
that all the seashore *Hymen, Hymenaee* sounds.

[*The Song of the Nymphs of Sebeto*]

1

The Muses sing the torch and bridal nights
of mighty gods, and Heaven's rites proclaim:
we sing you, Isabella, your delights;
your tender loves, O Sforza, we declaim.
The Muses bring to mighty gods no shame,
nor Naiad's song to you can blemish bring.
Parnassus too acknowledges our fame:
Sebeto proffers us his crystal spring.
Sing Hymen, Nymphs: let Hymen, Hymenaee ring.

2

Fresh torches, Lucifer! Shake their streaming light
abundant down that by their flakes of fire
your rising may, though late, compel the night:
haste your return, delay not love's desire.
As married lovers your return require,
as you return, though to their seeming late;
so wavering hearts of maids their fears inspire
whose secret longings your return await.
And the prime joys of night to you they consecrate.

3

Fortunate lad! for you the morning star
leaving old Ocean greets the glittering shore.
The pleasant couch of marriage from afar
he brings, and hymeneals evermore.
Sure from the right, when you your mother bore,
the bird of Jove clapped an applausive wing.
For Aragon's maid her pleasures holds in store
for you alone, and soon to you will bring.
Sing Hymen, Nymphs: let Hymen, Hymenaee ring.

4

Great-grandsire Atlas thousands rul'd in Spain
whom Iber numbers by his earliest stream.
Like gods her family, born like gods to reign.
Proud in those titles and that royal name,
she makes your coverlet and hers the same,
whom you receive in languid slumbering
whence those who come, remembering her fame,

boast themselves sprung from many a mighty king.
Sing Hymen, Nymphs: let Hymen, Hymenaee ring.

5

Your arms such snow-white loveliness will fill
as never by Eurota's stream was known,
nor virgin bands that roam Taygete's hill,
nor ancient heroes knew—nor them alone,
but never had we ken of such a one;
for Isabella dims our dancing ring
as fugitive stars by rising dawn outshone
or parting winter shent by new-come spring.
Sing Hymen, Nymphs: let Hymen, Hymenaee ring.

6

Whenas her mother's birth-pangs sent her forth,
fair Venus cradled her in warm embrace.
Honors she added of celestial worth,
beauty to beauty adding, grace to grace,
and said: "You shall the Foremost stand in place:
none others stand beside you rivalling
(save Venus' self) but all themselves abase."
Such gifts to her did goddess Venus bring.
Sing Hymen, Nymphs: let Hymen, Hymenaee ring.

7

Saturnian Juno came in proud estate,
stroking her infant limbs, and proudly spake:
"A scepter shall you wield of equal weight
as your grandsire's, your queenly progress take
through cities rich and powerful like your make.
Great Jove's great queen this augury doth propound
and pledges in this kiss, that none mistake."
And then the kiss was heard the room around.
Sound Hymen, Nymphs: let Hymen, Hymenaee sound.

8

Next gracious Pallas sings her choicest song
and choicest gifts with lavish hand doth strow:
"Maiden (she said) these gifts to you belong
—manners and mind severe, to make you grow
beyond your sex. Arachne skill'd to sew
shall yield, and I defeated shall resign."
The cradle with her tools doth overflow,

shuttles of gold and combs with golden tine,
in baskets not of gold, yet wov'n of wicker fine.

9

Samos of Juno, Athens of Pallas boast:
on Cyprus Cytherea's rites are due:
on Cynthus ridge is Phoebe worshipped most.
No single city makes her boast of you,
o Isabella. Sebeto claims you too;
Ticinus, Po, the Addus seaward bound,
raising their horned heads in proud review
will count themselves divine, being so renown'd.
Sound Hymen, Nymphs: let Hymen, Hymenaee sound.

10

Diana when she visits Delos isle
her native fields her joys to her restore.
At Eleusis Proserpina doth smile
to view the mystic rites she view'd before.
Now whence your self your blessed mother bore,
go virgin, worthy of such mother found:
both houses by this bond increas'd the more,
by bonds of wife and sister doubly bound.
Sound Hymen, Nymphs: let Hymen, Hymenaee sound.

11

Thus hymeneals sang they in such wise
for Rhea once, when Iris deck'd the bed,
Iris spectacular with a thousand dyes,
her fingers with ambrosia overspread.
With robes girt up the Hours hold their stead,
the heavenly host their joyous shouts redound
through Heaven's courts, below and overhead,
with "Io the Brother, Io the Bride" all round.
Sound Hymen, Nymphs: let Hymen, Hymenaee sound.

12

But now your chosen husband summons you,
claiming the laws of marriage, and his rights.
And we whose proper business hath to do
with riverflow, and dance, and floral rites
turn with the morning's sun to our delights.
Yet morning's sun brings less delight than pain
—as orphan'd calves that wander all their nights

through the deep woods do low, and grieve amain:
so we, that in our sun doth naught of you remain.

13

Our sportive shows, our songs will sound your name:
Our thyases we'll dance to your renown:
our odorous garlands first for you we'll frame
and in your memory leave them, hanging down
along your lotos tree whose dark-leav'd crown
on Sebeto's bank will flourish yet for thee,
that hasting sailors hasting past the town
may read this verse, grown larger with the tree:
QUEEN. ISABELLA'S. ROYAL. LOTOS. WORSHIP. ME.

14

But now the whispering wind and peaceful sea
call to make ready, and your lively crew
rebuke that these delays should longer be.
The captain from his deck is urging you.
Leave off embraces: make the journey due.
Delights await your prosperous voyaging
to dry your tears and never them renew,
but draw your passions from another spring.
Sing Hymen, Nymphs: let Hymen, Hymenaee ring.

15

High on the stern the maid waves to the shore,
the sailors cheer and lay the canvas on.
The hollow cannon flame with thunderous roar,
the ropes are coil'd, the anchor's up anon.
Her ship is under way, and now she's gone,
while still the echoes rive the air around.
So Thetis rides the waves by dolphins drawn,
so Venus sails her shell, for Cyprus bound.
Sound Hymen, Nymphs: let Hymen, Hymenaee sound.

16

Though vanishing sails have left our eyes behind,
baffled and weeping, as our chill'd hearts fail,
your voyage yet we travel in the mind:
past Gaeta's bay that shelters from the gale,
or Anxur heights, or shoals not safe to sail
by Ostian Tiber's mouth. Or passing these

(and Circe's straits where skill will not avail)
your pilot turns and with a favoring breeze
brings you to visit now the ports of Hercules.

17

Whether Port Argus foams beneath your oar,
or Ilva spreads her wealth of plundered mines,
or Populonia harkening Ocean's roar
down from her loftiest cliff her gaze declines,
or Nelean Pisa's hold arrests your lines,
or Father Magra by his margent steep
with all his Nymphs the voyager divines,
rearing his head where Lunar waters deep
their silent walls of white Carraran marble keep.

18

Liger at last receives her on his shore,
Liger the genius of her husband's realm
and first the new-come mistress to adore.
Yet not alone, for Venus takes the helm,
leaving Mount Eryx and his harbors calm,
to guide the maiden with divinity's hand,
forbidding wind to threat or waters whelm.
And at the last bids welcome them to land
a Tyrrhene progeny, the Nereids' holy band.

19

Nesaee, Spio, white Cymodoce,
Melite, Glauce, and Janira fair,
Doto the lovely and Amphinome,
Thoe, and Amathuse with yellow hair,
Opis, Pherusa, Halye—all are there.
Thetis their leader now forgets to grieve
but leads their troop that arching through the air
before the ships rejoicing swim and dive,
that in such merry mood at last at shore arrive.

20

The travell'd road so long, secure from harms,
thus with our prayers we follow in the mind.
But now you reach your husband's eager arms,
and grateful Night at last these lovers find.
Let Cypris send them mutual loves that bind,

Latona Queen their marriage bed befriend,
let Jove send health, and riches unconfin'd,
and length of years and princedoms let him send,
and fortunate be your house establish'd without end.

Sing Hymen, maids: Io Hymen, Hymenaee sweet,
Io Hymenaee, Hymen, let your song repeat.

APPENDICES

Appendix A:
The Chronology of Frederick's First Marriage

On October 26, 1474, Prince Frederick departed from Naples at the head of some four hundred soldiers and courtiers. After a leisurely progress through North Italian cities (Venice, Milan, Ferrara, and others), the company crossed the Alps in Easter week, 1475, intending to join the camp of Charles the Bold, Duke of Burgundy, the chief objective of the whole journey being to promote a marriage between Frederick and the Duke's daughter, Maria. On September 26, 1475, they finally succeeded in joining Charles, in Luxembourg, and over the next six months they lent assistance at the siege of Nancy (November–December, 1475) and the battle of Grandson (March 2, 1476), without gaining any commitment about the proposed marriage. Indeed, Ernesto Pontieri, who has traced the expedition's movements in detail (*Per la Storia del Regno di Ferrante I d'Aragona,* Naples, 1969, pp. 188 ff.), notes (p. 270, n. 117) that a Milanese dispatch actually speaks of Charles having signed his approval (May 6, 1476) of a marriage agreement between Maria and Maximilian, son of the Holy Roman Emperor, Frederick III—which marriage did eventually take place. Charles evidently said nothing to young Frederick of any such agreement, hoping presumably to have his assistance yet again as the campaign moved toward a third large battle (Morat, June 22, 1476). But on the very day before that battle Frederick appeared before Charles, requesting and receiving immediate permission to return to Naples. He departed that same day, spent a day or two at Gex, where Yolanda Duchess of Savoy (and sister of Louis XI of France) was in residence, and on June 25 went directly to the French court, then at Lyons, under a safe-conduct recently granted him by Louis. After a pleasant two months or so of feasting and hunting with Louis XI and his courtiers, the company at last embarked for Naples from Nice in late August or early September, visiting cities along the way, and finally arriving at Naples on October 21, 1476 (Pontieri, pp. 206–7).

Much of this circumstantial detail about a failed marriage-negotiation during 1474–76 seems relevant to the successful negotiation, during 1478–79, of a marriage contract between Frederick and Anna of Savoy, daughter of the dowager duchess Yolanda, and as niece of Louis XI brought up for most of her life in the French court. The question is twofold: why was the relationship with Charles abruptly severed? and is there a connection between that severance and the marriage of Frederick, almost three years later, to the niece of an inveterate enemy of Charles?

Ernesto Pontieri refrains, properly enough, from speculating on the cause of Frederick's abrupt departure. It is no wild leap of the imagination, however, to suppose that other people than a Milanese ambassador might have learned of Charles's sanctioning a match between Maximilian and Maria. Though we have no evidence that this occurred, we do have Commynes' assertion that Ferrante recalled his son: "Ledit prince print congié dudit duc le soir devant la bataille, en obeissant au mandement du roy son pere" (*Mémoires,* ed. Mandrot, 1.359). A few lines earlier, Commynes makes the same assertion, with some interesting additions:

> The prince of Taranto, called Don Frederick of Aragon, and his council, being dissatisfied with so many delays, sent a shrewd officer to the king of France, begging him to grant a safe-conduct to the prince, so that he might pass through his kingdom and return to the king his father, who had sent for him. (*Memoirs,* ed. S. Kinser, trans. I. Cazeaux, Columbia, S.C., 1969, 1.308)

We may add to this passage the plausible assertion by Augusto DeFerrari in DBI (s.v. Catone) that Angelo Catone wrote to Ferrante advising that Frederick be called home, Catone then following Frederick to the French court and eventually remaining there as personal physician to Louis XI.

It has always been known that Catone instigated Commynes' writing of the *Mémoires,* as Commynes himself acknowledges at the beginning of his work, so that what Commynes says about the rupture between Frederick and Charles is likely to be based on inside information. Put into sequential order, that account (supplemented by the DBI entry on Catone) seems to present: (1) dissatisfaction in Frederick's council with Charles's temporizing; (2) at some point, according to DeFerrari, a suggestion from Catone that Ferrante recall Frederick; (3) a recall dispatched by Ferrante; (4) dispatch of "a shrewd officer" to Louis XI by Frederick and his council, to request a safe-conduct; (5) the granting of the safe-conduct; (6) possibly, but not necessarily, a leak at some time about the Duke's secret signing (c. May 6) of a marriage agreement between Maria and Maximilian; (7) the open break with Charles, June 21, 1476; (8) a brief sojourn at Gex, where Yolanda of Savoy was temporarily in residence; (9) a journey by Frederick to the court of Louis XI, followed by two months of good-fellowship; (10) a journey by Angelo Catone, following Frederick to the French court, where he left Frederick's entourage to take up residence as court-physician to Louis XI; (11) in 1478, negotiations for a marriage agreement between Frederick and Anna of Savoy, followed by their marriage, apparently in March 1479 (see Luigi Volpicella, *Regis Ferdinandi Primi Instructionum Liber,* Napoli, 1916, pp. 221, 235).

We do not actually know that Frederick's brief stop at Gex had anything to do with Yolanda and her daughter, nor that Angelo Catone had anything to do with the council's decision to obey Ferrante's recall by arranging a lengthy visit at the court of Louis XI—although Commynes is careful to hint that his friend Catone deserves the credit, saying "There are some (my Lord of Vienne) [i.e., Catone] who affirm, that he left the army by your advice" (*Memoirs,* trans. Andrew Scoble, London, 1855, 1.314). But both Yolanda and Catone were in a position to help along the course of events that eventually turned the failed negotiations at the Burgundian court into the successful negotiations with Yolanda and her brother, Louis XI—with some degree of profit to both Yolanda and Catone.

The marriage itself is, in effect, suppressed by Sannazaro in his Elegy to Frederick (*Elegies* 3.1), and possibly for that reason it has been virtually suppressed by those who write about Sannazaro and Frederick. We know that in 1478 two Neapolitan envoys, Lancellotto Macedonio and Alessandro Antonio, were sent to France to arrange the marriage terms (Volpicella, p. 356), and that in mid-February 1479, Frederick sailed from Naples to be married in France (Volpicella, p. 234). And we can discover more from the travels of two eighteenth-century Benedictines, Edmond Martène and Ursin Durand (*Voyage Litteraire de Deux Religieux,* Paris, 1717–24). The two monks were allowed to examine the necrology of the Abbey at Issoudun (mod. Indre), transcribing a portion that includes the following:

> En 1480 en ce present jour [April 4] trépassa tres haute & puissante princesse Madame Anne de Savoye, femme de tres haut & puissant prince Monsieur Frederic d'Arragon prince de Tarente & seigneur d'Issoudun, laquelle trépassa en l'hôtel de Pauldy. (1.22)

An incidental bit of information here is that evidently a part of Anna's dowry was the signory of Issoudun (which ironically, having presumably reverted to the French crown after Anna's death, formed part of the dowry acquired by Cesare Borgia twenty years later when he married Charlotte d'Albret after being "energetically" refused by Anne's surviving daughter Carlotta, or Charlotte d'Aragon—for this, and further details of Anna's dowry, see René de Maulde la Clavière, ed., *Chroniques de Louis XII par Jean d'Auton,* Paris, 1889–95, 1.97, n. 2, and 291, n. 1). But more significant is the death date itself—probably no more than thirteen months after the wedding, and thus suggestive of a death from childbirth or from complications thereafter, although the Issoudun necrology does not specify that.

The details sketched thus far help to explain various aspects of Sannazaro's elegy addressed to Frederick: the vehemence against Charles the Bold, the rather curious elaboration of the return through the French countryside, with its almost incidental reference to nuptial torches, and the unfinished state of the rest of the elegy, as it passes over the marriage to Isabella, the four children from that marriage, Frederick's military activities on land and sea, and his eventual succession to the throne of Naples. The poem is at best a fragment, biographically speaking, and its fragmentary state was probably caused in part by the poet's embarrassment about what to say of that first marriage (and the surviving daughter), before the exile and death of Frederick made it more or less pointless to solve these problems.

The brief history of Charlotte d'Aragon has its own relevance to Frederick's closing years. After Anna's death, Frederick remained in France until he had made arrangements to leave Carlotta at the French court, whereupon he returned to Naples on May 22, 1482 (Volpicella, p. 235). We do not know that he ever saw his daughter again. By the end of the following year, most of the main actors in the foregoing sketch were dead: Charles killed in battle at Nancy, 1477; Anna dead in 1480; Yolanda of Savoy in 1478; Louis XI in August 1483; and even Maria of Burgundy dead (of a fall from her horse) in October 1482. But after twenty years the fortunes of father and daughter were to cross again. Having strongly supported his daughter in her refusal of Cesare Borgia (in 1499), Frederick promptly endorsed her marriage to the very wealthy Count Nicolas de Laval, on January 27, 1500 (d'Auton, *Chroniques,* ed. Maulde la Clavière, 1.286, n. 1; cf. 1.325–26). As Comtesse de Laval, Charlotte lived on the family estates at Laval, within about a hundred miles of Tours, Frederick's principal residence during his years in exile as Duke of Maine (for the terms of which exile, see d'Auton, ed. Maulde la Clavière, 2.60–95, 148, n. 2; 3.254, n. 1).

Charlotte d'Aragon survived her father's death less than a year, dying at twenty-five like her mother and probably of the same cause, since in this case we know that she died in giving birth, to her fourth child, on October 6, 1505 (L'Abbé A. Angot, *Dictionnaire Historique, Topographique et Biographique de la Mayenne,* Mayenne, 1962 repr., s.v. Laval, 2.579). One of those children, Anne de Laval, in 1521 married

François de la Trémoïlle, thus giving rise to later claims in that family to rights in the kingdom of Naples (see Charles Samaran, *Archives de la Maison de La Trémoïlle: Chartriers de Thouars et de Serrant,* Paris, 1928, pp. 4, 79, 228).

There are striking coincidences in this sequel to the ill-starred marriage in 1479: both mother and daughter dead at twenty-five, very probably from childbirth in both cases; the daughter living no more than a hundred miles from her father's place of exile, and dying at Laval less than a year after her father's death at Tours. One is inclined to empathize with Sannazaro's evocation, at the close of his elegy to Frederick, of a grim fate watching as princes and dukes act out their voyages and victories, their marriage feasts and funerals.

Appendix B:
An Unnoticed Imitation of Virgil
in *Paradise Lost* and *De Partu Virginis*

Imitation of classical authors can, of course, go beyond the echoing of
lines and phrases into such matters as narrative and dramatic technique—epic invocations, for instance, or the use of dramatic prologues,
or stichomythia. A good example of what can be done along these lines,
through imitation of a relatively subtle variation in narrative technique,
occurs when both Sannazaro and Milton choose to imitate the same
passage in Virgil.

In Book Eight of the *Aeneid,* Aeneas with a few companions visits
the prince Evander. As evening draws on, Evander's priests sing songs in
praise of Hercules. J. W. Mackail's translation accurately conveys the peculiar narrative technique with which we are here concerned:

> Then the Salii stand round the lit altar-fires to sing, their
> brows bound with poplar boughs, one chorus of young
> men, one of elders, and extol in song the praises and deeds of
> Hercules; how first he strangled in his gripe the twin terrors,
> the snakes of his stepmother; how he likewise shattered in
> war famous cities, Troy and Oechalia; how under Eurys-
> theus the King he bore the toil of a thousand labours by
> Juno's malign decrees. Thine hand, unconquered, slays the
> cloud-born double-bodied race, Hylaeus and Pholus, the
> Cretan monster, and the huge lion under the Nemean rock.
> Before thee the Stygian pools shook for fear, before thee the
> warder of hell, couched on half-gnawn bones in his blood-
> stained cavern; to thee not any form was terrible, not
> Typhoeus' self towering in arms; thou was not bereft of
> counsel when the snake of Lernus encompassed thee with
> thronging head. Hail, true seed of Jove, added glory to the
> courts of heaven! graciously visit us and these thy rites with
> favourable feet. Such are their songs of praise; they crown all

the cavern of Cacus and its fire-breathing lord. All the wood-land echoes with their clamour, and the hills resound. (*Aeneid* 8.285–305, trans. Mackail)

A third-person narration turns without warning into a second-person direct address to Hercules ("Thine hand, unconquered," and so on), with even a first-person reference to the singers themselves ("graciously visit us and these thy rites"), before returning to third-person narrative ("Such are their songs of praise"). Thus, without the usual prefatory announcement, Virgil has for a few lines presented his reader a direct transcript of the song of the Salii, returning to third-person narration as his verse paragraph comes to a close. There is no problem—only a slight peculiarity, one of the many stylistic devices with which Virgil embellished his poem. Slight though it be, the device did not go unnoticed by poets of the Renaissance. Sannazaro and Milton—and probably others—have employed it in their own heroic poems.

Sannazaro is, as we might expect, the closer to Virgil. In Book Three of *De Partu Virginis,* Sannazaro presents a panoramic survey of angelic activity in the skies over Bethlehem. One group is performing rather complicated military maneuvers in the air; a second is marching steadily through the clouds, singing and bearing various symbols of the Crucifixion; and a third is presented without visual detail, as follows:

> Others are singing the Father's unbounded praises and his mighty works—how he laid the first foundations of the new world and divided the earth from the shifting waters; how throughout heaven he hung her various lights, both moon and stars; how he brought forth the light of the mighty sun when the shadows had fled from the farthest Orient.
>
> O thou who art to be dreaded, you cast down the warring legions, you thrust them forth from heaven; you shatter with your thunderbolt their standards and their captain, and plunge them into gloomy Avernus, decreeing that they dwell beside Cocytus and her melancholy waters. Thee the twin poles sang, thee the earth most mighty, and thee in thy victory Ocean sang with his immeasurable surge. Mankind's betrayals have not escaped you, nor his unspeakable crimes, but you look upon mortal affairs with countenance serene, and comfort with your divinity an earth deemed worthy. Hail, great architect of Heaven, most mighty king of the gods, salvation of the earth and of mankind, thou whom the stars fear and the sun, the monarchs of the nether world and mighty Tartarus, thou whom mankind everywhere serves, who alone art ruler over all, and lovest all alike. Thine are a thousand

names, a thousand princely honors, a thousand royal. Hail, creator; hail, lord of unbounded Olympus; abide in peace with us and with the fallen earth. Let the clouds redouble our salutation and our voice be borne through the air to every quarter, and heaven's dome resound. (*De Partu*, 3.223–44)

The closing lines of the passage depart from the model, in that Sannazaro dispenses with any imitation of Virgil's "Such are their songs of praise" (*Aen.* 8.303), simply making an abrupt transition, after line 244, to the next section of his poem. But there can be no doubt that he is intentionally echoing the Virgilian passage in its presentation of a series in third-person narration, followed by an unannounced shift to a second-person address in praise of the deity's actions, and a further shift to a first-person reference by the chorus to itself. Ample evidence of deliberate *imitatio* is afforded by Sannazaro's providing a signature line at the point where each poet makes the abrupt shift from third-person narration to second-person invocation:

> . . . pertulerit. 'tu nubigeras, invicte, bimembris (*Aen.* 8.293)

> . . . protulerit. Tu belligeras, metuende, cohortes
> (*De Partu* Lat. 3.262).

In *Paradise Lost,* John Milton also appears to be employing this Virgilian technique, although his treatment is characteristically independent. Milton devotes very nearly fifty lines to rendering from varying points of view the contents of an angelic hymn of praise that responds to the Almighty's announcement in Book Three of His plan for mankind's redemption:

> Thee Father first they sung Omnipotent,
> Immutable, Immortal, Infinite, . . .
> Thee next they sang of all Creation first,
> Begotten Son, Divine Similitude. . . .
> Hee Heav'n of Heavens and all the Powers therein
> By thee created, and by thee threw down
> Th'aspiring Dominations: thou that day
> Thy Father's dreadful Thunder didst not spare,
> Nor stop thy flaming Chariot wheels, that shook
> Heav'n's everlasting Frame, while o'er the necks
> Thou drov'st of warring Angels disarray'd.
> Back from pursuit thy Powers with loud acclaim
> Thee only extoll'd, Son of thy Father's might,
> To execute fierce vengeance on his foes,
> Not so on Man; him through their malice fall'n,

Father of Mercy and Grace, thou didst not doom
So strictly, but much more to pity incline:
No sooner did thy dear and only Son
Perceive thee purposed not to doom frail Man
So strictly, but much more to pity inclin'd,
He to appease thy wrath, and end the strife
Of Mercy and Justice in thy face discern'd,
Regardless of the Bliss wherein hee sat
Second to thee, offer'd himself to die
For man's offence. O unexampl'd love,
Love nowhere to be found less than Divine!
Hail Son of God, Saviour of Men, thy Name
Shall be the copious matter of my Song
Henceforth, and never shall my Harp thy praise
Forget, nor from thy Father's praise disjoin.
    Thus they in Heav'n, above the starry Sphere,
Thir happy hours in joy and hymning spent.
(*P.L.* 3.372–417, ed. Merritt Hughes, who remarks, "Here,
as usual in his angel choruses, Milton puts himself into the
choir.")

The poet is moving with such agility among his *thee*'s and *thou*'s,
and *they*'s and *their*'s, that it seems unwise to remark here on every shift.
But clearly enough the general situation parallels the passage from the
Aeneid. The poet, in third-person narrative ("Thee Father first they
sung"), presents a chorus singing praises of the deity's actions, then
shifts to the singers' direct first-person invocation of that deity ("Hail
Son of God"), returns to the third-person narrative mode ("Thus they
in Heav'n"), and goes on to other matters.

Some of the oddities in Milton's passage have been noted by Allan
Gilbert in his bold and ingenious reconstruction of a hypothetical early
version of *Paradise Lost* as tragedy in the Greek manner:

> The hymn is so related to the subject of *Paradise Lost* that on
> first sight it seems well integrated. . . . The construction is,
> however, peculiar. The song begins by telling what the angels
> sang about the Father and then turns to direct address. The
> same method is used for the part on the Son (III.383–400).
> Then there is direct address to the "Father of Mercie and
> Grace," whose wrath is appeased by the Son. A slight change
> would render the structure normal; the poem might begin:
> "Thee Father first I sing"; and so might be treated the address
> to the Son. We then should have a lyric in which the speaker
> is not Milton himself, but perhaps an angelic singer in the

drama of *Paradise Lost*. Otherwise the lines in the first person must be thought an independent utterance by the poet, though they continue the hymn directly. (*On the Composition of Paradise Lost*, Chapel Hill, 1947, pp. 46–47)

It seems, however, quite plausible that Milton, like Sannazaro, is deliberately echoing Virgil's structure by introducing his angelic singers into a third-person narration, going on without prefatory announcement to a direct transcription of their song, and closing with the singers' affirmation of themselves and their relation to their deity ("Hail, true seed of Jove . . . graciously visit us"; "Hail, creator . . . abide in peace with us"; "Hail Son of God . . . thy Name shall be the copious matter of my Song henceforth"). Milton's use of first-person singular in 3.413–14 presents no great obstacle, in view of his regular practice in *Samson Agonistes,* throughout which drama the chorus refers to itself sometimes in the singular, sometimes in the plural, as did the choruses of Greek tragedy (cf. Gilbert, *Composition*, p. 14, n.7).

The entire passage artfully interweaves praise of the Father with praise of the Son, past action with present, and narrative mode with dramatic. We would not, therefore, be necessarily disturbed by the added complexity if for a moment the personae of the angels should appear to blend with the persona of the poet. But a simpler alternative suggests merely that Milton here is imitating the narrative technique of the Virgilian passage. And indeed, it seems wholly in keeping with Milton's poetic achievement, and his allusive, integrative imitation of classical poets, that the song of the angels in heaven should attempt to remind the reader for a moment of Virgil's Salii singing the praises of *their* Herculean hero.

These two Virgilian imitations are not brought together here to suggest that Sannazaro "influenced" Milton. There is no need for that. Both men obviously respected Virgil's artistry, and in Renaissance poetry it follows that they were both likely to pay him homage by appropriating his technique in presenting their choric praises of divinity. Admittedly Sannazaro's signature line (3.228) calls attention to what he is doing, whereas Milton simply incorporates the Virgilian peculiarity and leaves it there to be noted or missed by his fit audience though few. But this is a minor variation within the great underlying theme of the imitation of classical models.

Appendix C:
The Orange Grove at Mergellina

Sannazaro exercises a tactful restraint when speaking through his own persona at the beginning and end of *De Partu Virginis.* In his invocation of the Holy Spirit and the Virgin Mother, he makes no use of his customary stance as the shepherd-poet, even though he had ready to hand the example of great Virgil himself:

> Ille ego, qui quondam gracili modulatus avena
> carmen, et egressus silvis vicina coegi
> ut quamvis avido parerent arva colono,
> gratum opus agricolis, at nunc horrentia Martis
> arma virumque cano. . . .

> I am he, who once tuned my song on the slender
> reed, and leaving the woodland constrained the
> neighboring fields to serve the husbandman, though
> greedy of gain—a task pleasing to farmers: but
> now I sing the dread arms of Mars and the man.
> >   (*Aeneid* I.abcde, trans. Sidgwick,
> >   in *P. Vergili Maronis Opera,* Cambridge,
> >   1927, 2.137)

It seems worth comment that such a poem as *De Partu* should forego such an opportunity for reminiscence of well-known lines from Virgil. Sannazaro would have known that the early scholiast Servius had labelled these lines as rejected by Virgil's literary executor, but he may have refrained from using them simply because he thought that the proper reverence and humility would be better observed if no allusion were made at this point to his own poetical career, no matter how much classical precedent there might be.

On the other hand, a different kind of restraint is exercised in the closing paragraph of *De Partu Virginis,* as Sannazaro winds his poem down from the lofty heights of the heroic mode, down along the pleasantly shaded flanks of Posilipo to the deities of sea and shore, and on to his own villa by that shore, the haunt of the Muses, Mergellina, whose groves weave for him his own special crown. It is exquisite art, the verses flowing as splendidly resonant as those of Virgil himself, the presence of the poet growing stronger and stronger, called up by the very place names and deities that he has invoked so often before, until at the end the place itself is crowning him the poet of that place. Poet and place seem blended into one, and Sannazaro has skillfully but modestly suggested that he is retiring now from his attempt on the heroic to that level of pastoral where he has long since proved his right to wear the laurel crown.

But this crown is not laurel. Indeed, what is it? In books and articles of recent years, more than one English version has rendered Mergellina's *citria* as *cedars*, possibly under the influence of Italian translations (e.g., G. B. Casaregi, 1740), which can simply read *cedri*, leaving the reader to choose between cedars or some form of citrus tree, such as oranges or lemons, since *cedro* can mean any of these. Almost certainly, however, Sannazaro's *citria* denotes not cedars but citrus trees planted at Mergellina before his departure for France with his exiled king.

The concept of utilizing a garland from the grove at Mergellina, as a signature at the end of his major poem, might have come to him through Ovid. Pallas Athena, having completed her tapestry woven in contest with Arachne, "signs" her work with her own olive leaf—"and so, with her own tree, her task was done" (*Met.* 6.101–02, trans. Miller). And we may be sure that Virgil is also in Sannazaro's mind when the latter speaks of his trees at Mergellina "whispering tales of the Persians' holy groves," for Virgil had written of a "blest apple" growing in Media ("probably the citron," says Arthur Sidgwick, ed. cit., 2.74), and bearing very close resemblance to the laurel:

> ipsa ingens arbos faciemque simillimus lauro:
> et, si non alium late iactaret odorem,
> laurus erat

> The tree is large, and most like a laurel to view, and
> were a laurel but for the difference of wide-wafted
> fragrance. (*Geor.* 2.131–33, trans. Mackail)

These Ovidian and Virgilian overtones are interesting, and pertinent enough, but they are not central to deciding how to take Sannazaro's references to his *citria* at Mergellina. For that we need to turn to his friend and mentor, Giovanni Pontano, whose *De Hortis Hesperidum* appears decisive on this question, since it devotes almost twelve hundred hexameters to problems in the cultivation of *limones, citria,* and *citri* (lemon trees, and apparently two types of orange tree—cf.

De Hortis 2.180–230). Pontano, well acquainted with Sannazaro's grove at Mergellina, pictures his friend, the exiled Syncerus, making complaint to the uttermost poles while his orange trees are parched and the earth beneath his lemon trees lies lifeless (*Interea sitiunt citri ac limonide in umbra Torpet humus—De Hortis,* 2.297–308). The poet is gone; his faithful trees remain behind.

There they remained, in Sannazaro's memory, when on France's Atlantic coast he visited the shrine of his patron saint and offered him fresh garlands from summer's orange tree (*aestivam . . . citrum*), and virgin laurel, and the tender myrtle, and all the fragrances that Mergellina wafts from her neighboring shore (Epigrams 2.60, *Ad Divum Nazarium,* 57–60). The laurel and myrtle here may be a subtle return of compliment to Pontano, who specifically recommends, in discussing the cultivation of lemon trees, that the young tree be sheltered from cold and heat by a screen of laurel or rosemary, praising the plantation at Mergellina for providing such a screen of laurel, foxglove, and myrtle (*De Hortis,* 2.288–96). There the grove remained when Sannazaro in a codicil to his will left to an heir his "giardino dei cedri" at Mergellina (Pércopo, p. 100). And there it does *not* remain to this day, nor do we expect it, for readers of Sannazaro will have learned the lessons of Mutabilitie. But even so, at the end of the nineteenth century another great lover of Naples and her history, the youthful Benedetto Croce, promises that the traveller come to Mergellina will find here and there "tracce e frammenti," a stretch of ground that was once a garden adorned with statuary (*Storie e Leggende Napoletane,* ed. G. Galasso, Milan, 1990, pp. 224–25). "Anche un aranceto," he says. Also an orange grove.

Appendix D:
Mary's Magnificat
(*De Partu Virginis* 2.43–66)

Mary's Magnificat (Luke 1:46–55) is unmistakably an example of the inserting of essentially poetic material into a historical prose narrative. The practice is rare in the New Testament, although examples of this Hebraic literary tradition abound in the Old Testament (e.g., the Song of Moses, Exodus 15:1–19; David's Eulogy for Saul and Jonathan, 2 Samuel 1:17–27; Jonah's Lament from the Belly of the Whale, Jonah 2:2–9). Sannazaro has unerringly seized on the Magnificat as an opportunity for grounding his poem to some extent on an earlier poetic treatment of his subject, by echoing the very diction and phrasing of his historical source, prose though it be. Moreover, considered as Mary's psalm of praise to the Lord, the Magnificat provides his premier opportunity for balancing specifically Christian material from the New Testament against the bravura-piece of *imitatio* that brings Virgil's Messianic eclogue into his poem, under the guise of the Song of Lycidas and Aegon (*De Partu* 3.163–206).

It seems sufficient to demonstrate the poem's intention by simply listing (from *Biblia Sacra iuxta Vulgatam Versionem,* ed. Robertus Weber OSB, Stuttgart, 1983) all the active verbs in the Vulgate text in a column paralleled by the corresponding active verbs in *De Partu Virginis:*

Vulgate (Luke 1:46–55)	*De Partu* (Lat. 2.49–75)
1. Magnificat	1.
2. exultavit	2. exultant
3. respexit	3. respexit
4. dicent	4. dicar
5. fecit	5.
6. fecit	6.

7. dispersit	7. dispulit afflixitque
8. deposuit	8. dedit in praeceps
9. exaltavit	9. extollens . . . locavit
10. implevit	10. implevit
11. dimisit	11. reliquit
12. suscepit	12. suscepit
13. locutus est	13. promiserat

Some parallel nouns and adjectives could also be suggested, but the above paralleling of verbs is enough to move Sannazaro's treatment of his source into the realm of *imitatio.*

The point here is not merely to document the poet's use of Luke 1:46–55. That we would expect, *a priori,* and Sannazaro has, in any event, amply annotated in his own hand his uses of Scripture, in the mss. being prepared for the printing of the 1526 *editio princeps* (see Fantazzi-Perosa, pp. lxxii–lxxiii; lxxix). The central point to consider is, again, that of motivation: why does Sannazaro employ these surely deliberate and recognizable verbal echoes of the Scriptural Magnificat?

If Luke 1:49–55 is viewed as a psalm of praise to the Lord, I have suggested in my opening paragraph one motivation for Sannazaro's processing it as *imitatio*—i.e., to keep up the balance between sacred and profane materials as he fills out and extends the dimensions of his sharply limited central action. But the passage also is presented by Luke as historical narrative. Viewed in that perspective, Sannazaro's device of studding his version of the Magnificat with verbs from the Vulgate text looks innovative, anticipating a significant trend in Western literature. That is, he is deliberately importing into his poem recognizable fragments taken verbatim from a historical text. Within three-quarters of a century, one can find numerous examples of much the same impulse. Shakespeare at times uses the very language of historians in his own tongue, e.g., More and Holinshed; Ben Jonson translates from Cicero large portions of an oration against Catiline (reportedly at the cost of being hissed off the stage), and publishes his *Sejanus,* in 1605, with an overwhelming apparatus of marginal references to Roman historians. Closer to Sannazaro in genre, time, and culture, Torquato Tasso finds room in *Jerusalem Delivered* for several stanzas that are virtual transcriptions of passages from contemporary travel literature describing strange lands and customs (*Ger. Lib.* 15.41–43; 17.21–22). And of course, with the flood tide of interest in history and anthropology, in nineteenth- and twentieth-century poetry and fiction, comes a corresponding flood of similar examples.

One might instance Byron's pride in the authenticity of his shipwreck passage in Canto Two of *Don Juan;* or Browning's positive flaunting of "the old yellow book," especially in the middle portions of *The Ring and the Book;* or the incorporating of bits from newspaper stories, museum catalogs, local histories, and so on, into the work of such twentieth-century poets as William Carlos Williams, Marianne Moore, and Robert Penn Warren. It is true that my examples are blurring possible distinctions between imitation and translation, between poetry and history, between emulation of past masters and a growing awareness of "sources" in the archaeological and historical record. But it is interesting, and probably correct, to view the impulses of humanist *imitatio,* which may strike us as backward-looking and timorous, as yet another manifestation of the great groundswell of fascination with human history—which is in our time being transmuted into the still broader terms of Earth-history, and the survival or extinction of her flora and fauna.

Thus, considered as a poetic strategy, Sannazaro's use of the gospel of Luke in the passage under discussion not only appears surprisingly innovative, but innovative in the direction of a significant line of development in modern European literature. Admittedly he had no choice, his only source for his subject being its simple historical narration in the Gospels. Had his action been narrated by a great poet, such as David or Isaiah, no doubt Sannazaro would have unhesitatingly gone to that source, as he went to Virgil's Messianic eclogue. Still, he does plant evidence that he has quarried this portion of his poem out of the Gospel narrative's living rock, and in doing so he doubtless considered that, for all its fictive covering, his poem was being grounded on the rock of historical truth. That kind of concern—about the questionable validity of "lying" poetry, the advisability of choosing a subject from "vera istoria"—was to keep steadily increasing throughout the sixteenth century, and beyond. Hence we can view Sannazaro's utilization of Mary's psalm of praise in Luke as a poetic strategy in keeping with the concerns of his age, as he affirms the credibility of the Virgin's *mira fides* (her marvellous faith) by celebrating it in the very language of the most "privileged" of all texts. His poem, in a word, is Gospel Truth.

Appendix E:
The Lamb Twice Dyed
(*De Partu Virginis* 3.192–93)

Sannazaro's method of *imitatio* was doubtless beneficial to him, a steadying staff as he followed in the footsteps of earlier poets (*priorum . . . vatum vestigia, De Partu* Lat. 2.307–8). Many times too, no doubt, it surrounds the reader with the august presences of those poets, as if he were Aeneas sensing the presence of the departing gods as he threaded the streets of burning Troy. But there are times when the method fails, overloaded perhaps with reminiscences from divergent cultures or attempted allusions to conflicting symbols, so that a passage collapses into mere obscurity, uncommunicative and ineffective. Although that is a common kind of failure among poets, not to be attributed simply to the evil genius of *imitatio,* Sannazaro's prevailing practice of imitation does mean that when a passage fails we can have some confidence that the poet meant it to *be* allusive or imitative, even though we cannot see exactly how. Thus we can look with some confidence for causes when we find undue obscurity.

An interesting example occurs in the song of Aegon and Lycidas (*De Partu* 3.174–202), discussed in the General Introduction (see pp. 14, 17) as a segment of some 36 lines, of which about fifty percent are transcribed directly from Virgil's Fourth Eclogue. In 3.190–93, Aegon and Lycidas repeat verbatim two lines from the Pollio eclogue, and then venture on an expansion:

> Ipsae lacte domum referent distenta capellae
> Ubera; nec magnos metuent armenta leones:
> Agnaque per gladios ibit secura nocenteis:
> Bisque superfusos servabit tincta rubores. (Lat. 3.217–20)

Of themselves the goats will bring home their udders swollen with milk and the herds will have no fear of the powerful lions, and the lamb will go in safety among the

dangerous swords and twice-dyed will preserve the redness
that overspreads it. (3.190–93)

The first of these couplets is pure Virgil and offers no problem. The second, full of problems, appears to be meant to allude to a set of lines further on in Virgil's eclogue:

> nec varios discet mentiri lana colores,
> ipse sed in pratis aries iam suave rubenti
> murice, iam croceo mutabit vellera luto;
> sponte sua sandyx pascentis vestiet agnos.

> Wool will not learn to mock a variety of colors, but of him-
> self the ram on the meadows will change his fleece, one time
> with gently blushing purple, another with yellow saffron; of
> its own will, the scarlet sandyx will clothe the grazing lambs.
> (*Ecl.* 4.42–45, trans. Mackail)

Here we have lambs, at least, and a changing of one color to another,
though expressly not through the use of dye. No other passage in
Virgil's Pollio eclogue comes that close to being a model for Sannazaro's
second couplet (i.e., *De Partu* 3.192–93). Virgil's eclogue, however, is
not much help in our puzzling about Sannazaro's heaven-protected and
twice-dyed lamb. That is true, I think, because Sannazaro is trying to
make these two lines carry a considerable weight of Christian symbolism
and *Weltanschauung*—more weight perhaps than their eleven words will
readily bear.

Fortunately the ms. tradition offers assistance. The Fantazzi-
Perosa textual apparatus tells us that the poet in his own hand (cf. pp.
lxxii, lxxix) annotated 3.191 with a line from Luke [10:3]—*Ecce ego
mitto vos sicut oves inter lupos,* and also 3.192 with a cryptic *Virginum
martyria post Christi sanguinem.* In themselves, these annotations are not
very helpful. Their connection with the text is so loose that they might
just as well be in reverse order, associating the martyrdom of the virgins
with the herds that show no fear of lions, and the lamb that goes safely
among swords with the disciples sent forth like sheep among wolves.
But Renaissance poets are frequently unreliable in allegorizing details in
their own poetry, and we may content ourselves with having some as-
surance, from these annotations, that the lamb in line 192 is not Christ
himself, the sacrificial Lamb of God, but rather a Christian sent among
the perils of a wicked world—even though that lamb is appearing in a
song addressed directly to the Divine Child.

I labor this point because it is difficult to explain the *Bisque . . .
tincta* of 192–93, and potentially helpful to have this clue to the nature of
the lamb. Here the ms. tradition gives some further aid by supplying an

alternate reading for 3.220 which the Fantazzi-Perosa apparatus records as appearing in Codices N, S, and U:

nec repetita suos amittet lana rubores. (*De Partu* Lat. 3.220)

Repetita seems about as difficult here as *tincta,* but perhaps one might read: "And its fleece, being reclaimed, will not lose its redness." This tortured expression suggests a further line of speculation. *Repetita* is not precisely *redemptio,* but it is good Ciceronian language for reclaiming money or property. Are we speaking of a redeemed lamb that nonetheless will not lose its redness, the badge of human sin?

When Sannazaro replaced this line (as he replaced scores of others) his *repetita* became *bisque . . . tincta*—and it is reasonable to suppose that he took *tincta* as meaning *baptized,* a usage cited from Lactantius in the Lewis-Short dictionary: *Tinctus est ab Iohanne propheta in Jordane flumine* (Lactantius 4.15.2). If we read *tincta* so, the redeemed fleece has become baptized—twice-baptized, indeed. That is no problem, but something like confirming evidence, in the light of John the Baptist's proclamation to his disciples:

I indeed baptize you with water; but . . . he shall baptize you with the Holy Ghost and with fire. (Luke 3:16)

First by water and then by fire: *bisque . . . tincta* as a double baptism, by water and by the fire of the Holy Ghost, seems quite a plausible construction of the sense of this strange line. As for the *superfusos rubores,* the redness of shame is post-classical as a tropical extension of *rubor,* but not thereby impossible for Sannazaro. If the poet is suggesting that the baptized Christian will go in safety through the perils of this world, though still retaining the stain of original sin, the remaining difficulties are theological, not philological, and those deep waters we will avoid.

Thus we have taken a tortuous route to the explication of a tortured expression:

The lamb will go in safety among the dangerous swords and twice-baptized its fleece will preserve the redness of guilt that overspreads it.

A translator who would import that much interpretation into his rendering ought to blush with the guilt of his own original sin—but he might be heard to mutter to himself that the fault is not his alone.

Bibliography of Works Cited

Acta Sanctorum. quotquot toto orbe coluntur, etc. Paris, 1863–Brussels, 1940. 70 vols.

Alexandri ab Alexandro. *Genialium dierum libri sex.* Paris, 1586.

Altamura, Antonio. *Jacopo Sannazaro: con Appendici di Documenti e Testi Inediti.* Napoli, 1951.

———. *L'umanesimo nel mezzogiorno d'Italia.* Firenze, 1941.

Andrelini, Publio Fausto, et al. *Pia et emuncta opuscula.* Parisiis, 1513.

Angot, L'Abbé Alphonse. *Dictionnaire Historique, Topographique et Biographique de La Mayenne.* Mayenne, 1962 (reprint of 1900–1909). 4 vols.

Biblia Sacra Iuxta Vulgatam Versionem, ed. Robertus Weber OSB. Stuttgart, 1983. 2 vols.

Borghini, Vittorio. *Il Più Nobile Umanista del Rinascimento.* Torino, n.d.

Bridge, John S. C. *A History of France from the Death of Louis XI.* Oxford, 1929.

Butler, Allan. *Lives of the Saints,* ed. Herbert Thurston and Donald Attwater. New York, 1956. 4 vols.

Claudian. *Opera Omnia,* ed. N. L. Artaud. Paris, 1824. 3 vols.

Cognasso, Francesco. *I Savoia.* Milan, 1971.

Commynes, Philippe de. *Mémoires . . .* ed. B. de Mandrot. Paris, 1901–1903.

———. *Memoirs,* ed. S. Kinser, trans. I. Cazeaux. Columbia, S.C. 1969.

———. *The Memoirs of Philip de Commines,* trans. Andrew A. Scoble. London, 1855. 2 vols.

Contemporaries of Erasmus: A Biographical Register, ed. Peter Bietenholz. London, 1985. 3 vols.

Cosenza, Mario Emilio. *A Biographical and Bibliographical Dictionary of the Italian Humanists.* Boston, 1962. 6 vols.

Crinitus, Petrus [Del Riccio Baldi, Pietro]. *De poetis Latinis libri V.* Basle, 1532.

Croce, Benedetto. *History of the Kingdom of Naples,* trans. Francis Frenaye. Chicago, 1970.

———. *La Spagna nella Vita Italiana.* Bari, 1949.

———. *Storie e Leggende Napoletane,* ed. G. Galasso. Milan, 1990.

———. *Vite di avventure di fede e di passione.* Bari, 1947.

Curtius, Ernst Robert. *European Literature and the Latin Middle Ages,* trans. Willard Trask. Princeton, 1953.

D'Agostino, Guido. *La Capitale Ambigua: Napoli dal 1458 al 1580.* Naples, 1979.

Du Cange [Carolus Dufresne]. *Glossarium Mediae et Infimae Latinitatis.* Paris, 1845. 7 vols.

Gilbert, Allan H. *On the Composition of Paradise Lost.* Chapel Hill, 1947.

Greene, Thomas M. *The Light in Troy: Imitation and Discovery in Renaissance Poetry.* New Haven, 1982.

Herodotus. *Herodotus.* Loeb Classical Library, 1920.

Jaeger, Werner. *Paideia: The Ideals of Greek Culture,* trans. Gilbert Highet. New York, 1945. 3 vols.

Kennedy, William J. *Jacopo Sannazaro and the Uses of Pastoral.* Hanover and London, 1983.

Kidwell, Carol. *Sannazaro and Arcadia.* London, 1993.

———. *Pontano: Poet & Prime Minister.* London, 1991.

Marrou, Henri Irénée. *A History of Education in Antiquity,* trans. George Lamb. New York, 1956.

Martène, Edmond [and Durand, Ursin]. *Voyage Litteraire de Deux Religieux Benedictins.* Paris, 1717–24. 2 vols.

Maulde la Clavière, René de, ed. *Chroniques de Louis XII, par Jean d'Auton.* Paris, 1889–95. 4 vols.

Milton, John. *Complete Poems and Major Prose,* ed. Merritt Y. Hughes. New York, 1957.

Minieri-Riccio, Camillo. *Biografie degli accademici alfonsini detti poi pontaniani dal 1442 al 1543.* Napoli, 1880–82.

Moorman, John. *A History of the Franciscan Order . . . to 1517.* Oxford, 1968.

Muratori, Lodovico Antonio, ed. *Rerum Italicorum Scriptores.* Milan, 1723–38.

Ovid. *Fasti,* trans. Sir James George Frazier. Loeb Classical Library, 1931.

———. *Heroides and Amores,* trans. Grant Showerman. Loeb Classical Library, 1977.

———. *Metamorphoses, with an English translation by Frank Justus Miller.* Loeb Classical Library, 1960.

———. *Tristia. Ex Ponto,* trans. Arthur L. Wheeler. Loeb Classical Library, 1988.

Pausanias. *Description of Greece.* Loeb Classical Library, 1918.

Pércopo, Erasmo. *Vita di Jacobo Sannazaro,* ed. G. Brognoligo. Naples, 1931.

Petrarca, Francesco. *Le Rime,* ed. Nicola Zingarelli. Bologna, 1963.

Pliny. *Natural History,* trans. H. Rackham. Loeb Classical Library, 1950.

Plutarch. *Lives,* ed. A. H. Clough. Boston, 1875.

Pontano, Giovanni. *I Dialoghi,* ed. Carmelo Previtera. Florence, 1943.

———. *Joviani Pontani Carmina,* ed. Benedetto Soldati. Florence, 1902.

Pontieri, Ernesto. *Per la storia del regno di Ferrante I d'Aragona.* Naples, 1969.

Propertius, trans. H. E. Butler. Loeb Classical Library, 1912.

Quint, David. *Origin and Originality in Renaissance Literature.* New Haven, 1983.

Samaran, Charles. *Archives de la maison de la Trémoïlle: chartriers de Thouars et de Serrant.* Paris, 1928.

Sannazaro, Jacopo. *Arcadia & Piscatorial Eclogues,* trans. Ralph Nash. Detroit, 1966.

——. *Del Parto della Vergine ... tradotti in verso Toscano dal Conte Gio. Bartolommeo Casaregi.* Florence, 1740.

——. *De Partu Virginis,* ed. Charles Fantazzi and Alessandro Perosa. Florence, 1988.

——. *Opera Latina Omnia, & Integra* [annotated Jan Broekhuizen]. Amsterdam, 1689.

——. *Opere Volgari,* ed. Alfredo Mauro. Bari, 1961.

——. *Piscatory Eclogues,* ed. W. P. Mustard. Baltimore, 1914.

——. *Poemata,* ed. Josephus Cominus. Padua, 1751.

Sidney, Sir Philip. *The Countesse of Pembrokes Arcadia,* ed. Albert Feuillerat. Cambridge, 1912.

Statius. *Silvae IV, ed. with an English translation and commentary by K. M. Coleman.* Oxford, 1988.

Strabo. *The Geography of Strabo.* Loeb Classical Library, 1917.

Tibullus. *Carminum Libri Tres,* ed. J. P. Postgate. Oxford, 1959.

Vecce, Carlo. *Iacopo Sannazaro in Francia.* Padova, 1988.

Velleius Paterculus. *Res Gestae Divi Augusti.* Loeb Classical Library, 1992.

Virgil, trans. H. Rushton Fairclough. Loeb Classical Library, 1935.

——. *P. Vergili Maronis Opera,* ed. A. Sidgwick. Cambridge, 1927. 2 vols.

——. *The Aeneid of Virgil,* trans. J. W. Mackail. London, 1931.

Volpicella, Luigi, ed. *Regis Ferdinandi primi Instructionum liber.* Napoli, 1916.

Vulgate. *See* Biblia Sacra.

Glossary of Names of Persons and Places

This is not a complete index. Entries have been made, as a rule, when the name itself or its context seemed in possible need of explanation. Readers are reminded that the Introductory Notes to individual poems may contain information not repeated in this glossary.

*The asterisk denotes members of the Pontanian Academy who are mentioned in the poems in this volume. Many others are named by Sannazaro elsewhere, especially in the epigrams. Listings here are usually under the names adopted upon entering the Academy (e.g., Sannazaro would be listed as Actius Syncerus).

Acheron   DPV 1.206
One of the five rivers of Hades (Acheron, Cocytus, Lethe, Phlegethon, Styx). Hence, the infernal regions.

Achilles   DPV 2.139; Pisc. 1; El. 1.1, 6
Alexander's first act on invading Asia was to honor the burial mound of Achilles at Sigeum. The reference to Achilles' wife (El. 1.6) is obscure. Antiquity provided Achilles with more sons than wives.

*Acquaviva, Andrea   El. 1.11; 2.2, 10
See Introd. Note, El. 3.1.

———, Giulio   El. 3.1

Acroceraunia   DPV 2.156
A promontory on the northern coast of Epirus (mod. Capo Linguetta). See also Ceraunia.

Aegle   Pisc. 5
A name from Virgil (*Ecl.* 6.20).

Aegon   DPV 3.164; Pisc. 3
A Virgilian name (*Ecl.* 3.2; 5.72).

*Aelius   El. 1.11

Aemilia   El. 3.1
Territory south of the river Po, containing such cities as Ferrara, Parma, Modena.

217

Aetna   El. 1.2, 11; 2.6
Intermittently active volcano in Sicily.

Aganippe[an]   El. 1.11
A fountain on Mt. Helicon, supposed to inspire poets.

Alba   El. 3.1
The city founded by Ascanius, son of Aeneas (*Aen.* 1.267). It was succeeded by Rome, on a slightly different site.

*Albinus   El. 1.11
See Introd. Note, El. 1.5.

Alcides   Pisc. 4; El. 3.1
See Hercules.

Alcinous   DPV 2.157
His palace (*Od.* 7.81–132) was thought to be on the island of Phaeacia (mod. Corfu) in the Ionian Sea.

Alcon   Pisc. 5

Alecto   El. 1.11
In late Greek mythology the Furies, ministers of divine justice, are Alecto, Megaera, and Tisiphone.

Alexis   Pisc. 4; El. 1.1
See Corydon.

Allifae   El. 2.2
The reference is to Garlon's title as Count of Alife.

Alphesiboeus   Pisc. 4; El. 1.1
The name is Virgilian (*Ecl.* 8).

*Altilius   El. 1.11; 2.2
His epithalamion alluded to in El. 2.2 is included among the verse translations in this volume.

Amalfi   Pisc. 3
Town on the long peninsula at Naples, facing on the Bay of Naples.

Amanus   DPV 2.118
Mountain range between Syria and Cilicia.

Amathus   Sal.
Amathus and Paphos were cities in Cyprus, centers of worship for Aphrodite.

Amilcon   Pisc. 3

Amphitrite   DPV 1.182; Pisc. 1
Her son, by Poseidon, was Triton (q.v.).

Amyclae   El. 3.1
A town in Sparta, birthplace of Castor and Pollux.

Amyntas   Pisc. 1, 2
The name appears in Virgil's eclogues (2.35; 5.8).

Anas   DPV 2.174
The Guadiana river, in northern Spain.

Androgeo   El. 3.2
See Melisaeus.

Andromache   El. 3.2
Her husband was Hector, son of Priam.

Anio   El. 2.1
A tributary of the Tiber.

Antiphates   El. 3.1
For a moment S. is following Ovid's account of the Wanderings of Aeneas: "Antiphates terra regnabat in illa" (*Met.* 14.234). Ovid perhaps refers only to the town of Formiae, neighboring Gaeta, but it is natural to read the passage as Antiphates = Ferdinand I (Frederick's father). This has the peculiar result of equating Ferrante with the cannibalistic Antiphates (*Met.* 14.237–38), but S. might have taken some pleasure in so doing. His epigram *Ad Ferrandum Regem* (Ep. 2.8 in Padua, 1751) says: "Even though your name comes from iron, you are bringing in a Golden Age: for with you as king, nobody reaps any harvest."

Aonia   DPV 1.14; El. 1.11; 2.2, 4; 3.2
The district of Boeotia containing Mount Helicon and the Aganippean spring. Hence Aonides = Muses (q.v.).

Apollo   Pisc. 5; El. 1.5, 11; 3.1, 2
In El. 3.1 Apollo is linked with Delphi (and its oracle). All other examples of S's use of the name Apollo present the god as "the father himself and author of song" (El. 3.2). See Phoebus.

Appulia   El. 1.11
A province in south central Italy along the Adriatic.

Araby   DPV 1.121; El. 1.3
Arabia Felix (Araby the Blest) was renowned for the exotic and luxurious. Cf. Strabo, 16.4. 21 ff. Arabicus, like Assyrius, is often used for the rare and exotic (odors, fruits, gems, and so on) without much regard for geography.

Arachne   Pisc. 5

Famed for her weaving, she aroused Athena's jealousy and was transformed into a spider (*arachnid*) —*Met.* 6.5–145.

Aragon, House of

References to the Aragonese kings of Naples appear in Pisc. 4; El. 2.1; 3.1, 2, 3; and also 1.9 and 2.3. See also Antiphates.

Arar   DPV 2.172; Pisc. 5; El. 1.8

The Saône river, in eastern France, principal tributary of the Rhone.

Araxes   DPV 2.117

A river in Armenia, flowing east to the Caspian.

Arcady (Arcadia)   Sal.

Virgil (*Ecl.* 7.4, 10.31) set the fashion of picturing Arcadia as the homeland of pastoral poetry. The region was always a center of Pan-worship.

Arctos   DPV 2.13

Ursa Major and Minor, a double constellation in the vicinity of the North Pole.

Arethuse   El. 2.6

In *Met.* 5.487 ff., Ovid tells how Arethusa, born near Mt. Olympus, was pursued by the god of the river Alpheus. She fled underground and emerged as a fountain in Ortygia, an island forming part of the Sicilian city of Syracuse.

Argo   DPV 3.199

Jason's ship, piloted by Tiphys, in his quest for the golden fleece.

Ariadne   El. 2.5

Bacchus found her where Theseus had deserted her, on the island of Naxos. After her death Bacchus had her crown placed in the sky as a constellation.

Armenia   DPV 2.113

S. begins his counter-clockwise circuit of the Mediterranean at approximately the n.e. corner of the Roman empire.

Arno   El. 2.1

Etruscan river flowing past Florence to empty into the Mediterranean near Pisa.

Arsaces   El. 3.2

They are the kings of Parthia (cf. Matthew 2:1–12). S. is speaking here of composing DPV 2.389–93 and 3.110–206—not the Piscatoriae, to which he then turns in the lines following.

Arvernian   El. 3.1

I.e., in the French province of Auvergne.

Asbiti   DPV 2.202
Strabo says that their territory "reaches to that of Carthage" (2.5.33).

Ascanius   El. 1.1
See Alba.

Assyria   El. 1.3
See Araby.

Astraea   El. 1.8
See Introd. Note, El. 1.8.

Atestina   El. 3.1
The reference is to Ferrara's House of Este, supposedly descended from rulers of the ancient Atestini.

Atlas   DPV 2.181
The name usually is applied to a range of mountains, rather than a single peak, running through Tunisia, Algeria, and Morocco.

Aurora   DPV 2.14, 113; 3.6, 428
At DPV 2.113 not precisely a personification, but a general term for "the East." Elsewhere, the familiar Goddess of the Dawn.

Ausonia   El. 1.8; 2.1; 3.1
Frequent in the Roman poets for things Italian: people, cities, mountains, and so on. From a name for the original inhabitants, the Ausones.

Auster   DPV 2.392
Latin name for the south wind.

Avernus   DPV 3.231; Lam.; El. 2.4
In personifying Avernus (El. 2.4.61) S. may be following Servius's gloss on *Georgics* 2.164. Presumably the reference a few lines earlier to "the gloomy lake" is also to Lake Avernus ("without birds"), said to be so named because birds were killed by its fumes. Hence it was considered an entrance to the infernal regions, which are meant by the references in DPV and Lam. The grotto of the Cumaean Sibyl was close by.

Axius   DPV 2.146
A river in Macedonia, now the Vardar, joining the Aegean near Thessalonica.

Babylon   DPV 1.388; 3.370
The Judaeo-Christian tradition tends to use Babylon as a generic name for the proud and sinful metropolis. That seems not to apply at DPV 1.388.

Bacchus   DPV 3.390; El. 2.5, 8, 10; 3.1
Bacchus, god of wine and son of Semele and Jupiter, is "twin-mothered" because after Semele's death he was hidden in a pocket cut in Jupiter's thigh, and thus "mothered" twice (*Met.* 3.310–12). He is sometimes

"Father Lenaeus" by association with Gk. ληνός = winepress. The amethyst is an enemy to Bacchus because its name was supposed to derive from ʼα-μέθυστος = "not drunken" (Pliny, *Nat. Hist.* 37.41.121–24).

Baetis DPV 2.176
River in southern Spain (the Guadalquivir).

Bagrada DPV 3.167
A river north of Carthage, near Utica (Strabo, 17.3.13).

Baiae Pisc. 1, 4; El. 1.9; 2.4, 7
The most famous of the Roman seaside resorts, located just west of Naples.

Barcaeans DPV 2.194
Inhabitants of the Barca plateau, between Cyrene and Tripoli, in North Africa. Cf. Herodotus, 4.160; *Aen.* 4.43.

Bassarids El. 2.5
Dancers in the Bacchantic celebrations. For "perilous," see *Met.* 3.528–733.

Bauli Pisc. 3; El. 2.7
Roman resort between Miseno and Baiae.

Bellovaci Pisc. 3
Modern Beauvais. They appear frequently in Caesar's *Gallic Wars* as a powerful Belgian tribe.

Bistonia El. 1.5
The country of Thrace.

Bithynia DPV 2.140
See Carambis.

Bootes DPV 3.106
The Bear-keeper, a constellation.

Boreas DPV 2.23, 392; Pisc. 2; El. 3.3
Latin name for the north wind.

Briareus DPV 1.353
A sea-giant with a hundred arms. See Centaurs.

Butrinto El. 2.1
A Grecian city (anciently Buthrotum) on the mainland of Epirus. See Introd. Note, El. 2.1.

*Cabanilius Wil.; El. 1.11; 2.2
See Introd. Note to *Willows*.

Caieta El. 3.1, unnamed
Virgil tells us that the promontory of Caieta, north of Naples, was named for Aeneas's nurse, buried there (*Aen.* 7.1–4).

Callimachus   El. 2.1
Propertius himself acknowledges his debt to Callimachus (3.1.1).

Calliope   El. 1.5, 11; 3.2
She is the special Muse of epic poetry, but often represented more generally as aiding poets of all genres.

Calpe   DPV 2.390
Graeco-Roman name for the Rock of Gibraltar. See Hercules.

Campania   El. 1.9; 2.1; 3.1
The region surrounding Naples.

Cannae   El. 2.7
Hannibal's disastrous defeat of the Romans in southern Italy, at Cannae (216 B.C.).

Canopus   DPV 1.121
An ancient name for Lower Egypt, or Egypt generally.

Cappadocia   DPV 2.143
A country north of Cilicia, between the Taurus range and the district of Pontus.

Capri   Pisc. 4, 5
The island is about four miles offshore from the long peninsula separating the Bay of Naples from the Bay of Salerno, south of Naples.

Carambis   DPV 2.141
A city in the province of Paphlagonia, which lay between Bithynia and Pontus. All three provinces bordered on the Black Sea, constituting the extreme northern portion of Asia Minor.

*Carbo [Girolamo]   El. 1.11

*Cariteus   El. 1.11
He appears at greater length in S's *Arcadia*.

Carmel   DPV 2.213
Carmel forms a ridge, some 600 feet high at the Mediterranean shoreline and running about twelve miles southeast.

Carthage   DPV 2.188; El. 2.1
Its total destruction by the Romans (146 B.C.) marked the end of the Punic Wars. The site of the city was on the African coast at its nearest approach to Sicily.

Caspian   DPV 3.370
"Caspia regna" echoes Virgil's phrasing (*Aen.* 6.798) in Anchises' prophecies about the glories of Augustus.

Cassandra   Pisc. 5; El. 3.2

The first of the references in El. 3.2 (line 81) is to the Trojan priestess of *Iliad* and *Odyssey*. For the others, see Marchese.

Castaly   DPV 2.260; El. 1.5, 11; 2.1

The Castalian spring was on Mount Parnassus, sacred to Apollo and the Muses.

Catullus   El. 2.1

See Introd. Note, El. 2.1.

Caulon   El. 2.1

A city just north of Locri (q.v.).

Cayster   DPV 1.82; 2.129

A river in Lydia, flowing into the Aegean to the north of Maeander. The Homeric simile about its swans (*Il.* 2.459) and Virgil's adaptation of it (*Aen.* 7.699) were much imitated.

Celadon   Pisc. 3

κέλαδος: an outpouring of sound.

Celaenae   DPV 2.132

Town on the banks of the Maeander, in Phrygia. It is "Apollonian" because Apollo there contested with Marsyas on the flute.

Centaurs   DPV 1.354

Half man and half horse, the Centaurs lead off Virgil's list of the monsters of the infernal regions, followed by Scyllas, Briareus, the monster of Lerna [i.e., the Hydra], the Chimaera, Gorgons, Harpies, and the three-headed Cerberus (*Aen.* 6.286–89).

Ceramus   DPV 2.124

A coastal town in the province of Caria at the Gulf of Kos.

Cerastes   DPV 1.353

Not in Virgil's list of the monsters in Hades (see Centaurs). Statius associates them with the Furies (*Th.* I.103).

Ceraunia   El. 2.1

The Ceraunian heights are a ridge of mountains located in Epirus, as is also Butrinto (q.v.).

Cerberus   DPV 1.208 unnamed; 1.407

The three-headed watchdog of Hades. See Centaurs.

Cerretia   El. 3.2

See Introd. Note, El. 3.2. It. *cerro* = oak.

Chalcis (Chalcidean)   Pisc. 4; El. 2.1

A city on the island of Euboea, north of Athens. Its colonists came to Parthenope and built there a rival settlement, which became known as Neapolis ("new town"), later Naples.

Chaonian   El. 2.7
The Chaonian doves are from Virgil (*Ecl.* 9.13). They provided auguries in the oak grove at Dodona, in a district of Epirus known as Chaonia.

Chaos   Pisc., fragm.
See Erebus.

Charon   El. 1.9
The ferryman who transports the dead across the river Styx (*Aen.* 6.298 ff.).

Charybdis   Sal.; El. 1.2
Dangerous whirlpool near Sicily, shunned by Odysseus (*Od.* 12.235–45) and Aeneas (*Aen.* 3.420 ff.). Just opposite was the Siren Scylla.

Chimaera   DPV 1.354; Sal.
In *Iliad* 6.181, a tri-form fire-breathing monster. See Centaurs.

Chloris   Pisc. 3, fragm.

Chratis   El. 2.1
See Sybaris.

Chromis   Pisc. 3
The name appears in Virgil's eclogues (6.13).

Cilicia   DPV 2.119
Province just north of Syria. Its principal city was Antioch.

Cimmeria   Pisc. 4
Strabo links the Cimmerians with Lake Avernus (5.4.5).

Cinyps   DPV 3.168
The Macae (q.v.) lived on the banks of this river between the Lesser and the Greater Syrtis. Herodotus speaks at length of the fertility of its region (4.175, 198).

Circe   El. 1.1
Her island, Aeaea (*Od.* 10), was supposed by Virgil, among others, to have become the promontory on which Monte Circello was located, north of Naples (*Aen.,* 7.10 ff.).

Circello   Pisc. 3
See Circe.

Cithaeron   DPV 2.332
Boeotian mountain sacred to the Muses and to Bacchic revels—hence the reference to "that wicked old man" (see Silenus).

Claudius   El. 3.1
The name is arbitrarily assigned to Charles the Bold, Duke of Burgundy. See Introd. Note, El. 3.1; and Appendix A. Some readers may find interest in a lengthy description of the elaborate tomb of Charles (and his daughter

Maria) at the church of Notre-Dame in Bruges (Martène-Durand, *Voyage Litteraire*, 2.191).

Clearista   Pisc. 5
Sister of Herpylis the sorceress.

Clotho   Pisc., fragm.
An invented name for a sea-nymph—not one of the three Fates (q.v.).

Cocytus   DPV 1.408; 3.231; Lam.
See Acheron.

Colchian [the youth of Phacis]   El. 2.1
The reference is to Jason and the epic *Argonautica,* the chief scene of which is Colchis, near the Caucasian mountains. S's Phacis is a river in Colchis.

Colline   El. 2.1
A gate in the n.e. section of Rome's wall.

*Compater   El. 1.11
Pietro Gulino, called Compatre (Godfather) by the Academy. A fragment of S's long epigram on his death (in 1501) appears among the miscellany of verse translations in this volume.

Corus   DPV 3.403
Latin name for the northwest wind.

*Corvinus   El. 1.11

Corydon   Pisc. 4; El. 1.1
A Virgilian shepherd ("The shepherd Corydon burned for handsome Alexis"—*Ecl.* 2.1).

*Crassus   El. 1.1; 2.2

Crater   Pisc. 4
κρατήρ: wine bowl. A name for the Bay of Naples.

Crete   DPV 2.223, 330; El. 3.1
Jupiter was nurtured on Mt. Ida in Crete. In "that Cretan myth" Europa was borne by the bull from Sidon to Crete (*Met.* 2. 836 ff.).

Creusa   El. 3.1
Wife of Aeneas, whom he lost in the sack of Troy.

Cumae   DPV 3.176; Pisc. 2, 4; El. 2.4, 7, 8, 9
See Introd. Note, El. 2.9. See also Sibyl.

Cupid   El. 1.4 unnamed; 2.7 unnamed
The scarcity of references is an indication of S's general good taste. A few allusions to Love as a winged archer, however, have been omitted from this glossary.

Cyclopses   El. 1.11
They would be sent by Mt. Aetna because the Cyclopses forged thunder-bolts for Zeus in that volcano.

Cyllene   Pisc. 3; Sal.
Mercury was born on this mountain in Arcadia.

Cymodoce   Pisc. 1
A sea-nymph transformed from a ship into a nymph (*Aen.* 10.220 ff.).

Cymothoe   Pisc. 4, fragm.
A Nereid in *Aeneid* 1.144.

Cynthia   DPV 1.337; El. 3.3
Sister of Apollo and goddess of the moon, she and her twin were born on Mt. Cynthus in Delos. In El. 3.3 the Cynthian is Apollo (Cynthius). See also Phoebe.

Cyprus   Pisc. 3
Venus, or Aphrodite, was specially worshipped on the island of Cyprus. Hence she is sometimes called the Cyprian.

Cyrene   DPV 2.200
Principal city of Cyrenaica, in northeast Libya, bordering Egypt.

Cyrus   DPV 3.369
In the prophecy of Proteus, the Persian king Cyrus "stands for" worldly do-minion, more or less like Babylon (q.v.).

Cytherea   El. 2.8
The myrtle was sacred to Venus (the Cytherean), so called for her temple on the island of Cythera, directly south of Sparta.

Daedalus   El. 2.9
See Introd. Note, El. 2.9.

Damoetas   El. 1.1
The name appears in Virgil (*Ecl.* 2, 3, and 5).

Damon   Pisc. 4
A singer in Virgil's Eclogue 8.

Danube   DPV 2.167
See Ister.

Daphne   Wil. unnamed
See *Willows,* Introd. Note.

Daunia   El. 2.1
Poetic name for the Roman province of Apulia, in southern Italy, named for Daunus, father of Turnus, as in Virgil's Aeneid.

David DPV 1.212 unnamed
As shepherd, poet, and prophet, he may be considered a counterpart of Proteus (q.v.).

Delia El. 2.4
See Phoebe.

Delius El. 1.9; 2.9; 3.2
See Phoebus.

Delphi El. 2.7; 3.1
The most famous oracle of Apollo was located near this city lying beneath Mt. Parnassus.

Diana DPV 3.307; Pisc. 5; Wil.
In comparing epilepsy to "the wrath of outraged Diana" (DPV 3), S. probably alludes chiefly to Ovid's tale of Diana's punishment of Actaeon, thought excessive by some of the gods (*Met.* 3.174 ff.; also 8. 271 ff.). The other passages are standard references to the moon-goddess as huntress and protectress of the chaste.

Dicarchus Pisc. 3, 5
Roman Puteoli, modern Pozzuoli, called Dicarchus from the name of its founder (Statius, *Silvae* 2.2.95–135).

Dione El. 2.6
In most uses, Venus (or Aphrodite). See Eryx.

Dis DPV 1.352, 405
Roman name for Pluto; hence, the infernal regions.

Doris Pisc., fragm.
Wife of Nereus and mother of the Nereids.

Dorylas Pisc. 5

Dryads Pisc. 5; El. 2.8; 3.2
Wood-nymphs.

Drymo Pisc. 4
A Nereid in *Georgics* 4.336.

Duria DPV 2.175
The river Douro for part of its course marks the boundary between Spain and Portugal.

Dynamene Pisc. 4
The name is uncommon, but she is in Hesiod's list of the fifty Nereids (*Theogony* 240–64) and in a similar list (*Iliad* 18.43).

Ebro   [DPV 2.177]; Pisc. 4
A river in northern Spain. At DPV 2.177 transliterated as Iberus to emphasize the name's relation to the Iberian peninsula.

Elean   El. 2.6
See Jove.

Elizabeth   unnamed, DPV 1.155; 2.26 ff.
S. is obviously careful throughout DPV to avoid naming any human actors
in his poem. The sole exception is "Father Augustus" (2.105). Quasi-
historical characters such as Priam, Achilles, and Cyrus take no part in the
action.

Elysian   Pisc. 1; El. 1.3, 7
Technically, Elysium is the abode of the blest in the underworld. But overtones of the Christian Heaven are strong, in 1.7 especially.

*Elysius   El. 1.11

Ephyre   DPV 3.445
Virgilian name (*Georgics* 4.343).

Epirus   DPV 2.155
Province in n.w. Greece, part of what is now Albania.

Erato   El. 2.4
The Muse of lyric poetry.

Erebus   DPV 1.329, 361, 404; 3.52, 335; Pisc. fragm.
Erebus, god of darkness, was the son of Chaos and brother of Night. In
DPV, the name is used like Tartarus, as antithesis to Heaven.

Erigone   DPV 3.107
After her suicide for grief over the death of her father, Icarius, she became
the constellation Virgo.

Erythraea   El. 2.8, 10
The ancient world applied this name rather vaguely to the Red Sea, the
Persian Gulf, the Arabian Gulf, or even the Indian Ocean. "Erythraean
stones" (El. 2.8) is almost a "conceit," using the whiteness of pearls to allude to the Roman custom of marking a special day with a white stone. S. is
indebted here to Statius (*Silvae* 4.6.18).

Eryx   El. 2.6
A high mountain in Sicily. The nearby city of the same name had a famous
temple of Venus.

Eteocles   El. 2.1, unnamed
The allusion is to Polyneices and Eteocles, the sons of Oedipus, King of
Thebes. Hence to the Thebaid of Statius.

Ethiopes   DPV 1.231; El. 1.1
Renaissance painters regularly include a black king among the Magi. Virgil speaks of "the groves of the Ethiopes whitened with soft wool" (*Georgics*, 2.120).

Etruscan   El. 2.1; 3.2
"Many Etruscan things" (El. 3.2) refers to S.'s Italian sonnets. The word is often so used, in a sense extended beyond its more precise signification of the region north and west of Rome.

Euboides   Pisc. 5; El. 1.11
See Chalcis.

Euganean   El. 2.1
A region to the north of Rome (cf. Shelley's "Lines Written among the Euganean Hills").

Eumenides   DPV 1.349; 3.382
See Furies.

Euphrates   DPV 2.117
The Euphrates river flows through the mountain range of Taurus before turning east to terminate in the Persian Gulf.

Euploea   Pisc. 2; 4; fragm.
A promontory s.w. of Posilipo.

Eurus   DPV 2.22; 3.403
The southeast wind, in the Greek terminology.

Eurydice   El. 1.5
Married to Orpheus, she died on her wedding day. Orpheus gained permission to bring her back from the underworld but by looking behind when leaving he lost her a second and final time (*Met*. 10.1–77).

Eutychus   Pisc. fragm.

Fame   DPV 1.204; El. 2.1
A very frequent personification in Renaissance poetry and in Roman (e.g., *Aen*. 4.173–95). Perhaps significantly, S. shows little interest in her busy reporting of news and rumor.

Farfar   El. 2.1
A tributary of the Tiber. Virgil uses the form *Fabaris* (*Aen*. 7.715), but Ovid has S's *Farfarus* at *Met*. 14.330.

Fates   El. 1.6, 10
They are Atropos, Clotho, Lachesis.

Faunus   Wil.; El. 1.2; 2.4; 3.2
The Faunus who weeps for Morinna (El. 2.4.66) is possibly "the half-god goat, the half-goat god" who was pursuing her. More probably S. intends

the local deity listed by Virgil among the ancestors of the Latins (*Aen.* 7.47). The other passages seem to imply the more generic use of the name.

Flaccus   El. 2.1
I.e., Horace (Quintus Horatius Flaccus).

Furies   DPV 3.335; Lam.; El. 1.11
They are also known as the Eumenides (the "well-disposed," a prophylactic name). See Alecto.

*Fuscus   El. 2.3
See Introd. Note, El. 2.3. Possibly not a member of the Pontanian Academy.

Gabriel   DPV 1.52 ff.
Second to Michael in the angelic hierarchy, he appears as God's messenger in the Old Testament (Daniel 8:16) as well as in Luke 1:19, 26. S. of course emphasizes his similarity to Mercury in speech and bearing.

Gaeta   Pisc. 2, 3; El. 3.1
Ancient Caieta (cf. *Aen.* 6.900 ff.). See Introd. Note, El. 3.1.

Gaetulia   DPV 2.180; 3.165
A people of n.w. Africa, in modern Morocco. Strabo (17.3.2) specifies them as the largest Libyan tribe, and as living in the interior.

Galaesus   El. 3.1
A river near Taranto in Calabria (southern Italy).

Galatea   Pisc. 1; 2; 5
She appears in two well-known idylls of Theocritus (6 and 11).

Galaxy   DPV 1.391; El. 1.7
Via Lactea, or the Milky Way. Ovid set the fashion of calling it the high road to Heaven (*Met.* 1.168–76).

Galilee   DPV 2.213
To the south of Samaria, the district lies within sixty miles of Jerusalem.

Ganges   DPV 3.300; El. 2.5
This holy river runs through northern India bearing south and east to the Bay of Bengal. In El. 2.5 Ganges is mentioned because Bacchus carried his rites through all Asia (e.g., Euripides, *Bacchae* 17).

Garamantians   DPV 2.199
Herodotus describes them (4.174, 183) as dwelling inland in the African desert, far from the Syrtes (q.v.).

*Garlon   El. 1.4; 2.2

Garonne   DPV 2.173
Originating in the Spanish Pyrenees, the Garonne runs through southern France to join the Atlantic at Bordeaux.

Gaurus   El. 2.4
A mountain rising above Lake Lucrine outside Naples.

Genius   El. 1.4, 11; 2.2, 8
See El. 2.8, Introd. Note.

Glaucus   DPV 3.413; Pisc. 1, 2, 3
His transformation and love of Scylla appear in *Met.* 13.900 ff.

Gnidos   DPV 2.124
The city lies at the western tip of a very long peninsula jutting into the
Aegean. S. gives it mention because of its famous statue of Venus, by
Praxiteles.

Gonzaga   El. 3.1
The Gonzaga family were lords of Mantua in S's time.

Gorgon   DPV 1.354; El. 2.1
"Gorgonian waters" are from the spring of Parnassus, which broke forth
under the hoof of Pegasus, a winged horse generated from the blood of
Medusa. She and her sisters were called collectively "the Gorgons." See also
Centaurs.

Gradivus   Pisc. 3
See Mars.

Haemony (Haemonia)   Pisc. 5; El. 1.1
Poetical name in the Roman poets for Thessaly (or Thessalia), a country
famed for sorcery.

Haemus   DPV 2.146; El. 1.5
The mountain (and city) of Ismarus is in the Haemus, a range of high
mountains in Thrace. It was there that Orpheus charmed the wild beasts.

Halyachmon   DPV 2.148
Boundary river between Macedonia and Thessaly.

Halybes   DPV 2.144
S. evidently considered this name closely related to *Chalybes,* an iron-work-
ing race living in Pontus, east of the river Halys. See his fourth letter to
Seripando, in Fantazzi-Perosa, p. 95.

Halys   DPV 2.141
Boundary river between Paphlagonia and Cappadocia.

Hamadryads   El. 1.2; 2.4

Harpy   DPV 1.355
Virgil describes the Harpies at length (*Aen.* 3.216 ff.). See Centaurs.

Hebrus   El. 1.5
This Thracian river rises in the Haemus range, flowing down to the
Aegean.

Hecuba   El. 3.2
Wife of Priam in Homer's *Iliad*.

Helicon   El. 1.11; 3.1
The mountain of Helicon, in Boeotia, was traditionally the home of the
Muses (cf. Pausanias, 9.26–31).

Hellespont   DPV 2.137
Narrow point in the Dardanelles strait, famous for the story of Hero and
Leander (Ovid, *Heroides* 18 and 19).

Hercules   DPV 2.175; Pisc. 3, 4, 5; El. 1.5; 2.7
Born at Tiryns, Hercules was the grandson of Alceus (hence Alcides). His
famous twelve labors included the capture and herding of the bulls of
Geryon (Pisc. 4; El. 2.7), and setting up the Pillars of Hercules at the
Straits of Gibraltar (DPV 2.175). His death on Mt. Oetaea is the central
focus of the Trachiniae of Sophocles. See also *Met.* 9.134–279. References
to the cliffs of Hercules and the ruins of Hercules allude to the Roman resort of Herculaneum, destroyed along with Pompeii in the famous eruption of Vesuvius in 79 A.D.

Hermus   DPV 2.131; El. 1.1
A Lydian river carrying golden sands (*Geor.* 2.137).

Herpylis   Pisc. 5

Hesperia   El. 2.1
The name is allied to Hesperus, the evening star. Hence a country in the
West—Italy or Spain.

Hesperides   DPV 2.185; El. 1.9
The gardens guarded by the daughters of Hesperus were usually supposed
to be near Mt. Atlas. For aspects of special relevance to S., see Appendix C.

Hesperus   DPV 3.7
The evening star, whose daughters (in some versions) were the Hesperides.

Hounds [of Hell]   DPV 1.355
Aeneas hears the barking of the Hounds of Hell as Hecate passes by (*Aen.*
6.257).

Hours   DPV 3.100
The Hours [Horae] appear in classical mythology as a kind of Watch in
heaven (e.g., *Met.* 2.26, 118).

Hyades   DPV 3.105
A constellation of seven stars, supposedly the sisters of the Pleiades (Ovid,
Fasti, 5.165 ff.).

Hyale   DPV 3.256; Pisc. 2, 3
Of the nineteen daughters of Jordan (DPV 3.249–59), only Hyale's name is repeated significantly. The remaining eighteen are omitted from this glossary, excepting Dynamene (q.v.), Pherusa, and Rhoe.

Hydra   DPV 1.355
See Centaurs.

Hymen   El. 1.9
The god of weddings.

Hymettus   Pisc. 3
The mountain range whose shadow gave Athens its epithet of "violet-crowned." Hence, Athens.

Iberus   DPV 2.177
See Ebro.

Ida   DPV 2.133
The context here indicates the mountain near Troy, from which Zeus watched many battles of the Trojan War.

Idalian   DPV 3.146; El. 1.4
Myrtle was the tree of Aphrodite (Venus), who is called the Idalian goddess from Idalium, her sacred city in Cyprus.

Illyria   DPV 2.158
Country on the Adriatic seacoast, chiefly modern Albania, but extending inland toward today's western Yugoslavia.

Indus [Indian]   DPV 2.391; 3.299; El. 1.1
The river Indus flows generally s.w. through India to the Indian Ocean.

Insubria   El. 2.1
Region around Milan.

Iolas   Pisc. 3; El. 1.1
Virgilian name, from *Aeneid* 11.640.

Ionia   DPV 2.159
Here the seacoast of roughly the southern half of Italy, facing the Ionian Sea.

Iris   DPV 2.142
A river in northern Asia Minor, flowing into the Black Sea.

Isaurica   DPV 2.120
Country of a tribe living between Lycaonia and Cilicia (q.v.).

Ischia   Pisc. 2, 3, 4, fragm.
Volcanic island some sixteen miles west of Naples. S. consistently uses the old name, Aenaria or Inarime.

Ismarus   El. 2.5
See Haemus.

Ister   DPV 3.300
Classical name for the Danube (hence "its double name"). It runs east through Austria and Hungary to empty into the Black Sea north of the Dardanelles. Cf. Herodotus, 4.47–50.

Iulus   El. 3.1
Son of Ascanius (q.v.) and grandson of Aeneas.

Janus   DPV 2.105 unnamed; El. 2.3; 3.3
See Introd. Note, El. 2.3. The allusion to Janus's temple at Rome (DPV 2.105) is a reference to Christ's being born at the time of the Pax Romana.

Jordan   DPV 3.246 ff.
The Song of Jordan begins at DPV 3.290. For the daughters named in 3.250–59, see Hyale.

Jove   Pisc. 3, 4; El. 2.1, 5, 6, 7; 3.1
Jupiter, the supreme Roman deity. His weapon, like that of his Greek counterpart Zeus, was the thunderbolt. Nourished in infancy on Mt. Ida in Crete, he ruled from Mt. Olympus, in the province of Elis (hence Elean Jove). For references in S. to the Christian deity as Jove, see Jupiter Tonans.

*Jovian   El. 1.9, 11; 2.2; 3.2
Giovanni Pontano adopted Jovianus as his Academy-name. See Introd. Note, El. 1.9. He appears in S's poetry also as Pontano (El. 1.9) and as Melisaeus (El. 3.2).

Joyfulness   DPV 3.81 ff.
For this invention, see General Introd. p. 28.

Juno   Pisc. 3; El. 2.1 unnamed, 8
Wife of Jove, daughter of Saturn; hence "Jove's faithful consort and his sister," in El. 2.1, where the temple alluded to is presumably the one on the promontory of Lacinium, on the east coast of Bruttium, several miles north of Caulon. Juno was a special object of worship in the island of Samos, off the coast of Caria in Asia Minor. See also Introd. Note, El. 2.8.

Jupiter Ammon   DPV 2.202 unnamed
"The palm groves of Jupiter" would be the renowned temple of Ammon, also called Jupiter Ammon, in the date-palm oasis of Siwa, in the desert in n.w. Egypt, approximately 100 miles from the coast and very close to the boundary with modern Libya.

Jupiter Tonans [the Thunderer]   DPV 1.195, 396; 2.44; 3.17, 83; Lam.; El. 1.7; 2.1
In DPV the most frequent name for the Christian deity is the Thunderer, as in all passages cited here, except "Capitolian Jove" (El. 2.1), which might be taken either way. For the pagan deity, see Jove, and Jupiter Ammon.

Jura   El. 3.1
The mountain chain running roughly from the Rhine to the Rhone.

Lachesis   El. 1.3; 2.7
One of the three Fates, she cuts the thread of life.

Laestrygonians   El. 3.1
These ancient inhabitants of the region around Gaeta had a reputation for cannibalism. See Antiphates.

Lanuvium   El. 2.1
A town a few miles south of Rome on the Appian Way.

Laodamia   El. 1.6
See Introd. Note, El. 1.6

Lares   El. 1.9; 2.2
Deities who protect a particular dwelling or locale.

Latium   DPV 2.171, 189; Pisc. 4; El. 1.1; 2.3; 3.1
Specifically the countryside around Rome. Thus a road from Rome to Naples may be called the Latian Way. But frequently Latium = Italian.

Latona   DPV 2.225
See Phoebe, Phoebus.

Laurentian   DPV 2.190
The countryside around Ostia, at the mouth of the Tiber. S's phrasing is probably meant as a direct echo of Virgil's "Laurentia . . . arva" (*Aen.* 7.661–62).

Leleges   DPV 2.122
Early inhabitants of a variety of places in Asia Minor and Greece.

Leman   El. 3.1
The lake formed by the Rhone at Geneva.

Lemnos   Pisc. 3
Vulcan's relation to this Aegean island (*Iliad* 1.590–94) is familiar from *Paradise Lost* 1.740 ff.

Lenaeus   El. 2.8
See Bacchus.

Leonora   El. 3.1
Leonora d'Este, Duchess of Ferrara, was sister to Alfonso and Frederick of Aragon.

Lerna   Wil.
See Centaurs.

Lesbos   El. 2.5
This island in the Aegean, off the Lydian coast, was famous for its wine.

Lethe   DPV 1.216; Pisc. 1; El. 1.3, 6, 9; 2.7
The river of forgetfulness, in Hades. See Acheron.

Libitina   El. 1.10
Goddess of funerals; or, by extension, the apparatus of funerals.

Liburnians   DPV 2.158
People of Illyria, approximately western Yugoslavia.

Liger   Pisc. 3, 4; El. 3.1
The river Loire. For Frederick's death at Tours and burial on the banks of the Loire, see Appendix A.

Liguria   Pisc. 3, 5; El. 2.1
A section of northern Italy including Genoa and Milan.

Lingonians   El. 3.1
The Lingones inhabited the regions around modern Langres, in France.

Linterno   El. 2.2, 4
Minor river in Campania.

Liris   El. 1.1
A river to the north of Naples, between Mondragone and Gaeta (cf. Statius's poem on the Domitian Way, *Silvae* 4.3).

Locri[ans]   El. 2.1
Presumably these are the inhabitants of Locri Epizephyrii, on the east coast of Bruttium, very near the tip. It is probably being called "city of Meliboea" because its founders were colonists from Meliboea in Thessaly.

Loire   Pisc. 3, 4; El. 3.1
See Liger.

Lotos-eaters, land of   El. 2.1
In effect, the general vicinity of Carthage (Herodotus, 4.177).

Lucifer   DPV 1.265
The morning star, Venus; here, simply daybreak, or its harbinger.

Lucina   Pisc. 1; El. 1.4
Juno Lucina was protectress of women in childbirth.

Lucrine   Pisc. 3, fragm.; El. 2.4
A small lake about ten miles n.w. of Naples, near Baiae—but much larger before an eruption in 1539. In the fragment from the Piscatoriae, "Lucrine Venus" probably echoes Statius (*Silvae*, 3.1.150).

Lycabas   Pisc. 3
This Greek name is given to a fairly important figure in a famous passage in
Ovid (*Met.* 3.600 ff.).

Lycaeus   Pisc. 4
Arcadian mountain, a center of Pan-worship; hence a reference here to S's
Arcadia.

Lycaonia   DPV 2.121
See Lycia.

Lycia   DPV 2.121
Lycia and Pamphylia are districts along the Aegean coast of Asia Minor.
Lycaonia is in the interior, adjacent to them.

Lycidas   DPV 3.169; Pisc. 1
The name is assigned to an interlocutor in Virgil (*Ecl.* 9) and in the proto-
typical Theocritean pastoral, *Idyll* 7.

Lycon   Pisc. 2
A name in Theocritus (2.76; 5.8).

Lycotas   Pisc. 1

Lyda   Pisc. 2

Macae   DPV 2.194
African tribe in the region between the two Syrtes; i.e., between Carthage
and Cyrene approximately. See also Cinyps.

Machaon   El. 3.2
Generic name for physicians, from the Greek surgeon (*Iliad* 2.729).

Maeander   DPV 1.81; 2.128
Proverbial for its winding course, it flows into the Icarian Sea south of the
Cayster (q.v.).

Maenalus   Pisc. 5; El. 2.7
In Thelgon's song (Pisc. 5) the reference to this mountain in Arcadia, plus
those to the rivers Var and Arar, suggest that Thelgon is to some degree a
persona for S. himself.

Maeon   Pisc. 5

Maeonia   Pisc. 5; El. 2.1
Ancient name for Lydia. The "Maeonian springs" refer to the heroic style of
Homer, whose birthplace was claimed by Lydia among others.

Magnus Annus   DPV 3.177
S's phrasing is *magna . . . saecula,* echoing Virgil's *magnus . . . saeclorum . . .
ordo* (*Ecl.* 4.5). The translation uses *Magnus Annus* because Yeats's "Two

Songs from a Play" has given the term some currency in our time. The *locus classicus* for the concept of the Great Year is Plato's *Timaeus*, 39–40.

Magra   El. 3.1
River in north central Italy, joining the Mediterranean at Luna.

*Maius   El. 1.11; 2.7

Marchese, Cassandra   Pisc. 5; El. 3.2
See Introd. Note, El. 3.2.

Marius   El. 3.1
Gaius Marius improved his legions' supply route to Gaul by diverting the course of the Rhone, near Marseilles, to join the sea at a point deep enough for large ships (Plutarch, *Lives*, ed. A. H. Clough, 3.63).

Marmarica   DPV 2.203
The North African coastline just east of Cyrenaica.

Maro   El. 1.1, 9, 11; 3.1
Publius Virgilius Maro wrote the pastoral *Eclogues* and *Georgics* before his heroic *Aeneid*. His tomb (El. 1.1) was one of the sights for tourists in Naples.

Mars (Gradivus)   Pisc. 3; El. 2.1, 2; 3.1
The name Gradivus is conjectured to be related to *gradior:* i.e., one who marches. The commonplace dichotomy of Phoebus-Mars (El. 2.2, 10) is related to the broader theme of active life vs. contemplative life. See also Rhodope.

*Marullus   El. 1.11; 2.2

Massilia   El. 3.1; 3.2
The seaport now known as Marseilles.

Massyli   DPV 2.184; 3.166
Numidian tribe somewhat west of Carthage.

Mausolus   DPV 2.126 unnamed
The tomb at Halicarnassus (in Caria), erected by Artemisia for her husband Mausolus, was one of the Seven Wonders of the World.

Megaera   DPV 1.406
One of the Furies, born to the goddess Night in a multiple birth (*Aen.* 12.845–48).

Megaria   Pisc. 1
Apparently a part of the shoreline adjoining Mergellina.

Melampus   Pisc. fragm.
Here a kind of generic name for physicians, from a Greek physician of legendary skill.

Melanthius   Pisc. 4

Meles   El. 3.1
A river in Ionia, one of several places claiming to have been Homer's birth-place.

Meliboea   El. 2.1
See Locrians.

Melisaeus   Pisc. 2, 4; El. 3.2
In all three passages, the reader is expected to recognize Melisaeus as a per-sona for Pontano (cf. *Arcadia,* Eclogue 12). Androgeo and Opico are shep-herds appearing in S's *Arcadia.*

Melite   DPV 3.445
Virgilian name for a sea-nymph (*Aen.* 5.825).

Menalcas   DPV 3.206
See General Introduction, pp. 17, 26.

Mergellina   DPV 1.24; 3.447; Pisc. 1, 2
S's villa on the Bay of Naples, deeded to him by King Frederick in 1499.

Meroe   DPV 2.203
A triangular region in the Sudan, bounded by the Nile, the Atbara river, and the Blue Nile, was known in classical geography as the Isle of Meroe (Strabo, 17.2.2).

Merula   El. 3.2
Quite possibly a survival from Roman times, the place-name means "black-bird" in both Latin and Italian.

Methymnaea   El. 1.9
Birthplace, on the island of Lesbos, of the famous lyre-player Arion, res-cued by dolphins.

Milcon   Pisc. 1

Mincius   El. 3.1
Virgil was born in Mantua, beside the river Mincius, as Homer was in some versions born by the river Meles, near Smyrna.

Minerva   Pisc. 3, 4
The Promontorium Minervae was at the west end of the peninsula of Surrentum, south of Naples. As Pallas Athena, Minerva was worshipped at Hymettus (i.e., Athens).

Miseno (Misenus)   Pisc. 1, 2; El. 2.4
In *Aeneid* 6.156–235, Virgil explains the connection between the Promontory of Misenum (n.w. of Naples) and the drowning of Misenus, a trumpeter for the Trojan fleet. His spirit weeps for Morinna in El. 2.4.

*Montaltus　El. 2.6
See Introd. Note, El. 2.6.

Mopsus　Pisc. 3

Morini　Pisc. 3
A prominent Belgian tribe (*Aen.* 8.727).

Morinna　El. 2.4
S. specifies that she is a Naiad, but (like Nesis, q.v.) she is a huntress in the high country.

Muses　DPV 1.8; 2.261; 3.416, 446; Pisc. 1, 2, 3, 4, 5, fragm.; Wil.; El. 1.1, 5, 8, 9, 10, 11; 2.1, 2, 4, 5, 7, 8; 3.1, 2, 3
The goddess addressed at DPV 2.295 is the Virgin Mary, as in the prefatory lines, DPV 1.28.
Listed here are virtually all individual poems that speak of the Muses. Writer's block is a universal worry, whether goddesses are withholding their favor or "creative juices" are suffering from restricted flow.
See also Aganippe, Aonia, Calliope, Castalian, Erato, Helicon, Parnassian, Permessus, Pierian, Pindus, Thalia, Thespian.

Myco　DPV 1.117
Ovid speaks of "low-lying Myconos" (*Met.* 7.463). It is an island on the n.e. fringe of the Cyclades.

Mycon　Pisc. 1

Mysia　DPV 2.132
This province in Asia Minor, in modern Turkey, was just north of the province of Lydia, bordering the Aegean Sea.

Nabathea[ns]　DPV 1.235
A country in Petrine Araby; but, by extension, any exotic Oriental locale.

Naiads　DPV 3.436; Wil.; El. 2.3, 4, 10
In most passages the context suits their special designation as water-nymphs. That is distinctly not true for Morinna (q.v.).

Napaeans　DPV 3.355; El. 2.6
The name comes from νάπη, a woodland grove. In DPV 3.355–59 the banquet scene is possibly in such a grove, on the banks of Jordan. S. does not expressly identify Jordan's daughters with either Naiads or Napaeans— but he takes most of their names from Hesiod's list of the fifty Nereids (see Hyale).

Nasamones　DPV 2.195
An inland tribe near the N. African coastline (Strabo, 17.3.20, 23).

Naso　El. 2.1
I.e., Ovid (Publius Ovidius Naso).

Natalis [Natal Day]   El. 2.8
See Introd. Note, El. 2.8.

Naxos   El. 2.5, 8
Bacchus found Ariadne on this island, the largest in the group called the Cyclades.

Nebrodes   El. 2.6
Mountain range in Sicily.

Nemesis   El. 1.10; 2.1
The goddess who punishes human pride; hence, Tibullus's name for one of the mistresses addressed in his elegies.

Neptune   DPV 3.411, 444; Pisc. 2, 5
At DPV 3.411 he is personified, with his trident, and in Pisc. 5 conceived as a king hearing his subjects' complaints. In the other passages, simply "the sea."

Nereids   DPV 2.137; 3.410; Pisc. 1, 2, 3, 5, fragm.
Daughters of Nereus (q.v.). See also Dynamene.

Nereus   DPV 2.111; 3.445; Pisc. 1; fragm.
The sea, mildly personified in most passages, as husband of Doris and father of the Nereids.

Nesis   Pisc. 1, 2, 4
Small island between Naples and Puteoli (mod. Pozzuoli). See Posilipo.

Niphates   DPV 2.114
Mountain in the Taurus range, in Armenia, but near Assyria, as in Milton's "Assyrian mount" (*P.L.* 4.126; cf. 3.746).

Nisa   Pisc. 3
The name appears in Virgil (*Ecl.* 8.26).

Nisaea   Pisc. 1; El. 2.8
The name is applied by Ovid several times to Scylla, daughter of Nisus (e.g., *Met.* 8.35). Perhaps in Pisc. 1 only a sea-nymph, as in El. 2.8 the *Nisaeia turba* is a group of sea-nymphs.

Nomentum   El. 2.1
A city near Rome, to the north on the Nomentian Way.

Notus   DPV 2.22; El. 3.3
Greek name for the south wind.

Oebalia   El. 3.1
An alternate name for Taranto, as in *Georgics* 4.125. As second in line of succession, Frederick's title was Prince of Taranto.

Oedipus   El. 1.11

Oenomaus   El. 3.1
See Introd. Note, El. 3.1.

Oetaea   El. 1.5
See Hercules.

Olympus   DPV 1.4, 196, 392; 2.42; 3.2, 120, 183, 242, 381; Lam.; El. 2.6
In Elegy 2.6, the famous mountain in Thessaly. All other references are to
the Christian heaven.

Opico   El. 3.2
See Melisaeus.

Orcus   Lam.
Latin name for the underworld, or its god, or simply Death.

Orion   DPV 3.109

Orpheus   El. 1.5
See Eurydice.

Ortygia   DPV 2.225; Pisc. 3
A name for the small island of Delos, between Myco and Naxos, where
Latona bore the twins Apollo and Diana (Delius and Delia). See Phoebe.

Otranto   El. 2.3
In S's Latin text "Hydruntinas terras"; from Hydrus, or Hydruntum, the
Graeco-Roman name for modern Otranto, on the east coast of Italy. The
liberation of Otranto from the Turks (1481) was the major military success
of Alfonso II, at that time Duke of Calabria.

Pactolus   DPV 2.130; El. 2.3 unnamed
A river in Lydia reputed to have golden sands, as was the river Hermus
(q.v.). Both are at times identified with the modern Sarabat.

Paeon[ius]   El. 2.10
Pertaining to Apollo as god of healing (*Aen.* 7.769).

Palaemon   Pisc. 1
His virtuous mother was Ino (*Met.* 4.416–542).

Pales   El. 1.1, 2
The interest in rites of Pales seems a holdover from the *Arcadia* (Chapter
3).

Palladian   El. 3.3
Minerva (Pallas Athena) was a patroness of poetry, and of spinning and
weaving. Her leaf was the olive (*Met.* 6.101–2).

Pamphylia   DPV 2.120
Country on the southern Aegean coast of Asia Minor, with Lycia to its west and Cilicia to its east. See Lycia.

Panchaea   El. 1.2
A mythical island east of Arabia, in the Erythraean, with many spices and perfumes.

Panope   DPV 3.445; Pisc. 1, 4
See Palaemon.

*Panormita   El. 2.2
Antonio Beccadelli, called Panormita from his birthplace in Palermo, was the first head of the Neapolitan Academy, before S's time.

Paphos   Wil.; El. 1.4
See Amathus.

Paraetonium   DPV 1.252
A port along the North African shoreline west of Alexandria. By extension, Egypt.

Parcae   El. 1.6, 10
The Fates (q.v.).

*Pardus   El. 1.2, 11

Parian   El. 1.2, 9
A famous white marble quarried in Paros, an island in the Cyclades.

Parnassus   DPV 3.417; El. 1.9; 2.1; 3.1
The Castalian spring on Mt. Parnassus, above Delphi, was sacred to Apollo and the Muses.

Parthenope[a]   Pisc. 3, 4, 3 unnamed; El. 1.11; 2.1, 4; 3.1, 3
The original Cumaean colony at Naples was supposed to have been named Parthenopea, for a Siren whose tomb was located there. Hence the name frequently means Naples itself.

Penates   DPV 2.221
Guardian deities of the Roman household; by extension, a home, a dwelling-place.

Pergamum   DPV 2.133; El. 2.1; 3.1
Specifically the citadel at Troy; by extension, the whole city or even the whole race of Trojans.

Permessus   El. 1.11
A river rising in Mt. Helicon, and thus sacred to Apollo and the Muses.

Petrine   El. 1.1; 2.2

A locale near Sinuessa (q.v.). S's family had held land there that was evidently expropriated, presumably for political reasons. See Antiphates.

Peuce   DPV 2.170

Isle of Pines: a sizeable island formed by the Danube as it debouches into the Black Sea.

Phaeton   El. 3.1

Phaeton plunged into the Eridanus (Po), ending his disastrous attempt to drive the chariot of his father, the Sun-god Apollo (*Met.* 2.1–328).

Pharian   DPV 2.380

Egyptian (from Pharos, q.v.). Parian marble (q.v.) is more renowned. Perhaps the poet chooses a "brand" more likely to be familiar to Joseph.

Pharos   DPV 2.380; Pisc. 4

"Pharian columns" are presumably Egyptian, as was the lighthouse at Alexandria for which evidently a Neapolitan lighthouse was named (*Juv. Satire* 12.76).

Pharsalia   DPV 2.148

City in Thessaly, renowned for Caesar's victory over Pompey there.

Pherusa   Pisc. 4

Philippi   DPV 2.149

Octavian and his allies defeated Brutus near this Macedonian city. Philippi is "twice fatal" because there were two battles, Cassius committing suicide during the first engagement, and Brutus not until after the second was lost, twenty days later.

Phlegethon   DPV 1.350; Lam.; El. 1.11

See Acheron.

Phocaean   El. 3.1

Marseilles (ancient Massilia) was founded by refugees from Phocaea, in Ionia.

Phocian   El. 2.2

The Castalian spring (q.v.) was in the country of Phocis, between Boeotia and Aetolia.

Phoebe   Pisc. 3, 4; Lam.

Latona's twins, born on the island of Delos, were god of the sun (Phoebus) and goddess of the moon (Phoebe). She is patroness of the hunt and of chaste maidens.

Phoebus   DPV 2.261, 323; 3.419; Pisc. 4, 5, fragm.; El. 1.8, 9; 2.1, 2, 8; 3.1

Only once (DPV 2.323) does the name refer to the sun itself. Two passages (DPV 3.419; Pisc. 4) stress the prophetic power of poetry. All others cited here present the god as laurel-crowned leader of the Muses and inspirer of poets, as do the references to Delius (q.v.). See also Apollo, Phoebe.

Phoenix   DPV 2.357

Pholoe   Pisc. 3, fragm.

Phorcus   DPV 3.413
Like Glaucus, he was after his death changed into a sea-god.

Phrasidamus   Pisc. 4

Phrygian   DPV 2.381; El. 3.1
Province in Asia Minor, east of Lydia, whose weavers made a specialty of gold embroidery. The name was commonly applied to the Trojans. Thus Caieta speaks "in Phrygian phrase."

Phyllis   Pisc. 1; El. 1.2

Picentia   El. 3.2
A region south and east of Salerno, not to be confused with Picenum, a district on Italy's Adriatic coast. But cf. Strabo, 5.4.13.

Pierian   Pisc. 5; El. 1.5, 10, 11; 2.2; 3.1, 3
All such references (Pierian shades, waters, draughts, maidens) are to Mount Pierus, in Thessaly, sacred to the Muses (q.v.).

Pindus   El. 3.1
Virgil (*Ecl.* 10.11) seems to imply that the Muses favored this Thessalian mountain equally with Parnassus (q.v.).

Platamon   Pisc. 5
Mustard's edition of the Piscatoriae cites a passage from Pontano: "Also there are the caves of Platamon hollowed out along the shore and artificially created, which the passage of time and the salty washing of the sea has in large part consumed, places undoubtedly devised for pleasure and summer strolls and banquets" (De Bell. Neap., I.vi, cited in Mustard, pp. 87–88).

Pluto   DPV 1.355
A name for Hades, god of the classical underworld; hence, Satan in this poem.

Polybotas   Pisc. 2

Pomona   El. 2.10
Goddess of fruit trees.

Pontano   El. 1.9; 2.2
See Jovian.

Pontus   DPV 2.140
See Carambis.

Posilipo   DPV 3.443; Pisc. 1, 2, 4
Anciently Mons Pausilypus, a once-volcanic mountain s.w. of Mergellina. Pontano and S. constructed a myth that the island of Nesis was originally a nymph (Nesis) beloved by Pausilypus. See Benedetto Croce, *Storie e Leggende Napoletane* (Bari, 1948), pp. 290–92.

Praxinoe   Pisc. 2
Evidently an invented name.

Priam   DPV 2.134
Ruler of Troy when it was sacked by the Greeks. See Hecuba.

Priapus   El. 2.5 unnamed
He is the unnamed "garden god" in the opening segment of El. 2.5. S. discreetly ignores his most famous attribute, the phallus.

Prochyte   Pisc. 5; El. 2.7
See Procida.

Procida   Pisc. 1, 3, 4, fragm.
Island in the Bay of Naples, Lat. *Prochyte*—a form retained for euphony in Pisc. 5 and El. 2.7.

Prometheus   DPV 2.145
Prometheus was chained to his rock somewhere in the wild mountain range of the Caucasus, between the Black Sea and the Caspian.

Propertius   El. 2.1

Proserpina   El. 2.10 unnamed
Ovid tells her story in *Met.* 5.385 ff.

Proteus   DPV 3.292, 365, 425; Pisc. 1, 3, 4
As singer, prophet, shepherd of sea creatures, and master of metamorphic change, his figure had strong appeal for S. His prophecy constitutes almost the whole of the section that I have called The Song of Jordan (DPV 3.290–422).

Psylli   DPV 2.199
An inland tribe living near the Greater Syrtes. Herodotus (4.173) says that the entire tribe was already extinct in his day, swallowed up in a sandstorm while migrating through the desert. Thus we see S. here ignoring "verisimilitude" in favor of using a name that his readers might know.

*Pudericus   Pisc. fragm.; El. 2.2

Punic   El. 2.10

African (or "Libyan"). The word is formed from *Poeni*, the Phoenicians, who founded Carthage and dominated the whole of N. Africa.

Pylemon   Pisc. 1

Python   El. 3.3
A monstrous serpent, guardian of the cave at Delphi, killed by Apollo (*Met.* 1.438–44).

Quadriga Christi   DPV 1.362 unnamed
S's autograph ms. (Fantazzi-Perosa, 42–43) annotates this section as follows:
407 - Quadriga Christi [the chariot of Christ]
411 - Lucas [the Bull]
419 - Marcus [the Lion]
426 - Iohannes [the Eagle]
432 - Matthaeus [the Youth]
The conception is non-Scriptural, but of very early origin.

Rhodope   DPV 2.146; Pisc. 3
North Thracian mountain range, running down into the Haemus range. As a wild, rough country, Thrace was often spoken of as akin to Mars.

Rhoe   Pisc. 4

Rhoetaean   DPV 2.133
Rhoetaeum, a promontory near Troy; by extension, a Trojan.

Robert   El. 2.1
The allusion is to the success of Alfonso's surprise attack, in his campaign of 1485–86, against Roberto Sanseverino, a *condottiere* of the time.

Sabaean   El. 1.1, 6
Saba, in Araby the Blest (Arabia Felix), was famed for exotics such as myrrh and frankincense. The sisters who "offer Sabaean incense" (El. 1.6) are probably nuns.

Sabines   El. 3.1
Ancient Italian people adjoining the Latins.

Salentine   El. 3.1
The extreme s.e. tip of Calabria, the "heel" of Italy.

Samaria   DPV 2.214
The district was bounded by Carmel on the west and Jordan on the east.

Samos   Pisc. 3
Island off the coast from Ephesus, in Ionia.

Sarno   Pisc. 4; Wil.
Virgil's Sarnus (*Aen.* 7.738), to the south of Vesuvius, formed the port of Pompeii.

Saturn   DPV 3.178
Both S. and Virgil (*Ecl.* 4.6) are referring to the virgin goddess of Justice, Astraea (q.v.), and to the reign of Saturn in the Golden Age, preceding that of Zeus.

*Scala   El. 1.11

Scamander   El. 3.1
The river on whose plain the Trojan War was fought.

Scuccha   El. 1.11
Unidentified satirist(?).

Scylla   DPV 1.354; Wil.
As described by Homer (*Od.* 12.85–100), Scylla has six heads, and twelve feet dangling in the air. Her barking dogs are part of Ovid's vivid tale of her metamorphosis (*Met.* 14.59–67). See also Centaurs.

Sebeto   Pisc. 1, 5; El. 1.9; 2.3, 4
Sebeto, a small stream east of Naples, is the Sebethus of *Aeneid* 7.734. Both S. and Pontano mention the stream frequently.

Semele   El. 2.5
Her foolish request to see Jupiter "as Juno sees him" led to her instant death (*Met.* 3.273 ff.). See also Bacchus.

Serapis   Pisc. 5
The reference is obscure. Mustard (p. 88) annotates: "Perhaps an allusion to the so-called Serapeum at Pozzuoli."

Seriphos   DPV 1.117
A small island on the western end of the Cyclades.

Sibyl [Cumaean virgin]   DPV 1.87; El. 1.7; 2.7, 8, 9
The oracle at Cumae, most renowned of Roman oracles (cf. *Aen.* 6.42 ff.). Hence, prophets in general, or with specific reference to the prophets of the Old Testament (DPV 1; El. 1.7).

Sidonia   DPV 2.331; 3.438; El. 1.1
Sidonia, or Sidon (as in the Biblical "Tyre and Sidon") was a Phoenician city famous for the expensive Tyrian purple, or Sidonian dye. The ravishing of the Sidonian virgin alludes to the well-known myth of Europa and the bull (*Met.* 2.846 ff.).

Sigeum   DPV 2.134
A small town on a ridge near Troy, one of the standard place-names for alluding to that war. See also Achilles.

Silenus   DPV 2.334 unnamed; El. 2.5
Silenus is "that wicked old man" in DPV 2.334. He was often portrayed as a Falstaffian boon companion of Bacchus. See also Cithaeron, Priapus.

Simeon   DPV 1.236 unnamed
S. is virtually translating Luke's tale about Simeon (2:25–32).

Sinope   DPV 2.141
A well known Greek colony in Paphlagonia on the Black Sea.

Sinuessa   Pisc. 3, 5; El. 1.1
S.'s ancestral town, near Mondragone. Pliny calls it "the last town in the Extension of Latium"—i.e., just on the edge of Campania (*Natural History,* 3.5.59).

Siren   Pisc. 1, 3, 4, 5
The epitaph in Pisc. 1 and "the goldenhaired Siren" (Pisc. 4) are allusions to Parthenope (q.v.). The "fields that keep the names of the Sirens" (Pisc. 5) refer to Surrentum (mod. Sorrento). The "singing maidens" (Pisc. 4) are the sirens that Odysseus avoided (*Od.* 12). "Ye Sirens," in Pisc. 3, seems more general.

Sisyphus   DPV 1.409; El. 2.7
His punishment in Hades was to roll a stone uphill, repeating his effort each time it rolled down.

Sphinx   DPV 1.354
The sphinx had a woman's head, a lion's body, a serpent's tail, and an eagle's wings.

Stabiae   Pisc. 4
Roman resort, destroyed by Vesuvius along with Herculaneum and Pompeii. It was on the north slope of the long peninsula across the bay from Naples.

Stagira   El. 1.9
Birthplace of Aristotle.

Stoechades   Pisc. 3; El. 3.1
Islands off the southern coast of France, near Marseilles.

Strymon   El. 1.5
A river in Macedonia, near Thrace, running south to the Aegean.

Styx (Stygian)   DPV 1.75, 326; 3.201, 311; El. 1.7, 9, 11; 2.7
One of the rivers of Hades (see Acheron). Styx and Tartarus are S's commonest terms for the Hell of Christian tradition, as Olympus is his commonest term for Heaven. Most references are relatively vague (Stygian shades, waters, realms).

Subuncula   El. 3.2
See Introd. Note, El. 3.2.

Subura   El. 2.1
A busy quarter in the city of Rome.

Sybaris   El. 2.1
A town in Magna Graecia (i.e., lower Italy) on the river Sybaritis. Chratis is presumably the Crathis, which joins the Sybaritis just before they both enter the Gulf of Taranto.

Sylvans   Wil.; El. 2.4
Deities of the woods and fields, usually presented without specific attributes.

Syrinx   Wil., unnamed
See *Willows*, Introd. Note.

Syrtes   DPV 2.196
Shoals with dangerous currents and quicksands: Syrtis Major near Cyrene, Syrtis Minor at the other (western) end of the Bay of Tunis, not far from Carthage (Strabo, 17.3.17, 20).

Tabor   DPV 2.213
Mountain in Galilee, some six miles east of Nazareth.

Taenaris   El. 3.1
Taenaris is a mountain in Sparta, frequently used by extension for all Sparta.

Tagus   DPV 2.177; Pisc. 4; El. 2.3
A river in Spain and Portugal, with golden sands.

Tantalus   El. 2.7 unnamed
His punishment (*Met.* 4.458) was to thirst and starve within sight of water and fruits that shrank away so that he could not reach them.

Tarbelli   Pisc. 3
An Aquitainian tribe (*Gallic Wars,* 3.27).

Tartarus   DPV 1.33, 206, 348, 356; 3.239, 336; Lam.
S's standard name for the Christian Hell, presumably because Tartarus was reserved for the punishment of the specially wicked.

Taurus   DPV 2.119
A mountain range in the general area of Armenia, forming a kind of natural eastern boundary for the peninsular Asia Minor. See Niphates.

Tebenna   El. 3.2
See Introd. Note, El. 3.2.

Teleboeans   Pisc. 4, 5
They were the original inhabitants of Capri (*Aen.* 7.735).

Tethys   DPV 1.181; El. 2.6
Wife of Oceanus and mother of sea-nymphs and river-gods; by extension, the sea.

Thalia   El. 1.5
The Muse of comic poetry.

Thebes   DPV 2.224; El. 2.1, 5
See Introd. Note, El. 2.1.

Thelgon   Pisc. 5
See Maenalus.

Thermodon   DPV 2.144
A river in Pontus (northern Asia Minor), emptying into the Black Sea.

Thespians   El. 1.9, 11; 2.2
Thespiae is a village at the foot of Mount Helicon. See Muses.

Thetis   DPV 2.138; Pisc. 1
A Nereid, whose deep affection for her son Achilles is a recurrent theme in the *Iliad*.

Thisbe   El. 2.4
Her blood stained the white mulberry red (*Met.* 4.51, 165).

Thrace   DPV 2.145
A mountainous region extending north and east from Macedonia to the Black Sea, usually commented on as rough and wild.

Thunderer
See the entries for Jove and Jupiter Tonans.

Thyrsis   El. 1.1
A singing shepherd in Virgil's seventh eclogue.

Tibullus   El. 2.1

Ticinus   El. 3.1
River flowing past Pavia, which is the primary point of reference here.

Tiphys   DPV 3.199
See Argo.

Tirynthian   El. 1.5
See Hercules.

Tisiphone   DPV 1.34
One of the Furies in Hades. See Alecto.

Tityrus   DPV 3.174; El. 1.1
The line at DPV 3.174 would be readily understood by S's audience as a reference to Virgil himself (*Eclogues* 1.1; *Georgics* 4.566).

Tityus   El. 2.7
His punishment was a vulture that fed daily on his liver.

Tivoli   El. 2.1
Tivoli (ancient Tibur) is some twenty miles n.e. of Rome.

Tomi (Tomitanian)   El. 1.5
The poet Ovid was for unknown reasons exiled to this town on the Black Sea.

Toroentian   El. 3.1
Taurois, on the coast of Narbonne, was a fortified harbor for Marseilles.

Trinacria   El. 1.2
The Trinacrian shepherd is Theocritus, possibly a native of Sicily (called Trinacria for its three promontories: Pachynum, Pelorum, and Lilybaeum). Cf. *Met.* 5.346–51.

Triones   DPV 3.37
The constellation of Ursa Major and Ursa Minor; frequently by extension, as here, "the North" (cf. Isaiah 14:12).

Triton   DPV 3.167, 444; Lam.; Pisc. 1, 3, 4, 5, fragm.
The first reference in DPV is to the river, in western Libya. Elsewhere the reference is to Wordsworth's sea-god with his "wreathed horn" or, in the plural, to the "crowds of Tritons" (Pisc. 1), since the name became generic for the lesser deities of the sea.

Tritonia   Pisc. 3
A name for Minerva (or Pallas Athene, in Homer). Its origin is unclear. Here simply translated as Minerva.

Troy   El. 1.11
Troiano Cavaniglia (or Cabanilius) became lord of Troia, in the Neapolitan kingdom, late in his life (see *Willows,* Introd. Note), but he apparently always lived in the area. References to Homer's Troy, when under that name, are omitted from this glossary.

Turones   El. 3.1
This Gallic tribe lived near modern Tours, at which city Frederick died in exile.

Tusculum   El. 2.1
City in the hill country n.e. of Rome.

Typhoeus   Pisc. 4
A hundred-headed rebel against Heaven whom Zeus buried under Mount Aetna. But here, following Virgil (*Aen.* 9.716), under the island of Ischia (anciently Inarime).

Tyrrhene   El. 2.9
The Mediterranean between Naples and Sardinia.

Umbria   El. 1.9; 3.1
See Introd. Note, El. 1.9.

Varro   El. 1.9
M. Terentius Varro and P. Nigidius Figulus wrote on grammar and on many other topics in Cicero's era.

Varus   Pisc. 5; El. 3.1
The French river Var, flowing to the sea near Nice.

Veii   El. 3.1
One of the oldest cities of Etruria, a district in central Italy.

Vesuvius   Pisc. 4, 5

Vivula   El. 3.2
See Introd. Note, El. 3.2.

Vocontian   El. 3.2
S. uses the name of a Gallic tribe (the Vocontii) inhabiting what is now the region of Narbonne.

Volcae   El. 3.2
A powerful tribe in Narbonne.

Zacharias   DPV 2.67 unnamed
See Elizabeth.

*Zeno   El. 1.11
Rutilio Zeno.

Zephyr   DPV 1.77; 2.23; 3.403; Pisc. 2, 3, fragm.; Wil.
The west wind, normally with emphasis on its gentle nature. Frequently, any light wind.

Zephyraeus   Pisc. fragm.